BURMA'S PATH TO DEMOCRACY

BURMA'S PATH TO DEMOCRACY

THE MILITARY, AUNG SAN SUU KYI
AND THE ROHINGYA

TinTin Delphin

Algora Publishing
New York

Library of Congress Cataloging-in-Publication Data

Names: Delphin, TinTin, author.
Title: Burma's Path to Democracy: The military, Aung San Suu Kyi and the Rohingya/
TinTin Delphin.
Description: New York: Algora Publishing, [2020] | Includes
  bibliographical references and index. | Summary: "Burma is a country in
  transition: from monarchy to British colony, from independence to
  military dictatorships, and from the Generals to the Lady, Aung San Suu
  Kyi. This book traces one of the longest civil wars in history. It's
  about the Rohingya, one of the most persecuted people on earth. It's
  about pro-democracy uprisings, about sacrifice, and above all, the human
  resilience and capacity for hope. The book is based on true events and
  provides unique firsthand insights into key players in this enigmatic
  and troubled nation"— Provided by publisher.
Identifiers: LCCN 2020019066 (print) | LCCN 2020019067 (ebook) | ISBN
  9781628944198 (trade paperback) | ISBN 9781628944204 (hardcover) | ISBN
  9781628944211 (pdf)
Subjects: LCSH: Aung San Suu Kyi. | Rohingya (Burmese
  people)—History—20th century. | Burma—History—1962-1988. |
  Burma—History—1988– | LCGFT: Personal narratives.
Classification: LCC DS530.6 .D45 2020 (print) | LCC DS530.6 (ebook) | DDC
  959.105—dc23
LC record available at https://lccn.loc.gov/2020019066
LC ebook record available at https://lccn.loc.gov/2020019067

Printed in the United States

Dedication
>   To Ashley,
>   for pain and rapture, despair and pleasure.
>   You are the best I have on this planet.
>
>   and
>
>   To the people of Burma,
>   for their courage in the struggle against tyranny and
>   an unending hope for freedom and justice.

Acknowledgments

To the community leaders, veteran politicians, journalists, academics, and political activists who fearlessly granted me passionate interviews, shared their personal experiences and provided valuable insights, I am enormously grateful with sincere thanks, heartfelt if unspoken. They remain anonymous for safety and privacy.

Table of Contents

Acronyms

Acronym	Name
ABSDF	All Burma Students Democratic Front
ADC	Aide de camp, personal bodyguard
AFPFL	Anti-Fascist People's Freedom League
ARSA	Arakan Rohingya Solidarity Army
BBC	British Broadcasting Corporation
BCP	Burma Communist Party, or CPB
BEDC	Burma Economic Development Corporation
BIA	Burma Independence Army
BSPP	Burma Socialist Program Party, later changed to CEC, Central Executive Committee
CEC	Central Executive Committee
CPB	Communist Party of Burma
DSA	Defense Services Academy
DSI	Defense Services Institute
DVA	Democratic Voice of America
DVB	Democratic Voice of Burma
EAO	Ethnic Armed Organization
ICC	International Criminal Court, The Hague, Netherlands

IDP	Internally displaced people
KMT	Kuomintang, Chinese Nationalist Party
MEC	*Myanmar* Economic Corporation
MEHPCL	Economic Holdings Public Company Limited, formerly UMEHL, Union of *Myanmar* Economic Holdings Limited
MI	Military Intelligence
MNC	multinational company
MOGE	*Myanmar* Oil and Gas Enterprise
MP	Member of Parliament
NCA	Nationwide Ceasefire Agreement
NDF	National Democratic Force, split from NLD
NDSC	National Defense and Security Council
NGO	Non-Governmental Organization
NLD	National League of Democracy
NUF	National United Front
NUP	National Unity Party
OTS	Officer Training School
QMG	Quarter Master General, an officer in charge of army supplies
RC	Revolutionary Council
SEZ	Special Economic Zone
SLORC	State Law and Order Restoration Council
SPDC	State Peace and Development Council
UMEHL	Union of *Myanmar* Economic Holdings Limited, later renamed MEHPCL, *Myanmar* Economic Holdings Public Company Limited
UNDP	Union National Democracy Party, General Aung Gyi's party
UNHCR	United Nations High Commissioner for Refugees
UNSC	United Nations Security Council
USDA	Union Solidarity Development Association
USDP	Union Solidarity Development Party, successor of USDA
VOA	Voice of America

Glossary

Burmese term	Meaning
aingi	tight-fitted front-buttoned Burmese top
Bamar	Burman ethnicity
Bogyoke	General
Bogyoke Aung San Market	formerly known as Scot Market, with over 2000 stalls
chinthe	mythical lion with a dragon's head
Dagon Yeitha	General Aung Gyi's residence, also the official state guest house of the government
Daw	a woman, usually in a senior position
dhamma	six attributes of Buddha's teachings
gaung baung	silk hat worn by men
hpone	spiritual power
hpongyi or pongyi	monk
hpaya	Buddha
hti	umbrella, also tip of spire pagoda
kalar	dark-skinned people
Kayah	formerly Karrenni tribe or state

Kayin	formerly Karen tribe or state
Ko	a man, younger than U but older than Maung
Kokang	sub ethnic minority group
koyin	novice monk
kutho	merit or reward in heaven
kyat	Burmese currency
Kyaukphyu	a coastal town in Arakan state
longyi	wrap-around sarong
Ma	girl or young woman
Ma Ba Tha	radical Buddhist nationalistic group
Machanbaw	town in the northernmost tip of Kachin state
Mahn	Mr. in Karen language
Maung	boy or young man, or part of a name
Mingaladon	Rangoon airport
Myitsone dam	China's dam construction in Myitkyina
naga	mythical serpent with a dragon's head
nat	spirit
Naypyidaw	capital of Burma, means 'abode or city of kings'
Panglong Agreement	General Aung San's agreement to grant ethnic minorities the same rights as the *Bamar* people
peso	men's wrap around sarong
pewah	short lace shawl worn by women
sao	prince or lord in Shan language
sangha	Buddhist clergy
sawbwa or saopha	Shan chief or ruler
sayadaw	abbot of a Buddhist monastery
shiko	to bow with hands in prayer position as a sign of respect
suhn	prepared food offerings for monks
Tatmadaw	Burma's armed forces

Thakin	master, archaic Burmese
Thein Gyi Ze	local wet market for all purpose shopping
Thingyan	water festival (Burmese New Year)
Thura	brave, gallant, used as part of a name
U	an older man, usually in a senior position

Author's Note

On March 1, 1962, while my cousin and I were playing upstairs at *Dagon Yeitha* (Dagon House), General *Ne Win*, Brigadier General *Aung Gyi* and other high-ranking Burmese generals were meeting in the banquet room downstairs. The men were planning a military coup d'état the next morning that would take over the civilian government. Beginning with that coup, Burma — now known as *Myanmar* — was ruled for fifty years by a repressive autocratic army dictatorship, and for most of the period to 1988 by the General himself.

Within General *Ne Win*'s ruling party, the Revolutionary Council, was a soft-spoken, mild-mannered man, Brigadier General *Aung Gyi*. He was the General's right hand and confidant; his heir apparent. *Aung Gyi* wore many hats: he served as Vice-Chief of Staff of *Tatmadaw*, the armed forces; as second in command of the Revolutionary Council; Minister of Trade and Industry; and Minister of Defense; he was also my uncle.

Ideological and political differences led to *Aung Gyi*'s resignation, but he continued to be a champion for democracy for the people and the country he loved. For half a century the country was closed to the outside world while the xenophobic generals committed atrocities and plundered the country's bountiful natural resources to enrich themselves, their families and their inner circle crony friends. No one dared openly criticize the regime for fear of repercussion or danger to their families and friends. Now the truth must be told.

This is a narrative of five decades of under-reported horror. In 2011, Burma finally opened up to the world with a quasi-civilian government composed of former and retired army generals who swapped their decorated uniforms for civilian clothing. They appointed a retired general as President to lead the country, and things started to change. However, while some reforms have taken place to attract the much needed foreign investments and tourists, genuine improvements in human rights are far from reaching the expressed goals of the new 'civilian' administration. *Tatmadaw*, or the Burma army, continues to exert control over every level of government and most aspects of life and economy.

I myself was assembled in the US with parts from Burma. When Burma opened its doors to the world in 2011 after half a century of self-imposed isolation, I found a reawakening of my heritage and strengthening of my resolve and commitment to complete the narration of its untold story.

The tragedy of internal conflicts with ethnic nationalities has dominated the country for almost seventy years of civil war. Ethnic minorities have suffered discrimination legally, politically, religiously, and economically, while the Muslim minority population, internationally known as the *Rohingya*, has been stripped of all rights including health and education, and the bare necessities of human survival. Everyone suffered and many died fighting for freedom — students, monks, ordinary folks, farmers, villagers, minority ethnic nationalities.

This is a true story. It is not meant to be a scholarly contribution or an exhaustive investigative report but a reflection on personal life experience and observation of political themes through both Burmese and Western lenses. Sometimes I insert myself as a character, telling the story firsthand as the personal documentary of a thoughtful and concerned young observer rather than an agenda-driven storyteller.

Occasionally, especially in the first chapters, I present personal scenes that illustrate aspects of Burmese culture and the personalities of those who have shaped recent events; these scenes are set apart, indented, so as not to interfere with the main flow of the book.

My work is based on my recollection of real events, family dialogue, Uncle *Aung Gyi's* letters, awards and photographs, and interviews with Burmese veteran politicians and community leaders of the past era. It is written from the heart with compassion for the people of Burma who have sacrificed their lives in search of freedom. It is a story of extraordinary courage, tireless dedication and defiant struggle for human rights as citizens rise up in democratic uprisings against a merciless military regime. It is a story of powerful resilience and unending hope. It is a blend of memoir, reportage, and travel with a contemporary political backdrop. It includes a brief history of this exotic land of pagodas and an insight into Burmese culture, its friendly people, what goes on behind the scenes economically and politically, and their struggle for freedom and democracy. It is an objective exposé meant to uncover the truth about real events, and the atrocities perpetrated by the twentieth century's most notorious military dictators. It is about the value of freedom – a privilege we often take for granted, human resilience, and capacity for hope. It includes current events and an informed look into its past, present, and future through both Eastern and Western perspectives. It is my objective to enable readers to glean meaningful intellectual and cultural insight from this diverse and exotic land, hidden from the world for so long.

The book describes the dramatic changes that occurred following the coup in this Southeast Asian country. When the military dictatorship took over all government, businesses, banks, hospitals, schools, and every aspect of life, it also sealed off the country from the rest of the world, including foreign journalists. Fortunately my foreign-born mother was able to leave the country, taking us two children but leaving behind my high-profile Burmese father. He was not allowed to leave, being a relative and member of the family now in political opposition to the dictatorship. As a young woman, I endured life-changing psychological trauma, ripped away from my father, three generations of family, and friends, and I endured emotional upheaval with loss of loved ones, home and country. But I survived.

People of Burma may live in fear but they never give up hope. They believe there is an end to the drowning darkness. They hope for an end to poverty and hunger. They hope for a free Burma and a better life with the creation of jobs and improved healthcare and access to education. They hope for a happier society regardless of the name of the political system. They hope for a country where people are able to have independent thought and control their own actions. They hope for a government that can bring peace and prosperity to Burma as a new Asian center.

My father never saw my mother again, as she passed away shortly after we left. My young privileged life was terminated abruptly. Like many others have done, we lost our adolescence and were forced to grow up fast. There is no cute childhood photo as a baby or toddler to share with my own child, only memories of rupture. We left our former life behind, our past obliterated. My parents did not live to see a free Burma. But for the people living inside and outside of Burma currently, and for future generations, there is hope of an end to exile and displacement.

TinTin Delphin

Chapter 1. Royal Kingdom to British Colony to Independence

The Night before the Coup

"Quiet, children! Stop jumping on the sofa! You know the men are meeting downstairs!" called Captain *Kyaw Khine*. He was the trusted aide de camp or personal bodyguard of Brigadier General *Aung Gyi*, my uncle.

"Let's play a board game. Afterwards I'll tell you a story; then it's bedtime for you two."

In Burma, storytelling is a big part of children's life; family members and servants use stories to entertain, teach, guide, and discipline children. Bedtime stories may be life experiences, legends, folklore, tales of royal families, or teachings of Buddha. Bedtime stories told by Uncle's personal bodyguards would contain very impressive and heroic acts of real battlefield events. Bedtime stories from family members are different but just as entertaining. They are more legendary and mythical in nature, about princes and princesses, divine intercessions and interventions, treachery, bravery, love and sacrifice. We learn about the duality of good and evil, and good always prevails. We also learn about the history of Burma, the atrocities of war, and the courage and bravery of the soldiers fighting for Burma's independence from foreign domination.

The day was March 1, 1962. Dagon House is the official government guesthouse; it is also my Uncle's official residence. High level government meetings and state functions are held in the downstairs meeting rooms and banquet hall. The entire upstairs is private. This is where *TuTu* and I spend most of our time after school when visiting him. Our own family remains at the Victorian government mansion on *U Wizara* Road. *TuTu* and I would visit Uncle several times a week and often slept over.

Today the meeting went on long after we were put to bed. Later that evening I was awakened by a heated argument downstairs. General *Ne Win* was planning an army takeover of the civilian government, but Uncle *Aung*

Gyi was against it. Uncle left the meeting early to attend another state function.

After my uncle left the house, the rest of the officers went ahead in planning the coup. General *Ne Win* not only planned and organized the coup, he executed it personally by ordering every battalion of the armed forces to move according to his detailed plan, without the full knowledge and cooperation of his right-hand man, Brigadier General *Aung Gyi*.

Land of the Golden Pagodas

Burma has a long turbulent history encompassing wars and invasions by the Mongols, the British, and the Japanese, uprisings against Chinese communists, anti-Mao KMTs (Kuomintang), ethnic insurgencies, and half a century of military dictatorship. The country is a collage of serene landscapes, lush rice fields, carefree people, and timeless cultural and architectural beauty of towering pagodas and Buddhist temples.

A predominantly Buddhist country with strongly religious people, Burma is a land of love, compassion and goodwill. Burma is about the size of Texas, with an estimated population in 1962 of 27 million. By 2015–16, the population had more than doubled to an estimated 55 to 59 million. Burma is a peninsula about 1200 miles long and 575 miles wide, situated strategically between China in the northeast and India in the west, bordered by the Andaman Sea and the Bay of Bengal in the south. The Golden Land is fertile with abundant rain, sunshine and rich alluvial soil for agriculture, and it is neither overcrowded nor are its people underfed. It is well endowed with abundant minerals, oil and natural gas and valuable teak, mahogany and other exotic monsoon hardwoods from tropical rain forests. Burma is blessed with large deposits of gold, silver, tin, antimony, zinc, copper, tungsten, lead, coal, and limestone. Much of the world's most coveted pigeon-blood red rubies, blue sapphires and the most sought-after jade and amber are also from Burmese mines in the hilly regions in the north. The mighty Irrawaddy and its tributaries are the life-blood of the country, rising from the Himalayas in the Kachin state of northern Burma and meandering south for over a thousand miles before emptying into the Andaman Sea. The Irrawaddy yields abundant hydroelectric power and fertile and productive soil suitable for growing rice, beans and pulses, cotton, sugarcane, tea, rubber and other agriculture products. The Burmese coastal waters are rich with fish, prawns and other seafood as well as beautiful pearls.

Besides its rich natural deposits, Burma is highly bio diverse, both in species and ecosystems. Its dense tropical rain forests are home to hundreds of different types of exotic mammals, reptiles, birds and plants. Burma is also endowed with an astonishing array of landscapes ranging from jungle to the snow covered Himalayas where red pandas and tigers roam, to palm tree lined beaches on its western and southern coasts. The Upper Irrawaddy River is home to fresh water dolphins and the region contains lush rain forests, the prime source of legendary Burmese teak. Sun drenched emerald green paddy fields cover the Lower Irrawaddy River region and mangrove forests thrive in the Irrawaddy Delta. Here, the river splits into nine branches and a myriad of creeks and waterways, meandering southward and emptying into the sea. Southwest of the delta region is the unspoiled Mergui (*Myeik*) Archipelago with its spectacular marine wilderness, coral reefs, limestone caves and, hidden lagoons. *Myeik* Archipelago consists of more than 800 pristine islands in crystal clear water and virgin white sandy beaches.

Burma is appropriately called the Land of Golden Pagodas, rich in cultural heritage, an enchanted land of lost dreams. Children who seldom see foreigners, especially outside the big cities, will follow visitors, giggling and wide-eyed, full of curiosity. Unlike many commercialized tourist destinations, the people are not predatory but treat visitors with a kindness and curiosity that is refreshing. It is rare to be gouged by vendors, taxi drivers or common Burmese folks.

Religious People

Theravada Buddhism, the form of Buddhism that is closest to Buddha's original teaching, might have originated in India but it blossomed in Burma. This is also the religion of the people in Laos, Thailand, and Cambodia. Mahayana Buddhism is predominantly practiced in China and Japan. Although the majority of Burmese are Buddhists, the country is also home to Hindus, Muslims, Baha'is, Christians and animists who coexist in their communities. Christianity was brought into the country by missionaries from Europe and America around the 19th century. Many minority ethnic groups were converted from their traditional tribal beliefs to Christianity by missionaries who built schools in border states and taught them English. About 90% of the population actively practices Theravada Buddhism and its magnificent cultural heritage. Buddhism is not just a religion here. It is a way of life and an integral part of daily routine. It is a philosophy and influences customs, outlook on life, social and intellectual values, entertainment and political system. Buddhists conform to a comprehensive framework of religion to find meaningful interpretations of the world. The people accept and obey traditional religious beliefs and practices including self-control, toler-ance, forgiveness and generosity.

Concept of Hpone

Theravada Buddhism teaches the three gems — *hpaya* (Buddha), *dhamma* (scriptures), and *sangha* (the saffron-robed Buddhist clergy and monastic community). Buddhist scriptures teach about everyday life and how to cope with the events and situations common to all people such as pain, disease, fear, disappointment, loss, lust, sadness and anger. Burmese children must respect and honor parents; children and parents respect and honor teachers; children, parents and teachers respect and honor monks; children, parents, teachers and monks respect and honor Buddha. This has been the belief and practice of Burmese Buddhists since the beginning of Theravada many centuries ago.

Although men and women are treated equal in work and other aspects of life, in religious interpretation men are considered of a higher order. Men can be ordained as monks, a station in monastic life higher than that of nuns. In Buddhism only men are born with the spiritual aura called *hpone*. Men possess *hpone*, and monks possess a higher order of *hpone* than men, but women and nuns do not have it. This spirituality or *hpone* allows men and monks to reach enlightenment as Buddha did, while women lack this attainment.

Hpone must be respected and guarded, so women are not allowed to touch monks (*hpongyis*), not even young novices. It is also taboo for boys and men to walk under a clothes line hung with women's *longyis*, as that would negatively impact their *hpone*.

> Once, walking across an open field, my cousin Robert carried my folded longyi (sarong) as I was eating a juicy slice of watermelon. That was a serious transgression of his hpone and my big aunt, his mother, was outraged. I had to shiko[1] Robert three times to cleanse him and redeem his hpone.

Concept of Reincarnation and Kutho

Burma is blessed with abundant sunshine, rain and fertile soil, giving its people a simple and easy life of stability, contentment and an absence of want. Buddhists believe in reincarnation and the cycle of rebirth. There are no gods to pray to or ask for help because one's destiny is the outcome of one's actions during one's prior life. It is therefore important to do meri-torious deeds to obtain *kutho* and climb up to higher states of existences in future reincarnations. As a human, one has achieved a higher order of life than an animal, but the rest, life as a human, rich or poor, healthy or not, is

---

[1] To *shiko'* is to kneel down on the floor with both hands joined in prayer position and head bowed before a superior or an elder as a gesture of respect.

the result of your own doing. As devout Buddhists, Burmese people generously give alms or donations to the *sangha* (Buddhist clergy), meditate, pray and chant scriptures and incantation at places of worship on a regular basis to accumulate merits in the next existence.

For generations under authoritarian military rule the people of Burma have been subjected to non-Buddhist ideas such as discrimination, racism and radicalism, but they survive tyranny and crippling poverty with Buddhist spiritual resilience and remarkable tolerance. They learn to tolerate hardships and are generally contented, even with lower expectations of life. As practicing Buddhists, they are reluctant to take the life of any creature, even that of an annoying fly, a venomous spider, or a pariah dog, many of which roam the streets undisturbed. Unlike other religions, Buddhism teaches patience and endurance embracing all people and Buddhists do not try to convert anyone to their religion. This may be the reason there has never been any wars fought in the name of Buddhism.

Although my parents were Christians, they allowed us to visit pagodas and monasteries with relatives to learn Buddhist teachings. We grew up accepting both faiths and traditions. Grandma, aunts, and uncles all practiced Buddhism and there was a Buddha altar in the family home. The Buddha is honored with silver bowls containing water, rice, meat curries, and vegetable dishes offered daily as meals are freshly prepared. Often fresh flowers and fruits are included as offering to the Buddha. The servants wake up early to cook rice and curries for Grandma and aunts to offer to the monks when they make their morning rounds. The steam from fresh cooked sweet jasmine rice fills your nostrils, waking up your morning appetite. Barefoot monks clad in long robes arrive, holding their black lacquer alms bowls open. They walk in single file to accept food, chanting and giving blessings to the donors, as family members scoop out their first meal. Monks cannot consume food after 12:00 noon. Out of respect and veneration, the donated food is the best and freshest that families can afford. Good food is a big incentive for me to visit monasteries with Grandma and the aunts even though it meant sitting through lengthy Buddhist chant in ancient Pali or Sanskrit, never understanding a word. At my parents' house, there is no shrine or altar, but lots of artwork, some flowers, and a piano Mommy had arranged to ship in from abroad.

Homage to the Shwedagon

Growing up in Rangoon, one of my favorite adventures is to visit the mighty Shwedagon with TuTu and my aunts. The Shwedagon is one of the wonders of the world and the most sacred shrine in Burma. The majestisc stupa is 325 feet high, built on the hill near the Kandaw Gyi Lake, dominating Rangoon's skyline. My aunts told me that the Buddha's hair is enshrined in the stupa and the sacred dome is covered with 60 tons of pure gold. That would be valued at about $8 billion today! The spire at the top, or hti (pronounced 'tea'), is encrusted with big diamonds, rubies, emeralds, sapphires, jade and other precious stones from the mines of Burma. Grandma told me that the very tip of the top, the hti is crowned with a 76 carat diamond, larger than the Hope Diamond. According to history, Queen Shin Sawbu donated her weight in gold to enshrine the Shwedagon. Many Burmese monarchs throughout history and wealthy Buddhists people from all over the country have donated and continue to give money and gold to the Shwedagon to build and maintain the spectacular pagoda. The Shwedagon has four entrances each is guarded by a pair of two-story high mythical lions with dragon heads called chinthe. Each of the four entrances leads to a wide stairway consisting of about 130 steps. The western entrance is also equipped with a modern elevator for those who prefer a short cut to the main pagoda level.

As children, we prefer climbing the steps, as it is a journey full of stimulating sights, sounds and smells, with all sorts of vendors lined up on either side of the steps. The Shwedagon visit is not just paying homage to Buddha, it is an exciting bazaar shopping experience with colorful sights, sounds, flavors, and fragrances. Shop stalls sell flowers, candles, incense, toys, brass bells, gongs and cymbals, lacquer ware, gold leaf, and exotic puppets and toys. When we get hungry, we can stop, as there food stalls offering tasty Burmese specialties and exotic snacks. My aunts would buy flowers, candles and incense as offerings. A few times we bought brass gongs and cymbals for the family altar. On special occasions such as Buddhist Lent, they would buy gold leaf for donation. Gold leaf offerings are made of 24 carat pure gold that has been beaten paper thin; it is used to cover the glistening pagoda or to repair and maintain the gilded stupa/dome throughout the year. Over the years, hundreds or thousands of layers of gold leaf have been added on the pagoda dome and Buddha images. No one knows how thick the gold covering is today. The stairs are also lined on either side with giant murals with graphic portrayals of life on earth, heaven and hell. These over-sized colorful murals and paintings depict Buddhism principles, tales and folklore, palace and court costume and pageantry, temple and court scenes. Life in tranquil Nirvana is also portrayed, contrasted by fires, fierce looking mythical creatures, and boiling cauldrons and brimstone tortures of hell. The adults will embellish these painted murals with elaborate tales detailing how disobedient kids end up being swallowed by Mother Earth or are fed to the scary mythical creatures.

We have arrived at the main level of the Shwedagon. The terrace is surrounded by elaborately gilded stupas, shrines, and decorated pavilions. There are eight shrines on the main level, because Burmese astrology recognizes eight days in a week, with Wednesday divided into two parts. The shrines are placed around the eight corners of the octagonal stupa. Worshipers can pick their birth-date shrine to pray, pour water, and offer incense, candles, paper umbrellas and flowers. The shrines include animals, as each day is associated with a different animal. Monday is tiger, Tuesday is lion, Wednesday morning is tusked elephant, afternoon is tuskless elephant, Thursday is mouse, Friday is guinea pig, Saturday is dragon serpent and Sunday is a winged gryphon, a legendary creature with the head and wings of an eagle and the body of a lion. My birthday is Saturday and the shrine with the mythical dragon serpent is called naga. The Burmese name for a person born on a Saturday must begin with a 'T', as in TinTin.

Ethnic Nationalities of Burma

Burma is a beautiful and unspoiled exotic land with its mosaic of 135 distinct ethnic tribes and sub tribes, each with its own culture, language and religion, and many have their own armies. They practice ancient traditions, mores and faith and wear colorful clothing decorated with silver coins, bracelets and anklets.

About two thirds of the population are of the *Bamar* race, a Burmese-speaking people. The *Bamar* originally came from the north and occupied the upper and central plains near the Irrawaddy River. Today they live predominantly in the Irrawaddy River basin but also occupy the central seven divisions of the country. The *Bamar* people are of Tibeto-Burman origin and 90% are Buddhists and their language, Burmese, is also the official language of the country.

In 1989 the military government under dictator General *Than Shwe* changed the name of the country from Burma to *Myanmar* and the capital Rangoon to *Yangon*. Arakan state is now *Rakhine*. Cities, streets and other landmarks with colonial English names were also renamed with Burmese-language names. Both names are internationally recognized and are used in this book, with Burmese names and words italicized or in parenthesis for clarity. For example, the Karen people are now called *Kayin*.

Burma is divided into seven states representing seven major ethnic nationalities — 8% Shan, 7.5% *Kayin* or Karen, 3% *Rakhine* or Arakanese, 2% Mon, 1.5% Kachin, <0.75% Chin, and 0.05% *Kayah or* Karenni. With the exception of Arakan state on the western coastal region, the ethnic states are located in resource-rich hilly regions bordering the country. Most Kachin, Chin, Karen and Karenni are Christians due to Western missionary presence building churches and schools and teaching Christianity, English and Western thinking to the locals. They also provided free education and health services in these ethnic regions. The Arakanese are predominantly Buddhists living with a minority Muslim group, now internationally known as the *Rohingya*.

An estimated 6–7 million Shan live in Shan State in eastern Burma but smaller Shan communities also live in Kachin State to the north, and bordering countries of China, Thailand and Laos. The Karen people number around 6.5 million and live in Karen state in the southern and south eastern part of the country, but thousands live across the border in Thailand as refugees or in a state of limbo. An estimated 3 million live in Arakan, western Burma, along the Bay of Bengal, most are Arakanese Buddhists. Of the estimated 1.5 million Muslims who lived in Arakan, more than half now live in refugee camps in Bangladesh. They are not recognized as an official ethnic minority group by the government of Burma. Mon State is situated in the southern part of Burma and borders *Bago* (formerly Pegu) Region, *Tanintharyi* (formerly Tenasserim) Region and Karen State. It has access to the Andaman Sea. An estimated 2 million people live in Mon state. The Mon are considered to be one of the first peoples in Southeast Asia and the earliest group to settle in Burma. They were responsible for spreading Theravada Buddhism in Burma and Thailand. The Kachin, estimated to number between 1 to 1.5 million, are traditionally hill dwellers subsisting on rotational cultivation of hill rice. About 500,000 Chin live in Chin State in the northwest which separates Burma from India and 300,000 live in *Kayah* or Karenni state located between Karen and Shan state along Burma's border with Thailand.

The Seven-Decade Civil War

Burma has experienced colonialism, communism, fascism, and socialism, among other ideologies and movements, creating a highly complex multi ethnic, multi-racial and multi religious country. The country has a history of continuous political unrest and wars against foreign domination, fighting the British, then the Japanese, followed by battles with communists and the nationalist KMTs (*Kuomintang*) of China. Even after independence, its long history of wars continues with diverse armed ethnic minorities in bordering provinces who want autonomy from the central *Bamar* government rule. As the dominant group of the country, most of the military and the central government is ethnically *Bamar*. The ethnic minority groups took up arms against the *Bamar* ethnic dominated central government to protect their territorial rights to ancestral land. The fight to control natural deposits and deep-rooted cultural and religious differences also contributed to almost seven decades in armed struggle of civil war as these ethnic regions are well endowed in raw material deposits.

Under British rule, the tribal groups favored the colonizers as they were viewed as protectors from the Burmans/*Bamar* army. When World War II broke out *Bogyoke* (General) *Aung San* led the *Bamar* army to join the Japanese army to push the colonialists out, the ethnic minorities (Karen, Kachin, and Chin, and Karenni) fought alongside the British against the joint forces of the Japanese and the *Bamar* fighters. The Japanese promised independence once the British were pushed out. When the Japanese occupied the country but failed to grant Burma independent rule, *Aung San* switched sides and aligned the Burmese army with the allies to drive the Japanese out of Burma. After the war, *Bogyoke Aung San* wrote the *Panglong* Agreement to grant ethnic minorities the same rights as the *Bamar* people and to be autonomous with the right to rule their own regions. Unfortunately, General *Aung San* was assassinated before Burma received its independence, and the country was left in war ravaged chaos. Gone were the promises of *Aung San's Panglong* Agreement which were never honored by any subsequent civilian or Burmese military governments. So the ethnic groups took up arms and rebelled against the central government, and the fighting continues to this day. This is one of the longest civil wars in the history of mankind, lasting almost seventy years as of this writing.

While each minority ethnic group is different, they have one thing in common — they have all been oppressed by the *Bamar*-dominated military government. The junta exploits the resources of the minority ethnic regions and controls mining and extraction of minerals and gems by confiscating ethnic land and forcing villagers out of their homes, frequently displacing whole communities. The human rights abuses committed by the Burmese armed forces against the tribal people include sexual harassment, kidnapping, torture, mutilations and arbitrary killings. *Tatmadaw*, the armed forces also loot and burn villages and use child soldiers and lay land mines that kill or cripple civilians. Hundreds of thousands of villagers have fled to neighboring countries like Thailand seeking asylum. Most end up in disease-stricken refugee camps and many die of malaria, typhoid and other infectious diseases.

Royal Kingdom to British Colony

Burma was ruled by monarchies and various dynasties since the 9th century. The royal kingdom of Burma ended when the last king of Burma, King *Thibaw*, was defeated by the British in 1885 and exiled to India.

Burma has suffered under many foreign hands, with conflicts between rival kingdoms, invasion by Genghis Khan and the Mongols, the Anglo–Burmese wars, and the Japanese occupation. Bordering countries also have interest in Burma and its natural resources and many wars have been fought with neighboring Thailand and China. The country suffered during the two World Wars and was invaded and occupied by two imperial powers, the British and the Japanese. There were three brutal Anglo–Burmese wars over sixty years, in 1825, 1852 and 1885, at the end of which the British colonized the country in 1886 and annexed it as a province of the greater British Indian Empire. They set up a colonial government in Rangoon that ruled until the outbreak of World War II. The British wanted access to teak forests, oil wells, mineral deposits, and ruby, sapphire, amber and jade mines as well as access to the vast Chinese market through its northern border.

At that time Burma was ruled by a monarchy and was easy prey. King *Thibaw*, the last king of Burma, was only 28 years old. The British traveled up the Irrawaddy River to Mandalay, then the capital, and attacked the palace, capturing the young monarch and his queen. The king was overthrown relatively easily by the British in 1886. King *Thibaw* and Queen *Supayalat* were exiled to British-ruled India. They were carted away in bullock carts like common criminals. Burma became a colony of Britain in 1886 and it stayed that way for six decades.

The people of Burma deeply resented this colonization and the disrespectful treatment of their monarch. The British looted the palace artifacts, priceless treasures and crown jewels, and plundered the land. The British also shot, beheaded and hanged many Burmese who fought them, armed only with swords and machetes. For decades following the British takeover, armed resistance brewed but was crushed by the better armed foreigners.

When World War II started, Germany formed an alliance with Italy and Japan and became Britain's archenemies. This provided an opportunity to fight the British and push them out of Burma. The Burmese resistance groups immediately joined the Japanese who invaded the colony, with the agreement Burma would be free once the British were driven out. However, the Japanese did nothing of the kind. It is therefore no surprise that Burmese armed resistance switched sides and fought with the allies against the Japanese. After the war the people were tired of foreign invasion and plundering; a nationalist movement developed and the resistance leader General *Aung San* negotiated and received independence from the British in 1948.

Colonial Rule

When the British annexed Burma to the British Indian Empire in 1862, a flood of Indians immigrated to Burma to take advantage of the post war boom. The colonial government made huge sums of money selling teak, petroleum, metal, precious stones, and other extractions from Burma, but the Burmese people remained poor and did not benefit from the growing economy.

The British built roads, railroads, river transport and ports to move raw material deposits out of the country. They built commercial buildings, churches and other cultural and religious centers, Victorian mansions for their families, cinemas, private golf, polo and tennis clubs, and sports stadiums for their entertainment and pleasure. It is therefore natural for the people of Burma to harbor strong distaste for colonialism and want to be free from such foreign domination and exploitation of their country's natural wealth.

The British denied administrative jobs to the Burmese and instead, recruited Indians to fulfill important government posts as they did in India in the name of the British Indian Empire. They encouraged migration of Indians to Burma. Hundreds of thousands of Indians came to Burma and the Indians even outnumbered the Burmans (*Bamar*) in some key cities. In

Rangoon, then the capital, half the population was Indian and only about a third Burmese. Many Indians who migrated into the country on the coattails of British colonialists prospered, owning real estate and business enterprises at the expense of the local *Bamar* people. During the colonial era, given the favorable treatment by the British, the Indians ran much of the country's finance and commerce and were disliked by the local *Bamar* for this unfair competitive edge.

The Indians began to prosper and owned much of Rangoon, everything from corner betel nut shops to large factories, including banks, businesses and big bazaars. They worked as criminal court judges, government administrators, pharmacy dispensers and prison wardens. The working class labored on farms and mines, tailored clothes, or worked as housekeepers, cooks, drivers, and gardeners. Indians were everywhere. Consequently, economic grievances and hostility brewed. The British also recruited and trained the Indians as soldiers to reinforce the British army and recruited non *Bamar* ethnic nationalities of Kachin, Chin and Karen into its local imperial army and formed ethnic battalions.

To alleviate the labor shortage and to provide the needed manpower, the British encouraged immigration of not only Indians but also Chinese, rather than train locals. The Burmese began to suffer mounting unemployment and poverty under the British rule. Dislike and anger grew and opposition to British rule began to build among Buddhist monks and university students. One of the Rangoon University students was *Aung San*, who later led his Thirty Comrades and fought for Burma's independence.

Meanwhile, the Indian and Chinese immigrants built businesses, and English-proficient Indians worked as civil servants and construction workers. They thrived economically, dominating commercial life in the country, opening shops and businesses. Many Indians prospered through their association and connections with the British. Resentment grew. As the Burmese people were devout Buddhists, there were also cultural conflicts. Foreigners refused to remove their shoes when entering sacred places such as pagodas, temples, and monasteries; this was seen as disrespectful toward Buddhism. Foreigners began to marry Burmese women or kept them as mistresses, as well, causing anti-Chinese and anti-Indian sentiment and periodic riots.

During the colonial era, Western missionaries arrived and built churches. The missionaries were especially successful at converting ethnic minorities like Kachin, Chin and Karen people to Christianity. They also built schools and hospitals, providing education and healthcare in the tribal communities.

As the post war economy flourished, Burma became a major rice exporter of the east and Rangoon became a cosmopolitan city where churches with towering steeples now sprinkled the skyline amid the pagodas, mosques and temples. Colonial Rangoon was also a commercial hub and trading center for agricultural products, Burma's largest export. The country was one of the region's wealthiest nations of the time.

Independence

Meanwhile anti colonialism sentiment brewed and Burmese nationalism increasingly grew among the university students and the Buddhist *sangha*, monk community. As a young student from Rangoon University, *Aung San* began to organize a resistance movement to fight against the colonial rule.

In the 1930s a group of young nationalists led by *Aung San* known as Thirty Comrades or Thirty *Thakins* (Masters), formed the Burma Independence Army, BIA. They joined the Japanese army and forced the withdrawal of the British. The Japanese invaded Burma to close off the Burma Road, the main supply line to Southern China. With the support of the Japanese forces, British and Indian soldiers were pushed back to the jungles and mountains of the eastern Indian border in mass retreat. Once Burma was free of the colonialists, the Japanese took over the country.

They failed to keep their agreement with General *Aung San* to return the country to the people of Burma. Instead, the Japanese soldiers brutally tortured the Burmese, molested the women and plundered the cities. The soldiers burnt homes and shops, looted and raped Burmese girls and women, and tortured anyone who dared to resist their demands. The Japanese masters were worse than the British, so General *Aung San* created the Anti Fascist People's Freedom League, AFPFL, to fight the Japanese. When World War II broke out and the Japanese dishonored the agreement, General *Aung San* switched sides and joined the US and allied forces and pushed the Japanese out of Burma.

General *Aung San* and his comrades successfully fought two wars, first against British imperialism and later against Japanese fascist military rule. In 1947 General *Aung San* went to England and negotiated with the British for independence. With a national united front as AFPFL, General *Aung San* led the group towards freedom from foreign domination and exploitation to independence.

Just prior to independence, General *Aung San* and his cabinet members were gunned down in the bloodiest assassination in the history of Burma. The following year, on January 4, 1948, the British lowered their Union Jack for the last time as the new flag of the Union of Burma was raised in front of the Secretariat Building in Rangoon, which, for over half a century, had been the seat of the British rule. Burma is now an independent parliamentary democracy free from foreign rule and domination. *U Nu*, one of General *Aung San's* patriotic colleagues, inherited the leadership responsibility following the assassination.

Independence Day, January 4, is celebrated with parades, music, dances, and feasts throughout the nation. The army celebrates with a show of land, air and naval power and military might of *Tatmadaw*.

> The army tailor made two children-sized female army officer uniforms for TuTu and me. We were excited to be Tatmadaw soldiers for the day, in our olive green skirts, khaki shirts, and matching green berets. They were exact replicas of the ladies' army uniforms and we wore them with pride and saluted like Tatmadaw officers. Due to Uncle Aung Gyi's hectic schedule attending multiple official functions, his ADC, Captain Kyaw Khine, took us for a ride in the army helicopter. It was our first experience to see the city of Rangoon in full view under our feet. The boys, my brother Albert and my cousin Robert, got a ride in a twin-engine twin-fan high speed lift helicopter that carried soldiers into the battlefield and was used as a specialized gunship. All of us were treated to the panoramic aerial view of the parade. Later that day we toured a military training camp where the soldiers took us for a ride in a real battle tank. The tank plowed through some rough jungle terrain with felled trees, deep ditches and trenches with a smooth rolling motion as if it were sailing over the waves in the ocean. It was a day of adventure and stunning impressions for the four cousins.

Post-Independence Turmoil

Prior to independence but after the war, General *Aung San* was the head of a transitional government. He demanded total political and economic freedom from the British, who signed an agreement guaranteeing Burma's independence within a year. *Aung San* also negotiated the *Panglong* Agreement on February 12, 1947, with Shan, Chin, and Kachin ethnic leaders and signed the agreement that guaranteed them the freedom to choose their own political destiny after independence. The Agreement would give minority ethnic nationalities equal rights as the *Bamar* people and political autonomy and equality without discrimination. However, the *Panglong* agreement was not fulfilled. While a political conference was in session, the communists, led by *Galon U Saw*, armed with machine guns, broke into the Secretariat Building in Rangoon and gunned down General *Aung San* and his eight cabinet ministers. *Galon U Saw* had been the Prime Minister during the colonial era and had obtained weapons from a British army officer.

Galon U Saw was executed by hanging. Meanwhile, trouble also brewed within the political party of AFPFL. The communist faction of the AFPFL nearly split the group but in the end decided to shelve their ideology and unite in a combined resistance against the enemy, foreign influence and domination. AFPFL held together during the crisis and *U Nu*, one of General *Aung San's* patriotic colleagues and the chairman of AFPFL, was elected prime minister after independence. General *Aung San*, the father of independence, is revered as a national and independence hero.

Unlike other British colonies around the globe, Burma did not become a member of the commonwealth after independence. General *Aung San* had negotiated for complete freedom from the British without any dominion status. Burma became an independent republic named the Union of Burma. From 1948 to 1962, Burma had a full-fledged democratic parliamentary government, with *U Nu* as the first Prime Minister to lead the fragile new parliament and war ravaged country.[1]

Other young political figures of the time stepped in as prominent nationalists and leaders of the newly independent Burma. Among them were General *Ne Win*, who later became chief of staff, and Brigadier General *Aung Gyi*, who later became vice chief of staff of Burma's army. Other notable generals and politicians were Brigadier *Maung Maung*, Brigadier *Aung Shwe*, *U Kyaw Nyein*, and *U Ba Swe*. Following independence, the country was experiencing widespread conflicts and constitutional disputes among different political groups. Various factions of political parties including socialists, communists, nationalists and ethnic minority groups rose up against the new fragile government of *U Nu*.

Civil war also erupted due to internal conflicts between *Tatmadaw* and various armed regional ethnic nationalities who sought greater autonomy. They felt betrayed when General *Aung San's Panglong* agreement was not honored after independence. Ethnic nationalities also wanted their own independence and took up arms against the new central Burman or *Bamar* government of *U Nu*.

The Shan, Karen (*Kayin*), Kachin, Chin, Karenni (*Kayah*), Mon, and Arakan (*Rakhine*) all wanted self-determination and had always aspired to control of their respective regions. They remembered World War II when the Japanese betrayed General *Aung San* and refused to turn over the country after the British were defeated. Many ethnic nationalities, including a large group of the Karens, had fought alongside the allies and General *Aung San* against the Japanese to drive them out of Burma. After independence, when General *Aung San's Panglong* agreement was not addressed, the ethnic people felt their sacrifice was not repaid and their loyalty betrayed.

---

[1] Burmese honorific titles precede names the way Sir or Lady, or The Honorable, are used in English. Examples include *U, Ko*, and *Maung* for men, and *Daw* and *Ma* for women. Prime Minister *Nu* is therefore called *U Nu*.

Fighting from several factions was also widespread inside the newly independent state. Mao's persistent Chinese communist insurgents and US-backed anti-communist KMTs (*Kuomintang*) rebels, both from across the border, were invading northern Burma. The drug lords and rebels, equipped with powerful war weaponry, continued internal wars with *Tatmadaw* in the remote poppy-growing regions of the Golden Triangle which borders Burma, Thailand and Laos, as they operated the lucrative opiate, heroin and amphetamine trade. Burma is the second largest opium producer in the world after Afghanistan.

After Burma regained independence and the British left, armed insurgencies broke out from the ethnic nationalities. The Burma Communist Party, BCP, also wanted to overthrow the new fragile government. Former Burmese revolutionaries, Chinese communists, hard line socialists, defectors from the Burma Independence Army and other communist sympathizers joined BCP and took their operations underground and continued power struggle with *U Nu's* new administration.

The country was left war torn and shattered with most of the cities burnt to the ground by World War II air raids and bombings. Burma's new leaders were faced with the monumental task of leading and rebuilding a war-ravaged country, with political insurgents and armed ethnic nationalities who threatened to break away from the central government. Adding to the challenge was a severe shortage of well trained and educated political and business leaders. Most government and civil positions had been held by Indians, and many of them fled when the British left, fearing repercussions from the new Burmese government. Rampant lawlessness also prevailed, especially in the remote areas, due to readily available weapons left from World War II.

> I met Prime Minister U Nu twice during my childhood. We had dinner at his house with his wife Daw Mya Yi. U Nu had a round face and lopsided smile when he talked. I saw him again at our house when my parents reciprocated their hospitality. He was a religious man and wouldn't hurt a fly, as it was against Buddhist principles to kill any living creature.

U Nu was a pious and devout Buddhist and ruled the country based on Buddhist principles of trust and tolerance rather than a definitive political ideology. He devoted his energy to promote Buddhism and placed religious issues above political and economic crises. He traveled throughout the country, preaching Buddhist principles and way of life to all citizens. People held his sandals when entering pagodas and monasteries just as the Indians did for Mahatma Gandhi. Women waited in his path and spread their long hair for him to walk on. He devoted more time to meditation and religion than to resolving political dissent and the deteriorating national situation. With blind faith in an idealistic dogma, he made Buddhism the state religion causing more friction with ethnic minorities, many of whom were Christians or had preserved their traditional tribal beliefs and practices. The ethnic groups also felt betrayed as the 10-year secession clause of the *Panglong* agreement was not addressed by *U Nu's* new government. They took up arms and began to seek support from neighboring China to wage war against the Burmese government and to secede from Burma.

Thus by the early 1960s, Burma was troubled by a widespread insurgency, ethnic unrest and the invasion of Chinese communist forces in the north. The newly independent country was in disarray and was on the brink of disintegration. *U Nu's* political party AFPFL began to fall apart due to a split into two rival factions, the yellow Clean AFPFL faction under *U Nu* and *Thakin Tin*, and the red Stable AFPFL faction under *U Ba Swe* and *U Kyaw Nyein*.

Moreover, the Communist Party of Burma was infiltrating *U Nu's* administration through the National United Front, NUF, led by *Thakin Than Tun*, General *Aung San's* brother-in-law. Prime Minister *U Nu* was deeply guided by Buddhist principles of trust and tolerance. But these principles could not defeat the communists or armed ethnic insurgents in the bordering states nor could they tame unruly and corrupt politicians of his administration. Eventually, *U Nu's* government found itself in the midst of the civil war with armed ethnic minorities.

Chapter 2. Military Coup

The Day of the Coup

The trampoline-style sofa hopping and Chinese checkers game at Dagon House ended with dinner and a bedtime story. The next morning, as we were being taken to school, I saw army tanks and trucks rolling into the streets and armed soldiers were everywhere. When the driver picked us up to go home, I saw more tanks and trucks in the streets and soldiers in government buildings, city hall, Rangoon University, and the Presidential Palace.

There was no television in Burma until the 1980s but the radio repeatedly broadcast the announcement, "Tatmadaw has taken control of the country with a military coup. President U Win Maung, Prime Minister U Nu and all cabinet ministers have been put under house arrest and the constitution has been abolished by the armed forces led by General Ne Win."

The Burmese army took the reins from an ineffective and corrupt civilian government. The military coup was supposed to be bloodless, but a student from our school was shot and killed by the army. He was seventeen-year-old Mimi Thaik, a classmate of my brother Albert. Mimi's father, Sao Shwe Thaik, was the sawbwa (chief) of the Shan tribe and nationality; he became the first president of Burma when the country got independence from the British in 1948. Mimi was fatally shot at his house by a Tatmadaw soldier when he tried to protect his father from being arrested by the soldiers.

School as Usual

Our parents kept life at home as routine and normal as possible to help us feel secure in times of chaos. We focused on school, with after-school programs like piano or language lessons and swimming practice. Both my parents had received a Western education and spoke English fluently. Papa went to St Paul's Boys School and Mommy went to an American school abroad. Living in Rangoon, colonial era imports like Horlicks and Ovaltine,

Cadbury chocolates, and English biscuits were staples at our house. Papa enjoyed Johnny Walker more than local fermented-palm toddy and Mommy preferred shopping at Rowe & Co over Thein Gyi Ze wet market. Everything from air conditioners to automobiles, toothpaste and toilet paper were imported as Burma was primarily an agriculture country. Ballet shoes, tutus and all our party dresses were purchased abroad. Being musically inclined, Mommy made sure I learn to play a musical instrument. She had a piano imported from Hong Kong. We continued our music and dance lessons in the midst of the crisis in the government. The days following the army coup, soldiers were everywhere, inside and outside buildings and on the streets. The new military government announced the establishment of 'the Burmese Way to Socialism'. The adults began talking about the army taking over this business and that hospital, police headquarters, airport, central rail, and seaports. We were told not to visit Uncle at Dagon House for several days as he was busy running the affairs of the country.

Grandma, the Matriarch

Like many Asian cultures, Burmese families extend beyond the nuclear family, including grandparents, aunts, uncles, and cousins living in one household. Our extended family in Rangoon included three generations living together. The government provided our family a colonial mansion on a tree-lined boulevard named U Wizara Road. Papa's grandma's ancestors were direct descendants of Dalaban, a Mon Knight and warrior of the royal kingdom of the Mon tribe. During King Alaungpaya's reign, Dalaban was the most respected and feared warrior of his time. Mon people were the first ethnic group of people that came to Southeast Asia and were the major source of influence on Burmese culture, spreading Theravada Buddhism into the country. Papa remembered his grandmother, Daw Thet, who owned the petroleum oil distributorship of Burma Oil Company. She also owned distributorships for Western-made cigarettes and iron hardware. She passed away long before I was born. Great-grandma Daw Thet prospered and the family business expanded into various sectors including agriculture and ownership in rice paddy plantations.

Papa's mother, my grandma Daw Kyin May, and her sister Daw Kyin Pu, were notorious for their dowager strength and business acumen as entrepreneurs. Through their intuitive skills and joint ventures the family enterprise grew from rice paddy fields to other crop plantations. Papa told me stories of how his aunt Daw Kyin Pu, armed with pistols, used to travel by boat with her fleet of barges carrying unmilled rice (with husks) along the Irrawaddy River. She and her convoy would stop at rice mills along the river and its remote meandering tributaries, delivering unpolished rice to the mills and collecting large sums of cash from the sale. She was a fearless and enterprising business woman even by today's standards. She never married and remained a lifelong career woman. Grandma and her pistol-toting sister Daw Kyin Pu owned land and other properties. It is quite common for women to own and operate businesses in Burma. Grandma Daw Kyin May was the matriarch of Papa's family. Papa's father died during the war and grandma raised six children single-handed. She was the unchallenged authority of the family and everyone respected and honored her wishes. Once, when grandma was ill, she wanted oranges but none were available as oranges were not cultivated on a commercial scale. However, within a few days the army delivered cases of large juicy oranges for her. Where did these big, beautiful, succulent oranges come from, each stamped with an English name? Years later I recognized the same big bright oranges in a supermarket in California, marked with the same stamp: 'Sunkist'.

Burmese women and men have equal rights under the law. As far back as the past dynasties of the Burmese monarchy, women were always granted equal rights in inheritance, marriage and divorce. They enjoyed equal legal rights as property owners and in the event of a divorce were entitled to half of the property accumulated during the marriage. When one generation passes, inheritance rights are also equally divided among men and women heirs. Burmese women keep their birth names after marriage. Burmese culture shows no preference towards boy babies. Girls are encouraged to attend school just as boys are, and education and the path to any profession are open to both equally. However, economic hardships would push families to choose to send boys over girls away from home for better opportunities in education and employment. In general Burmese women seem to be able to enjoy more freedom than their counterparts in some neighboring countries.

Thanaka

Thanaka is a natural organic beauty aid for girls and women, and even young boys use it as sunscreen. It is a light yellow cream made by grinding the bark or roots of thanaka tree (Murraya paniculata) with water. It has a pleasant, fragrant aroma and is applied to the face and arms as a skin conditioner and make-up foundation. Besides giving smooth and beautiful skin, thanaka also has a cooling effect on the skin and acts as both sunblock and astringent. The active ingredients in thanaka are anti-fungal and control oiliness by tightening pores and are known to help prevent pimples. Women who work in paddy fields planting rice seedlings in the hot summer months wear thick layers of thanaka on their faces and arms. Frequently, young girls are made up with thanaka on their faces in beautiful floral designs.

Grandma developed a restorative routine involving thanaka. While she was taking a shower, one of the servant girls would start grinding a thanaka root on a round stone slab with an indented channel around the rim to hold the water. She would grind the thanaka in circular motion using water from the channel until a creamy paste was formed. After the shower, she would help Grandma apply the thanaka on her face, arms and legs. She then gave Grandma a massage and invariably Grandma would drift into a relaxing slumber for hours.

The family house on U Wizara Road was an old Victorian mansion of the British era. There was a roundabout on U Wizara Road with the statue of U Wizara on top of a tall tower which I saw twice a day on my way to and from school. U Wizara was a famous Buddhist monk who opposed the British rule. He was arrested for protesting the colonial government's regulation against wearing of Buddhist robes in prison. He died after staging a hunger strike for 166 days.

Our family compound was secured and heavily guarded by Tatmadaw soldiers. Behind the main house was a row of housing for servants, cooks, gardeners, drivers, body guards and soldiers. After middle aunt passed away, Uncle moved to live at Dagon House. Once the estate of a Chinese tycoon, it now belonged to the government as the official state guesthouse that would host visiting dignitaries and other official guests of the government. My parents also maintained their own private residence in Park Lane near the Polish embassy. We had many pets. During General Ne Win's caretaker government, thousands of mangy diseased stray dogs were destroyed using poisoned meat. We were heart-broken when our dog was poisoned accidentally. She was pretty smart — she loved to chew gum and knew exactly when to spit it out. Albert also raised tropical fish in large concrete tanks in our yard and kept a poultry coop for his chickens. My hobbies were simple and low maintenance: playing and eating. From May through October, tropical monsoon brought heavy rain and wind. When it rained at night I could hear the mangoes dropping from our trees — thud — thud — thud, and in the early morning I would be the first one up with a bucket to run out and collect the delicious fruit. Sweet, juicy, tree-ripe mangoes are my favorite, besides durian, a distinctively pungent custard-like fruit with a spiky, alien-looking husk. In the garden there were three coconut palm trees giving us a source of fresh coconut water. Once, our mahli (gardener) climbed up the palm tree with his machete in hand but came sliding back down quick as lightning due to a snake encounter. Most Burmese vipers, such as like king cobras, are poisonous.

Uncle Aung Gyi

As young army officers Aung Gyi and Kyi Shein were colleagues and best friends within Tatmadaw, composed of the Army, the Navy and the Air Force. Captain Kyi Shein was married to my big aunt, Robert's mother. They met at Defense Officer Training in Mingaladon where Captain Kyi Shein was an army instructor. When the young, handsome Aung Gyi was introduced to my middle aunt, who was 12 years younger, he was smitten by her beauty and instantly fell head over heels in love. Colonel Aung Gyi's many years of persistent courtship and devotion paid off. They married and Aung Gyi's military career took off, rising rapidly from Captain to Colonel, to Brigadier, and Brigadier General.

Uncle Aung Gyi was mild-mannered and soft-spoken with high morals. He did not gamble, curse, or womanize. He was well-liked, respected and revered by the ordinary people of Burma as well as the soldiers and army officers. Although in the military rough language generously sprinkled with profanity was usual, even among the high ranking officers, no one ever heard Uncle use any swear words. Uncle had served in Tatmadaw from its beginning during the British colonial days until 1963 when he resigned from the Revolutionary Council, the supreme governing body of the time.

During the war he and General Ne Win worked together as close comrades in Burma's 4th Rifles, the elite military regiment fighting for Burma independence. After the military coup of 1962 Uncle became the economic czar of Burma. The country prospered under his leadership and his belief in private industry and market-oriented principles. Uncle rose to become a four star Brigadier General. He soon became second in command of the ruling Revolutionary Council following the 1962 coup staged by General Ne Win. He also served as Vice-Chief of Staff of Burma army, Minister of Trade and Industry, and was Chairman and Chief Executive Officer of the military established Burma Economic Development Corporation, BEDC. He was the regime's second most powerful man and was considered 'heir apparent' of the dictator, General Ne Win.

The Funeral

As children we never thought about mortality. My first experience with grief was the loss of my middle aunt due to pregnancy related complications. She was Uncle Aung Gyi's beloved, beautiful wife and TuTu's loving and devoted mother. Uncle's grief was insurmountable and I was overwhelmed.

Auntie was only 28 years old and had been studying at Rangoon University medical school. There were no funeral parlors or mortuaries, and it was customary to bring the body home from the hospital for a home funeral. Auntie was laid on a bed at U Wizara Road family home, dressed in traditional attire consisting of a pink silk longyi or sarong and a tight-fitted white lace Burmese style blouse, or aingyi. A white lace veil covered her face; she looked like Sleeping Beauty. Grandma was weeping so hard she had to be physically supported by two servants to keep her from collapsing. The house was filled with hundreds of people grieving, crying, and talking. President U Win Maung, Prime Minister U Nu, other cabinet ministers, Tatmadaw generals, foreign diplomats, and other VIPs came to pay respect and condolences. Although Uncle Aung Gyi had introduced us to many politicians at various state functions, I had never met President U Win Maung till now — although we frequently swam at his indoor pool at the Presidential Palace.

Everyone of Rangoon high society attended Auntie's funeral, dressed in black Burmese jackets, white shirts, and colorful silk longyis. Their wives were adorned with woven silk longyis and jewelry from head to toe that would make even a Windsor jealous. Beautiful flower wreaths and breathtaking floral arrangements had to be stacked on top of each other for lack of space. The army brought a couple of trucks to carry them. The servants and helpers served the guests a feast of colored rice and chicken, various meat curries, vegetable sides, and all sorts of traditional Burmese delicacies. I ate several times that day. The funeral procession was the longest anyone had seen in recent Burmese history. It consisted of a motorcade of several hundred VIP limousines, cars, trucks some carrying flowers, army soldiers in jeeps and lorries, and security police on motorcycles. TuTu and I rode with Uncle Aung Gyi in a black limousine behind the hearse carrying Auntie's white coffin with gold hinges, followed by several other black limos carrying the rest of the family. Next the army trucks carrying the funeral flowers followed the motorcade and it continued with the VIP cars and their bodyguards behind them. Soldiers with rifles in army trucks and jeeps also escorted the funeral procession to guard the generals. Sections of some of the streets including U Wizara Road leading to the cemetery were closed and guarded by military police with special arm bands on motorbikes. It was a long day and TuTu and I fell asleep during the ceremony at the cemetery.

Memories of Childhood

As a single parent, Uncle Aung Gyi remained very close to his daughter and we accompanied him to numerous official government functions. Uncle built strong relationships with both the East and the West. He welcomed the royal family from England and cultivated friendship with Thailand's King and Queen. He developed close personal relationships with the Prime Ministers of China and Japan. We were taught to curtsy when meeting Princess Alexandra of England, and King Bhumibol Adulyadej Rama IX and Queen Sirikit of Thailand. (King Bhumibol Adulyadej passed away in 2016 after 70 years' reign as monarch of Thailand.) I can still remember the Queen, who was stylishly and tastefully dressed, like Mommy. We learned to bow to welcome Prime Minister and Mrs. Ikeda of Japan. Uncle was a skilled negotiator and a master of policy implementation with an unusual attentiveness to the details and nuances of diplomacy. He negotiated an agreement with Prime Minister Ikeda for several hundred million dollars of war reparations to cover the damage and injury inflicted on Burma and the Burmese people during the Japanese occupation.

When Prime Minister Zhou En Lai of China came to visit Rangoon the first time, TuTu and I met him briefly and shook hands with him. Burma's relationship with China was strengthened through Uncle's personal relationship and friendship with Prime Minister Zhou En Lai. Uncle had visited China on state duty more than a dozen times. Zhou En Lai's gift to Uncle was a 12-foot-long hand-painted Chinese silk scroll with two long-legged cranes on the edge of a pond in the midst of pink chrysanthemums, with jagged mountains in the background. Uncle gave the scroll to Mommy, who loved art and home decorating. The Chinese scroll hung from ceiling to floor on our living room wall. On his second trip to Rangoon, Zhou En Lai brought his daughter NaNa with him; TuTu and I became instant friends with her. Uncle Aung Gyi also traveled to the USSR and USA on official government business and formed strong personal relationships with many heads of states and dignitaries like Nikita Khrushchev, and Marshal Tito of Czechoslovakia.

TuTu and I were always dressed in matching outfits when accompanying Uncle to state dinners and government functions. Hong Kong, then a British colony and tax-free haven, was Asia's shopping paradise and many Western businessmen and tourists would have their suits and shirts custom tailored by world-famous HK tailors. Mommy would order dresses, can cans, and shoes for us with exquisite designs of satin bows, ribbons and laces which I helped cut out from Western magazines. Since there was no local facility, such items had to be shipped back to HK for dry cleaning. Music and dancing were my passion, but playing the piano — especially practicing scales — was not. When the Chinese National Ballet Group visited Rangoon on an exchange goodwill mission, we accompanied Uncle at the opening ceremony, seated in front row. They performed Tchaikovsky's Swan Lake. When the performance ended, we went on stage with dozens of red roses for the dancers and posed with them for the photographers and the press. Every night for the remaining three weeks, TuTu and I were at the ballet, front row seats, mesmerized.

When the Russian naval commander came to visit in their World War II submarine, Uncle took us to welcome the commander and his crew. All four of us cousins got a tour of the submarine. The marines were well built, tall and robust, and greeted us with ear to ear smiles. The chef and his helpers were peeling potatoes for dinner. The narrow galley kitchen was well-stocked with supplies including cases of vodka. The sub was narrow and much longer than I expected; I felt claustrophobic so we had to cut short the diplomatic tour representing our country. Inspecting gem extraction mines with Uncle in bordering states of the country was more fun.

One summer when school was out TuTu and I accompanied Uncle to Shan and Kayah States during his visit to inspect the Biluchaung hydroelectric power plant. The journey to the hilly north east of Burma to Taunggyi, the capital of Shan state took several days. We traveled in a caravan of olive green military vehicles, mostly filled with security guards in jeeps in front and heavily armed soldiers in a convoy of army trucks behind our air-conditioned army Land Rover. We made multiple stops in many towns and villages to stretch and eat along the way. The villagers were very friendly and welcomed us by waving their hands or small Burmese flags. There were many prearranged official welcome stops too. We were delighted to be offered cool beverages and I went straight to the snacks while Uncle delivered his speeches. At Taunggyi we stayed at a government house, a stately colonial mansion built by the British, and feasted on local juicy oranges, apples, cherries and strawberries grown in the cool climate of the hilly region.

Back in Rangoon Uncle enjoyed long walks in the park with his ADC while TuTu and I ran, chased each other, played hide and seek, laughed and sang at the playground. But life was about to change. After the military coup, the army began to take over businesses, factories, shops, schools and clinics in the name of nationalization. I often heard Uncle say he believed the army take-over should be temporary and once the corruption was cleaned up the military should let the civilian government run the economy and the country. He was not interested in personal power. He only wanted to effect meaningful political, social and economic change for the people and the country he loved. As the years passed, I got a deeper understanding of what he stood for and the true meaning of his statement. It not only reflected the perceptiveness of a devoted revolutionary but the intuitive wisdom of a pragmatic and prudent statesman.

The Caretaker Government

All this time the Burmese army kept out of politics while U Nu's government, unable to restrain unruly and corrupt politicians, found itself in the midst of the civil war with the communists and armed ethnic minorities. The deteriorating situation could no longer be ignored. Two young colonels, Aung Gyi (later to become the second in command of Burma's army as a Brigadier General), and Maung Maung, went to see U Nu and told him the army could not tolerate corrupt politicians, unruly rebels and communist insurgents. They advised U Nu to transfer state control to the military to restore order, stating that Tatmadaw would not stage a coup but "neither would it tolerate violations of the constitution by politicians, nor would it permit them to make deals with the communist insurgents"[1].

So in October 1958, after having announced over the Burmese radio that he was asking General Ne Win, Chief of Staff of the Burma armed forces, to assume charge of the Burma government, Prime Minister U Nu resigned. The army took over the government, led by General Ne Win who promised to hold a free election two years later. Burma was rescued, not a moment too soon, from political chaos and economic disaster. The people supported the transition.

The caretaker government accomplished miracles during its 18 months in power as young, tenacious, and fiercely patriotic soldiers took over the country's administrative, political and legal systems with unprecedented zeal. General Ne Win's energetic officers, most of them under forty, faced the problems with national pride, efficiency and strict military discipline. The military government cleaned Rangoon of slums, uncollected garbage, and thousands of stray dogs. A campaign was set up to "cleanse with sweat" the filthy areas of the capital. Hard laborers (called coolies) as well as businessmen, with brooms and shovels, enthusiastically disposed of the two-decade accumulation of litter. Thousands of squatters were relocated to new satellite

---

[1] *Southeast Asia.* Life World Library. Author: Stanley Karnow, New York: Time Incorporated, 1962.

---

towns of *Okkalapa* and *Thaketa*. The army also removed corrupt politicians of *U Nu*'s administration and intensified fighting against the communists, tribal and vandal guerrillas. Crime was reduced, and law and order was restored. The army also arrested 'disturbers of the peace' and hundreds of communists were deported including NUF, National United Front, founder *Aung Than*, older brother of General *Aung San*, to Coco Island. On the economic front, the army increased agricultural and industrial production and export trade, raising Burma's much needed foreign exchange reserves. Postal, railway, bus, and shipping services were reorganized. Foreign traders who transgressed against economic controls were deported. Price controls and restrictions against high profits and hoarding helped to reduce living costs. Port facilities were modernized, and streets were repaired after decades of neglect. The cabinet of young officers was very successful in reducing crime, tidying up Rangoon, reducing the rebellions in bordering ethnic states, increasing agricultural and industrial production, and strengthening exchange reserves. It seemed General *Ne Win*'s army regime had run the government better than *U Nu*''s civilian government.

Contrary to the fears of many, power had not gone to General *Ne Win*'s head, so far, and the army government had worked heart and soul to set Burma back on its feet again. The Burma army returned the government to the civilians in 1960 as promised. An election was held and *U Nu* rode back into power over his opponents by an overwhelming popular support and vote. Once again, *U Nu* was Prime Minister.

Two years later, in 1962, Burma was falling back to the disintegrating situation of 1958 that brought in the military government. *U Nu* and his ministers seemed to be unable to run Burma's affairs effectively. Ethnic minorities and other opposition groups reemerged making the country politically unstable. *U Nu*'s government sought to make compromises with minorities, insurgents and communists, in return for their eschewing violence. Once again the religious Premier was afflicted by trade deficits, crop failures, dissident tribesmen, and myriads of other forms of economic stagnation as what the Rangoon press refers to as his '16,000 problems', quoting a Burmese proverbial saying[1]. The communists and other opposition factions were infiltrating the government through corrupt politicians. The Shans, Karens, and Kachins were threatening national unity. A military rescue was again imminent and this is where our story really begins.

---

[1] *Newsweek*. "Problem No. 16,001", March 12, 1962, 52.

The Military Coup

As described above, the senior generals of *Tatmadaw* met at Dagon House to discuss plans for the military takeover of *U Nu's* civilian government, but the two top leaders, Generals *Ne Win* and *Aung Gyi*, could not reach an agreement. *Aung Gyi* left the meeting first, to attend a state function, and *Ne Win* joined him later, but there was no further discussion of the coup.

Aung Gyi was blindsided by General *Ne Win* the next morning. On March 2, 1962, in the early hours, the Burma army headed by General *Ne Win* staged a coup d'état. *Ne Win* had planned the minute details and executed the coup without involving Brigadier General *Aung Gyi*, his second in command. General *Ne Win* woke up Brigadier General *Aung Gyi* at Dagon House with the news that he had taken over *U Nu's* government. Other army officers *Kyaw Soe, Than Sein, Bo Hla Myint, Bo Saw Myint, Bo Ba Ni*, and *Bo Lwin* came to Dagon House that morning to report that the coup had been totally successful, with only the one casualty already mentioned — the son of Shan President *Sao Shwe Thaike* was shot and killed at their residence.

General *Ne Win* immediately assigned Brigadier General *Aung Gyi* to organize a ruling military junta, dubbed the Revolutionary Council, to handle the change-over of the government. Brigadier General *Aung Gyi* was stunned at the hasty, reckless and audacious move. He immediately called all heads of ministries to meet at Dagon House, his residence, and instructed them to remain calm and continue normal functions of their ministries until a new cabinet was formed. Brigadier General *Aung Gyi*, Vice Chief of Staff and General *Ne Win's* No 2 man, was assigned to run the day-to-day management and the affairs of the Ministry of Defense.

The new government declared that they had acted for national security reasons. The army cited four key reasons for the coup: (1) the concern over the growing power of *U Nu's* left wing politicians, (2) the threat of the dissident minorities to break away and secede, (3) the responsibility to prevent the threat of communists, and (4) the general economic stagnation of the country. Thousands of soldiers in tanks and trucks rolled swiftly into Rangoon and seized the police stations and the airport[1]. President *U Win Maung*, Prime Minister *U Nu* and his cabinet ministers, the chief of justice, and other key politicians, tribal princes and numerous dissident leaders in the states were arrested and put in detention. The constitution was suspended, parliament was dissolved, and the nation put, for the second time, under military rule.

---

[1] *The Reporter.* Stanley Karnow: "A Second Chance for *U Nu*", March 30, 1966, 29-33.

The Revolutionary Council

At first the army's takeover was accepted with a certain relief, and student organizations, Buddhist monks, veterans, labor unions, and others welcomed the return of General *Ne Win's* government. Brigadier General *Aung Gyi* said that the army take-over had saved the country from a political crisis again. General *Ne Win* assumed positions as Head of State, Prime Minister and Defense Minister. Brigadier General *Aung Gyi* became Head of the Cabinet and Trade and Commerce Minister. Other generals were assigned positions heading up various ministries. *Aung Gyi* and his generals were instantly over-burdened, serving multiple positions and running the new government.

After the overthrow of the civilian government, General *Ne Win* announced, as the new president and prime minister, the formation of Burma Socialist Program Party and the creation of the ideology, Burmese Way to Socialism. A 17-member Revolutionary Council was established and it assumed all power in the country. It took over all government offices including the Secretariat and the High Court. Everyone had to work double and triple duty in their current posts within *Tatmadaw* as well as their newly created positions in the new administration.

Within months of the coup, Brigadier General *Aung Gyi* was running almost all government functions with his team of young army officers. The generals of the new ruling government, Revolutionary Council, were more comfortable reporting to him and expressing views more freely working with him than General *Ne Win*, who tended to be short tempered, abrupt and sometimes irrational. As time went on, General *Ne Win* became more isolated and autocratic. He was never liked by *U Nu's* politicians, who had ruled the country since independence. *Ne Win* and many of his generals were also suspicious of the ministers of *U Nu's* deposed government as they were Western-educated during the colonial rule. The generals disliked their condescending attitude and their Western superiority complex. Eventually, these elite bureaucrats of the Burma's upper class defected to the West or to neighboring countries.

Burmese Way to Socialism

The 1962 military coup staged by General *Ne Win* was not a voluntary takeover like the caretaker one in 1958. Thousands of soldiers in tanks and trucks rolled into Rangoon. The army seized the airport, sea ports, police stations and important buildings including the Secretariat, Government House, and the High Court. The civilian president, prime minister and the cabinet members were stripped of their titles and positions and taken into detention (described as political custody). The 1947 constitution, the first since independence, was suspended and parliament was dissolved. The coup purged the bureaucracy of the elite ministers who were replaced with younger military officers who were more energetic, loyal, and patriotic. A one-party state was created as Burma Socialist Program Party, BSPP, as the only political party allowed to exist. The Revolutionary Council claimed to pursue independent neutrality with all countries. Burma kept on friendly terms with China, who shares the 12,000 mile northeast border.

The Burmese Way to Socialism was an ideology composed of a xeno-phobic mixture of Marxism, Buddhism and Burmese nationalism sprinkled with anti-Western sentiment, isolationism and socialism. General *Ne Win* began to seize all private businesses and made them state owned against the advice of his No 2, Brigadier General *Aung Gyi*, who favored a moderate approach to governance and market based economy. For the coming decades under General *Ne Win*'s rule, his policy devastated one of the richest econo-mies of the region. Burmese way to Socialism plunged Burma into poverty for decades to come. It affected not only the economy but the quality of educa-tion and healthcare, and lowered the living standards of the people of Burma to prewar era level.

Although *Tatmadaw* was founded during the struggle for independence, its role changed after the 1962 coup. In addition to defense, *Tatmadaw*, under General *Ne Win*, took on a leading role in politics, economics, legal and all aspects of life in Burma. A provision to guarantee that privileged position for the military was added to the constitution. Under *Ne Win*'s rule, Burma became totally militarized. English language instruction was removed from all schools and foreign aid organizations, like the Ford Foundation and World Bank, were dismissed from the country. Entry visa restrictions were imposed on foreign journalists and business people, and ordinary citizens were restricted travels especially to Western countries. Often, a limited number of state scholars were sent abroad to be trained as scientists and technicians, but they were only sent to Soviet Union and Eastern Europe. All publications and media were censored or banned and only government owned newspapers were permitted that published regime's propaganda news.

Against the recommendations of Brigadier General *Aung Gyi*, General *Ne Win* nationalized all businesses and industries — agriculture, banking, communication, utilities, construction, transport, import export trade, wholesalers, brokers, mining and extraction, rice, rubber, and timber. All private firms were taken over including department stores, hotels, restau-rants, bars, shops and gas stations. As businesses closed down, licenses issued to foreigners to operate bus and taxi services were withdrawn. The regime also took over the sales agencies of all foreign airlines. Private law, medical clinics and pharmacies were also confiscated. The oil industry, dominated by the US and UK, were closed down and operations taken over by government-owned Burma Oil Company, which monopolized oil extraction and production. Everything was seized and controlled by the soldiers, qualified or not.

My parents lost their companies and business ventures like everyone else; they were taken over by the military regime without compensation. All business owners, regardless of nationality, were ruined. Tens of thousands Indians who worked in these industries had to leave the country as soldiers took over their jobs. Many of the Indian and Chinese people who had dominated Burma's economy since the colonial days left the country in a mass exodus.

The impact of all-out nationalization and subsequent mismanagement by the regime was devastating. Corruption propagated every level, shortages were widespread, prices escalated, black market mushroomed, rice and other exports diminished, and foreign exchange reserves plunged. The fertile soil of the Irrawaddy delta had made Burma the largest rice grower and exporter in the region, but now rice mills were taken over by the government and as the sole buyer of rice from farmers, created a monopoly in rice market. Production plummeted. Black markets flourished. Within a few years of the military coup, a country that had been the largest exporter of rice was unable to feed its own people.

The Resignation

After the coup policy and ideological disagreements began to brew in the inner circle of the Revolutionary Council over how economy should be run, government monopoly or free trade. Pro-communist Brigadier General *Tin Pe* favored total state control of economy while pro-democracy Brigadier General *Aung Gyi* advocated open competitive market based economy. General *Ne Win* had many long discussions on economic policy and other strategic issues with Brigadier General *Aung Gyi*, his closest comrade in arms who had stood alongside him since the underground days fighting for liberation from the British colonial rule and the Japanese occupation. As Minister of Trade and Commerce responsible for Burma's economy, Brigadier General *Aung Gyi* explained the concept of a mixed economy of state and private owned institutions to his boss. Without private enterprises, there would be no competition. State owned companies would become monopolies and that would be the ground to breed corruption, shortages, price increases, black market, and inflation. Brigadier General *Aung Gyi* said free and open market competition was necessary for the national economy to grow and raise the standard of living of the people. However, General *Ne Win* remained unconvinced and supported his economic monopoly and one party rule pursuing total isolationism and established a xenophobic military government under his Burmese Way to Socialism. General *Ne Win* opted for full control and all out nationalization of the economy.

Brigadier General *Aung Gyi* knew that personal rivalries or rifts between the top generals would disturb cohesion, morale and unity within the *Tatmadaw* he had helped create and train, and which was dear to his heart. He believed that bloodshed must be avoided at all cost, the interests of the people served, and the security of the whole country must be protected. Thus, to the shock and dismay of the nation, Brigadier General *Aung Gyi* resigned from the Revolutionary Council and left the army.

With the departure of the only military man with an understanding of economic principles, the country accelerated its decline toward economic devastation. The country was left under the control of an army of soldiers with no experience or skill in governing or any understanding of economic principles. This was the beginning of authoritarian military dictatorship which would last for the next half a century, plunging the people of Burma into destitution. Burma was cut off from the world.

Chapter 3. General Ne Win Era 1962–88

Military Rule

For five decades, a series of military regimes managed to hang on to power, control and material rewards and privileges, by using repression, plundering, brainwashing and propaganda. They ruled ruthlessly by means of force, numerology and superstition. Students, monks, and anyone who opposed the regime was harassed, jailed, tortured, or killed. Burma's military junta ruled from 1962–2010 starting with General *Ne Win* and ending with General *Than Shwe*, plundering the country to enrich the generals and their crony friends and allies. They drove the people into crushing poverty. The armed forces became a ruthless dominating force rather than protector of the people and country. In response, the people have stood up in major protests in 1962, 1967, 1970, 1974, 1988, 1996, and 2007 with untold thousands of lives lost. And the world was silent.

> Most of these dictator generals came from humble backgrounds, with limited education. Some rose through the ranks in the army, some were low-level clerks. Their ignorance and obscurantism led some of them to rely on superstition, numerology and astrology. For example, the Burmese currency *Kyat* was denominated in units of 9, as that was a lucky number. The new capital, *Naypyidaw* ('city of kings'), was built on the advice of an astrologer. The generals surrounded themselves with a tight-knit circle of loyal military men, cronies and allies. Enormous personal power was retained by purging rivals, betraying friends, and keeping followers constantly fearful and off-balance with intimidation under watchful eyes of military intelligence, MI. They were ruthless in purging and eliminating rivals or anyone suspected of disloyalty. They promoted and rewarded those who agreed with and carried out their wishes. Lower rank subordinates, followers, and 'friends' were kept on their toes with intimidation, fear, and 24/7 spying by MI and paid

plainclothes informants. *Tatmadaw* rewrote the constitution so they would not be legally held accountable for crimes against the people of Burma. Meanwhile, they indulged in a lifestyle of excess, surrounded with opulence, including extraordinarily extravagant weddings for their daughters. Ending with Senior General *Than Shwe* in 2010, this was the longest military dictatorship on earth.

General *Than Shwe*'s era began with SLORC, State Law and Order Restoration Council and the SPDC, State Peace and Development Council, from 1988 to 2011. During his 24-year reign, corruption and cronyism reached new heights. Freedom and democratic life disappeared, including the political parties, the media, the trade unions, health and educational institutions, civil society and foreign investment. The generals were embittered nationalistic fanatics who despised colonialists and foreigners, and they sealed off the country to the rest of the world.

Over the decades, the army grew bigger and stronger from 180,000 men to over 400,000. Little was spent on education and health care but a whopping 40% of GDP went to supporting *Tatmadaw*. A huge amount was spent to support its vast network of informants, military intelligence, and spies placed in offices, schools, factories, tea houses and other public places. After the 1962 coup and the establishment of the Revolutionary Council, the Burma Socialist Program Party was formed in 1964 as the only political party allowed in the country.

In 1988, the State Law and Order Restoration Council, SLORC, was created, which then changed to the less militant name of State Peace and Development Council, SPDC, in 1997. The junta also created the Union Solidarity and Development Association, USDA, in 1993, as the only recognized politico-social organization, which was dissolved later and replaced by the Union Solidarity and Development Party, USDP.

Shortly before Burma opened its doors to the international community in 2011, many high ranking generals resigned to become 'civilian' candidates for the military-backed USDP, which, to no one's surprise, won the elections held in 2010. Although the name of the ruling party changed from time to time, the power and control remained in the hands of the same handful men who shaped how democracy is defined in the country today.

The General Ne Win Era, 1962–88

General *Ne Win* was born *Shu Maung* in 1911 in *Paungdale*. He attended Rangoon University, planning to become a doctor, but did not complete his education after failing major exams. He left the university and worked as a postal clerk. Through friendship and close association with old colleagues who wanted to liberate Burma from the British, he joined *Aung San* and became one of the 'Thirty Comrades' trained in China to help the Japanese push the British out of Burma. Like many of his comrades, he adopted a new war name or *nom de guerre*. *Ne Win* means 'Radiant Sun'. He fought in many wars alongside *Aung San* until independence was won from the British in 1948.

Ne Win was always suspicious and resentful of the educated, especially Western-educated. Since independence, tension and dislike existed between *U Nu's* cabinet ministers, many of whom were British educated and trained, and the officers of *Tatmadaw*. Conversely, the British-trained former civil service bureaucrats looked down on the military men as monastery-educated intellectual light-weights.

Ne Win did not want Marxism or follow *U Nu's* Buddhism but wanted to pursue a political ideology that incorporated Buddhist tenets, isolation, anti-foreign sentiment and superstition for the country. This was his idea of the Burmese Way to Socialism. With the coup of 1962, General *Ne Win* stripped the ethnic Shan *saophas* (also known as *sawbwas*) or princes of their feudal powers in the ethnic province bordering the country. He abandoned *Aung San's Panglong* Agreement and seized control of the raw material deposits of both the Shan and the Kachin states. The minority groups took up arms against *Ne Win's* central government, the Kachin in the north, the Shan in the east, and the Karen and Mon to the south, erupting in constant armed conflict and threatening civil war.

General *Ne Win* ruled the country from 1962 to 1988 as a general, then as self-appointed president, and later as a political kingpin. During his 26-year reign, hundreds of unarmed university students were killed for anti-regime protests. The historic Rangoon University Student Union, which was a symbol of colonialism as well as Burma's independence struggle and a landmark celebrating the end of British colonial rule, was destroyed by dynamite. Civilian politicians educated during the colonial era were arrested, including former Prime Minister *U Nu* and Brigadier General *Aung Gyi*. He created the most feared military intelligence service, MIS, spying and intimidating past and present politicians, students, monks, ordinary citizens, and their families, even distant relatives and friends. Damages to economy, health, education, communication and infrastructure were monumental and decay and destruction of human resources were unfathomable.

Ne Win was street smart, playing close to his chest but not afraid to take risk, and sometimes, almost reckless. He operated with sticks, not carrots, and peaceful protests by unarmed citizens were always violently suppressed with brutal killings. When riots broke out in Rangoon University, the military opened fire on student demonstrators. All colleges and universities were then put under strict government control to discourage mass gatherings and anti-government activities, propelling student activists to go underground. Similar student protests erupted in 1975, 1976 and 1977 and were similarly brutally suppressed; then Rangoon University was closed for months and years combined. In 1988 the most prominent uprising in Burmese history broke out, led by students and reinforced by the *sangha*, the Buddhist clergy, and supported by the broader population, threatening anarchy in the country.

After Brigadier General *Aung Gyi's* departure from the military government in 1963, *Ne Win's* regime took an abrupt turn to hard line radical socialism and began to nationalize all remaining private businesses, large and small. The oil industry was seized and rice mills and agriculture production were taken over by the state. The army confiscated private property and turned them to military run state corporations. People began to feel the impact of high speed nationalization in their daily life living with shortages, long lines, increasing prices and growth of everything black market. All means of production, transportation, communication, and all aspect of life were under the control of the military government. People were thrown out of work as *Tatmadaw* soldiers, although unskilled, untrained, and inexperienced, took over businesses, shops and all types of jobs. Every aspect of the country including economy, education, and healthcare was now in the hands of *Tatmadaw*. Within the first couple of years of General *Ne Win's* rule full scale nationalization took place at an unprecedented accelerated pace according to the Burmese Way to Socialism.

Every few days the Revolutionary Council issued new rules and regulations reflecting increasing socialistic authoritarianism with a strong military focus and bringing about drastic changes in the country based on General *Ne Win's* superstition, xenophobia, and increasing military control. Trade unions were banned and all political parties outlawed. To establish incontestable power the RC dissolved potential focal points of opposition such as the Buddhist Council and the Rangoon University Council that constituted two of the strongest potential political forces, namely Buddhists monks and university students. All political, religious and social parties that had potential opposition force were dissolved, declaring BSPP as the one and only legal political party in the state. In a staunch Buddhist country like Burma, the monks represent a powerful group but the regime tried to reduce their influence with criticisms in newspapers attempting to smear their reputation. The unarmed monks retaliated and staged peaceful demonstrations against General *Ne Win's* government, burning the newspaper in public and distributing anti-government pamphlets. They were brutally shot down.

When protests by the university students periodically erupted into riots, the army opened fire on the unarmed students, killing many and wounding many more. Rangoon University closed down numerous times for periods ranging from weeks to months and even years. The RC then abolished the Supreme Court and established a State Court and special courts empowered to impose the death sentence to anyone interpreted by the authority as guilty for acts of insurrection and what it deemed to be crimes against public safety, property, and national security.

To limit the influence of foreigners, all technical and financial aid from foreign private institutions were terminated, declaring all foreign aid programs would be accepted only on government to government basis. Foreign citizens were dismissed from governmental positions, and direct contact with foreign diplomats were discouraged and restricted. Burmese officials were intimidated or harassed to avoid intimate association with foreign nationals and Ne Win's party members began to shun contact with the press and limit contacts with foreign diplomats. Foreign journalists and news media were either denied permission to enter the country or granted only 24 hour stays and entry visas were severely limited.

Local people were not allowed any international contacts and all books, magazines, newspapers, and media were censored and controlled by the military. Foreign multinational corporations and foreign entrepreneurs have accumulated immense wealth as millionaires and billionaires during the colonial era and under Prime Minister U Nu's rule. Ne Win ordered the RC to review all contracts and licensing agreements with them to expose bribery and corruption accusing them of exploitation of Burma's rich natural resources by using powerful Burmese connections to promote their interests. Trade agreements and commercial contracts with foreign institutions were no longer deemed valid and terminated. Foreign business people were deported. Foreign aid workers were asked to leave the country and higher education scholarship programs from the West were terminated.

Due to Ne Win's suspicion and hostility toward educated people, hundreds of colonial-era educated and trained professionals, many had studied in the UK and US, were fired from top positions. Unwelcome and now out of work, doctors, lawyers, engineers, businessmen, entrepreneurs and teachers left the country in droves, creating a severe brain drain and a lost generation to come as the last educated and trained generation dies. The loss of educated and high skilled people had long term dangerous negative consequences to the economy leading to decline in productivity and living standards for decades to come.

To promote austerity, horse-racing, beauty contests, and dance competitions were banned. Currency was demonetized and people lost their life's savings overnight as the *kyats* (Burmese currency) became worthless paper. In a cash economy with no reliable rudimentary consumer banking system, people kept cash at home, hidden in jars, earthen pot and under mattresses. Without any warning, the government wiped out people's life's savings.

Transfers of money into and out of Burma became impossible. Only selected state scholars could go abroad for study and training and these were students from families of the generals or those well connected to them and the junta, and they were generally sent to communist or socialist countries of the military government's choice.

All banks and private schools were nationalized and renamed People's Banks and People's Schools or State School. A government-controlled propaganda based curriculum was imposed in schools throughout the country terminating English language instruction and establishing Burmese language instruction mandatory. Medical and technical phrases and terms did not always translate well into Burmese, but they were awkwardly changed into Burmese anyway, with some loss of meaning and many cumbersome phrases.

Everything from rice to rubies was nationalized, owned by the state and managed by unskilled and untrained soldiers, creating unprecedented shortages, stagnation and a booming black market. The shelves of retail shops (confiscated and renamed 'People's Stores') became empty — as predicted by *Aung Gyi*. Only bribes to the staff would bring the merchandise out from storage in the backroom. State owned stores were unable to provide even the basic necessities and perpetually faced shortages. Long queues for rations of rice, cooking oil, gas and other basic goods became widespread. Prices escalated.

To survive, the people began trading stolen Burmese art, Buddhist relics, antiques and valuable timber like teak for food, clothing, medicine and soap with the neighboring countries of China and Thailand.

The government also took over agencies of all foreign airlines. The pace of nationalization in Burma amazed even the Russian and Chinese diplomats in Rangoon. General *Ne Win's* regime drove out most of the resident aliens who had dominated the country's commerce. Rangoon, once the commercial center in the region, declined rapidly. The riches of the country were in the hands of a handful of army generals and their business cronies. Widespread corruption was rampant and bribery became necessary to get anything done. Corruption permeated daily interactions between the administration and the public. Doctors doing autopsies were swayed with under the table money to write false reports; police were paid off to destroy evidence or produce fake evidence; and judges were bribed to pass lenient sentences. This was the beginning of the long downward spiral that would even intensify with the next dictatorship under General *Than Shwe*.

Within a few years of General *Ne Win*'s rule, all economic institutions and private enterprises and all aspects of society, businesses, media, education, and health were under the control of *Tatmadaw*. Burma quickly became one of the world's most impoverished nations.

This was not the Burma General *Aung San* had envisioned. People lived in fear as spies and military informants were rampant in schools, businesses, communities and all public places. People began to mistrust one another and even members of the same family for fear of retaliation. The unhappy majority began to realize the course of events and complained, though more in private grumbling than in open criticism for fear of retribution. General *Ne Win*'s reign was characterized by extreme xenophobia and anyone or anything foreign, especially Western, was suspect and unwelcome.

General *Ne Win* loved horse-racing, gambling, alcohol and women. He was officially married six times but kept a series of mistresses. He was secretive, hot tempered and ruled the country with an iron fist. He made frequent trips to London to attend Ascot races and loved being entertained by the Queen. He suffered from severe paranoia and other psychological illnesses and had received multiple treatments for schizophrenia in Vienna from the famed Austrian psychiatrist Dr Hans Hoff. *Ne Win* the playboy became a control freak. He bankrupted the nation while he bought mansions in London and Tokyo. Crushing poverty, illiteracy, and diseases shot up throughout the country. Commercial, industrial and agricultural production deteriorated. The legal system was abolished and all rule of law destroyed. With no government training or prior experience, General *Ne Win* and his soldiers ruled the country as an ill prepared paranoid autocratic regime driving the nation to the ground while the rest of Asia flourished.

Dynamite Explosion

Shortly after the coup, in July 1962, protests by the university students against General *Ne Win*'s policies erupted into a riot. The army, armed with assault rifles, gunned down the peaceful demonstration, killing over a hundred unarmed students and arresting more than 3,000. Official government announcements downplayed the massacre and reported the death toll at 15 –17 and 27 wounded.

The RC established a special State Court empowered to impose the death sentence on anyone for 'crimes' as it deemed fit. The university became the site and testament for suppressed political activism and anti military rule and authoritarianism. Since this event, university students were regarded by *Ne Win's* regime as enemies of the state and a great threat to his rule.

The day after the riot, the historic Rangoon University Student Union building, which symbolized the anti-colonial nationalism since the 1920s, was dynamited by the soldiers. The monument representing Burma's struggle for independence from colonialism was destroyed forever. Who gave the order for this? No. 1 General *Ne Win* categorically denied giving the order to shoot and to flatten the Student Union building, conveniently making *Aung Gyi* the scapegoat. In fact, *Aung Gyi* was visiting his older sister in *Kemendine* township who was ill at the time. Many officers were issuing conflicting reports and orders in the chaos and disclaiming responsibility.

Later, the dynamite purchase order was traced: it was signed by General *Kyaw Soe*, and the order to detonate was also signed by him, as Minister of Home Affairs and Chairman of the Security Council. The wiring and planting of the explosives was done by Major *Tun Yi*, of the engineering department. Just before the explosion, Colonel *Min Thein* — who was taking his early morning walk — arrived while the soldiers were hunting for a senior officer as required to sign the order. At Major *Tun Yi* 's request for the needed signature, the colonel signed off on the order without studying it properly. In the chaos no one knew for sure who gave the troops the final green light, but the battalion commander who ordered the troops to fire that day was Lieutenant Colonel *Sein Lwin*, the same military man who ordered the firing on unarmed civilians in the famed 8.8.88 massacre two and a half decades later, killing hundreds of unarmed students.

Immediately following the slaughter and the explosion, *Ne Win* ordered the dead and the injured moved to erase any trace of the mass killing. The regime closed down Rangoon University for four months.

Division at the Top

The resentment of businessmen grew and so did the uproar among peasants and farmers, outraged over the land grab and collectivization of agriculture. General *Ne Win* admitted the all-out nationalizations had caused problems but he reiterated that the system would move forward as planned.

A split in the power center resulted, with two different fractions and opposing views: those who favored a moderate democratic rule with free market and the hard line opposition faction who wanted an iron clad controlled economy. Brigadier General *Aung Gyi* was a moderate and a supporter of free markets who believed General *Ne Win's* economic policies would lead to chaos and bankruptcy. He believed in market-oriented economics and felt that soldiers should be soldiers — meaning that the army should return the power to a civilian government.

General *Ne Win* came increasingly under the influence of the Brigadier General *Tin Pe*, who favored a radical communist-inspired approach to the economy with centralized state control, nationalizing everything from banks to bananas.

Productivity began to plunge and black markets sprang to life. The impossibility of reconciling their ideological and policy differences began to split the Revolutionary Council. The division within *Tatmadaw* intensified rifts within the top tier. A fierce feud ensued between the leftist hard liners *Tin Pe* and *Ba Nein*, and the moderate open market seekers led by Brigadier General *Aung Gyi*, threatening the army on the brink of a split-up.

Due to their wide range of differences, Brigadier General *Aung Gyi* felt he could no longer be part of General *Ne Win's* authoritarian regime. These radical policies were against his personal principles, values and commitment to the people. As a soldier who has fought for his country's independence *Aung Gyi* knew he must avoid a potential bloody civil war and save his country from total disintegration. As a devout Buddhist, he abhorred bloodshed and always advocated diplomacy over guns as political solutions. Perceiving a potential break up within *Tatmadaw*, Brigadier General *Aung Gyi* submitted his resignation and asked General *Ne Win* to relieve him of his duties in the armed forces so he could return to civilian life.

In February 1963, Brigadier *Aung Gyi* resigned as Vice Chief of Staff of *Tatmadaw*, Minister of Trade and Industry, Chairman of the Burma Oil Company, and Acting Chairman of the Revolutionary Council (a role he filled during General *Ne Win's* absences). He had been General *Ne Win's* right hand and heir apparent.[1]

General *Ne Win* became more and more xenophobic, barring foreigners from entering the country, Burma soon faded from the world's view.

Brigadier General *Tin Pe* was not only a hard line leftist with militant hardcore socialist ideology, he had previously co-founded the left coalition party National United Front, NUF. Driven by ambition to be *Ne Win's* closest yes man, he had been finger pointing and spreading fabricated accusations against the mild mannered Brigadier General *Aung Gyi* even before ideological and policy differences began to splinter the RC.

BEDC, Burma Economic Development Corporation, was set up to assist retired army personnel and their immediate families. Since independence, Brigadier General *Aung Gyi* had managed BEDC as Chairman. Under his lead-

---

[1] *Time.* "Burma: Army Socialism", Friday, Feb. 22, 1963, 32.

ership, BEDC became the most successful business enterprise of the Burmese government in modern history. It started with a loan of 600,000 *kyats* (about US $513) from Defense Services Institute, DSI, and grew rapidly under Brigadier General *Aung Gyi*. BEDC invested funds by purchasing many companies, banks, hotels and ocean vessels. BEDC maintained funds and assets in UK and Europe to take care of retired *Tatmadaw* officers, their families, and for their medical treatment abroad when needed.

Brigadier General *Tin Pe* and his pro-communist colleagues *Kyaw Soe, Ba Nyein, Than Sein,* and the NUF communist clique began to stir up trouble. They alleged that *Aung Gyi* had siphoned off money from BEDC and set up accounts in Geneva, Switzerland, and Thailand; that he bought mansions in London and Japan; and that he had plans to assassinate No. 1 and take over the country.

BEDC books were audited and no one could find evidence to support the absurd claims. What they found was that the Geneva account was maintained for investment of the Five Star Line by BEDC, the Thailand account was for the sale of fresh fish, the house in Ginza was for a BEDC office, and the London house was purchased with Oppenheimer's investment by BEDC. Brigadier General *Aung Gyi* was squeaky clean. The audit also uncovered a hidden statement of an unauthorized withdrawal of 2000 Sterling pounds by no other than Brigadier *Tin Pe* himself for personal expenditures without the knowledge and authorization of BEDC Chairman *Aung Gyi*.

The books not only confirmed Brigadier General *Aung Gyi's* forthrightness and honesty, but finger pointing turned to *Tin Pe*, who then accused *Aung Gyi* of forging *Ne Win's* signature on state documents in an attempt to take over as head of state. In reality, as No. 2, Brigadier General *Aung Gyi* had to fill in as acting Chief when General *Ne Win* was abroad for medical treatments or golf outings which he did rather frequently. Buddhists believe it was *karma* that Brigadier General *Tin Pe* was involved in a car accident and sustained severe injuries to his spinal cord. As a compassionate practicing Buddhist with high moral principles, Brigadier General *Aung Gyi* was sympathetic even to a colleague with malicious intentions who had tried to bring him down in the past. As BEDC chairman, he approved *Tin Pe's* travel expenses and medical treatment abroad with funds from BEDC's overseas account. Instead of retiring *Tin Pe*, as he was medically unfit to serve in the army, Brigadier General *Aung Gyi* recommended *Tin Pe* be promoted and given a desk job as QMG, quartermaster general in charge of supplies and equipment. *Aung Gyi* did what he believed was right and honorable.

By now the Burmese Way to Socialism and rapid nationalization were in high gear and total inefficiency and corruption crept in at every level imaginable within state owned and operated institutions. Burma, once the biggest rice exporter, now suffered rice crisis as exports of all agriculture products, timber and other raw material fell to record lows and foreign exchange reserves dwindled. The country was literally broke. Although he has left the military, Brigadier General *Aung Gyi* continued to urge General *Ne Win* to turn around his national economic and political policies. He warned *Ne Win* that increasing economic hardship among the people will result in a revolt and uprising against the government and indicated that a healthy sustainable economy was needed as the foundation to build a stable country. General *Ne Win* also received wake up calls from leaders of other countries who, having observed the shocking events of student massacre and accelerated monopolization process, also encouraged him to change course. But General *Ne Win* did nothing. Instead he intensified his control in the name of the Burmese Way to Socialism and became more paranoid of foreigners. General *Ne Win's* hard line economic policies devastated the country and drove its people into crippling poverty. Burma went into a tailspin for the next fifty years while the rest of Southeast Asia prospered.

Brigadier General *Aung Gyi's* resignation stunned the military. His colleagues within *Tatmadaw* pleaded with him to reconsider. *Aung Gyi* believed the authoritarian control General *Ne Win* had chosen would not only alienate the people from *Tatmadaw* but the people would suffer as the economy plunged. The global community was also jolted by his sudden departure. General *Ne Win* was just as stunned.

Within hours, *Ne Win* sent a team — Colonel *Saw Myint, Ko Saw U, Ko Chit Hlaing* and Captain *Thaung, Aung Gyi's* old bodyguard — by Burma Air Force plane to ask him to reverse his decision. *Aung Gyi* was firm and reiterated that as long as major fundamental policy differences existed, he could not in clear conscience retract his resignation. General *Ne Win* also visited *Aung Gyi* at his residence in Dagon House, returning his resignation letter and asking him to burn it. In the decades following his resignation, *Aung Gyi* wrote many letters strongly criticizing the government's Burmese Way to Socialism and warning General *Ne Win* of possible social unrest and uprisings. *Ne Win* put *Aung Gyi* in prison, feeling threatened by the popular former Brigadier General whom the people continued to respect and admire.

Over the decades of his rule, General *Ne Win* expressed regret at letting Brigadier General *Aung Gyi* leave the military. On several occasions he offered *Aung Gyi* the position of US Ambassador, residing in Washington DC. Each time, *Aung Gyi* said his decision was irreversible and rejected the offer. He could not represent policies that he opposed and for which he had paid the high price of seven years arduous prison life. It was customary for General

Ne Win to offer overseas positions as ambassadors or embassy attachés to ousted, former, and retired high-ranking military officers. All had gratefully accepted these retirement perks except Brigadier General *Aung Gyi.*

Ne Win also expressed his regrets for allowing ideological and policy disagreements to come between them and their lifelong friendship. He knew his insecurity and irrationality allowed him to harbor unfounded fears that *Aung Gyi* would rise up in revolt against him as other former political colleagues had tried to do. His paranoia had cost him his closest friend, his comrade since the days of the struggle for freedom and independence, and his right hand and heir apparent. In his peculiar way, perhaps driven by guilt, General *Ne Win* occasionally would make goodwill gestures to the retired General *Aung Gyi.* At one time *Ne Win* offered his help when the retired general ventured out as a private citizen to open a tea house. As expected, *Aung Gyi* thanked No.1 and gracefully declined.

Back at *Tatmadaw* and the junta's Revolutionary Council, replacing Brigadier General *Aung Gyi* as the new Trade and Commerce Minister was none other than the 'Red' (communist) Brigadier General *Tin Pe,* whose only business experience was working as a warehouse clerk taking inventories. As *Ne Win's* puppet, he got promoted within the army due to his blind loyalty. Over the next five years under the direction of the Red Brigadier every sector of the economy was under military control, driving the country to potential starvation. The Ministry, faced with delays, shortages and non deliveries resulting from incompetence, mismanagement and corruption, deteriorated quickly and the national economy collapsed, as predicted by Brigadier General *Aung Gyi.* As the people's protests got louder and the student unrest continued, former Brigadier General began to write open letters to his old boss warning him and suggesting major economic reforms. In 1970, for health reasons, *Tin Pe* was forced to retire, but the negative effects of the gross mismanagement of the economy continued for decades.

With Brigadier General *Aung Gyi*'s departure, other high ranking generals and officers who shared his ideology and economic policy also departed from *Tatmadaw,* leaving General *Ne Win* alone at the top. He became obsessed with safeguarding his supremacy. National building and economic development were no longer on his agenda. As the economy collapsed, corruption created a generation of people that had to do whatever needed to survive. No one trusted anyone. Stealing, looting, cheating, and bribing became part of life. The social fabric ruptured, moral values collapsed. Jails and prisons were filled to capacity with arrests ranging from petty theft to national threat of espionage, some offenses real, others imagined or perceived by General *Ne Win* and his junta.

The Old Man became increasingly xenophobic and his paranoia grew as he became more isolated. His anti foreign sentiment also intensified. No visitors were allowed into the country. Foreign businessmen, civilian workers, professionals, educators, and charity workers who provided overseas aid were expelled. Foreign missionaries and teachers were forced to leave the country and entry visas to Burma were banned to everyone except a few diplomats.

Last Days of MEHS

When General *Ne Win* took over the country, we were attending Methodist English High School, an elite private school in the then capital. It was the school of the privileged and old money Rangoon aristocracy offering comprehensive ten year primary and secondary education. The children of General *Ne Win*, past presidents, prime ministers and diplomats, and *Aung San Suu Kyi*, the Nobel laureate, attended MEHS.

General *Ne Win*'s daughter Sanda and TuTu were close friends and classmates for ten years at MEHS and later both attended Rangoon University medical school and became physicians. Since General *Ne Win* implemented the Burmese Way to Socialism, or more properly the Burmese Way to Isolationism, there was no more rock n roll, pop music, Western music, bands or concerts, no trendy clothing or dyed hair. We just hung out with friends after school. In those days, you did not need appointments for play dates or to see friends. You just showed up. If they weren't home, you went to a different friend's house. It was quite simple and hassle free.

With General *Ne Win*'s private school nationalization, MEHS was renamed Dagon State School No. 1, and English was no longer the language of instruction. My middle school education abruptly ended. Our parents lost their companies, businesses, employees and friends. I don't think they suspected they were about to lose each other.

By now the government had completely closed the country. Burmese citizens were not permitted to leave. There were armed military intelligence and soldiers everywhere. Immediately after independence, every soldier shared the same goal, to serve the country and rebuild Burma. In the years following the coup under General *Ne Win*, the generals tasted power and now wanted more. General Aung Gyi was glad he was no longer part of the regime. Immediately following his resignation from Tatmadaw Uncle flew to Machambaw in the remote hills of northern Kachin State for solitude and seclusion.

Papa and Mommy

Papa was a colonial era son with British education and Mommy had studied abroad in an American school. English was their common language and was spoken at our home. When World War II broke out, Papa and his father escaped the bombing and crossed the border into China. With proficiency in English, both my parents volunteered as interpreters for the allies. After the war, they married and Papa brought his bride to Burma. At first

Mommy was lonely as she had no family or friends and spoke no Burmese. Mommy was born and raised in China; both her parents were physicians.

My mother grew up with the social graces and rituals of the upper class culture of 5,000 years of Chinese history. Her marriage moved her to a drastically different environment, requiring a traumatic period of adjustment for a decade and a half. Life in Rangoon must have been a culture shock — foreign language, strange religious beliefs of animism, coconut worship and spirit possession, unfamiliar customs and food with people eating with their fingers. As a foreigner, she received a lukewarm welcome from her in-laws. Mommy was always impeccably dressed, either in Western suits or Chinese cheongsam (qipao), the tight fitted traditional dress. She wore pumps and high heels often with stockings — even in the tropical climate. Few locals knew or had seen nylon stockings. Papa's two sisters wore flip flops. They were well-built full-figured women and fairly outspoken. They would make less than flattering comments about Mommy's slender figure, her foreign style of dressing, or the way she ate with utensils. She was too refined and delicate for their taste. To her they were unpolished hillbillies. Neither was wrong. It is customary for Burmese people to eat with their fingers and chew with their mouths open, accompanied by slurping to indicate enjoyment — the louder the slurp, the tastier the food. They use their right hand for eating. The left hand is usually reserved for personal hygiene. At our house we used forks and spoons, but Mommy was usually served with a bowl and chopsticks. I often went to the kitchen and ate with the servants, using my fingers and slurping like the locals. All of Papa's family at U Wizara Road, including Grandma, aunts and uncles, would eat that way. The cook prepared different dishes at home, Burmese for Papa, Chinese for Mommy, and Albert's favorite was Indian food. I ate everything.

Being Roman Catholic in a family of staunch Buddhists, Papa was a non-traditional Burmese son. The Catholics from Portugal were the first missionaries to arrive in Burma in 1554. They built churches and schools. Papa was sent to study in an English Catholic parochial school in Rangoon. He was baptized as a Catholic and Friday was always fish day at home. To add insult to injury, he married a foreigner. Although he was a disciplinarian, Papa was very generous with friends. He loved to entertain, treating friends and business associates and paying for elaborate meals. Papa was witty and articulate with a funny bone, always ready with a joke. He made people laugh everywhere he went and was well liked for his generosity, love of life and sense of humor. Much of his passion for life diminished when Mommy, Albert and I left Burma. Mommy passed away a year later, never having seen him again.

Goodbye Burma

When conditions in Burma deteriorated following Uncle's resignation, my parents arranged for us to leave Burma. The idea was that Albert and I could complete our education abroad; Mommy was not a Burmese citizen and so was able to leave the country with her two minor children. As a relative of General Aung Gyi, Papa was not allowed to leave Burma. Was the military junta afraid that Aung Gyi's family member would organize anti-government campaigns outside of Burma, possibly with the help from the West? Papa said to me, "You must go with Mommy, you are strong and you will have a better future abroad." My roots were in Burmese soil and my mind wandered into the past, seeking the comfort of the good old days. General *Ne Win*'s Burmese Way to Socialism sundered families and robbed the people of freedom.

The day arrived too soon when the three of us were to board the airplane. Mingaladon Airport was full of soldiers, armed with rifles and bayonets. No one leaving the country was allowed to take any gold, jewelry or precious gemstones like rubies, sapphires and jade. They opened all our suitcases and searched the contents thoroughly. They snatched my dolly away from my arms and ripped her open head to toe to search for hidden gems. Mommy held me tight as I was shaking like a leaf. As I walked toward the plane holding her hands, I turned around to have one last look at Papa, TuTu, cousin Robert, my family and friends. I felt a lump in my throat. I waved back, clinging to Mommy's hand, fighting hard to hold back my tears of shock, sadness, anger, and confusion. It felt like I had been ripped apart like my doll.

Chapter 4. Burmese Way to Socialism

The End of the Burmese Way to Socialism

Following his resignation, *Aung Gyi* had urged General *Ne Win* to implement economic reforms, but instead, *Ne Win* made more arrests, fearing attempts by the monks and university students to organize political opposition. He also arrested *U Nu* and other former prominent political leaders without a charge.

Meanwhile rumors spread, suggesting that former Brigadier General *Aung Gyi* would soon return and save the people. *Aung Gyi* began to write letters to General *Ne Win* warning him that the economic crisis of the country would result in violent protests and uprising with potential for a civil war.

Aung Gyi had traveled to many countries, including two trips to the US, and he was stunned by the level of technological and economic progress he witnessed abroad. His letters criticizing the government and how the country has been misguided into economic ruins were widely distributed, even among the foreign diplomatic circle. Fearing the monks, the students and the people, *Ne Win* arrested *Aung Gyi*, his followers, and many politically literate monks and university students who sympathized with him. Prime Minister *U Nu*, other former prominent political heads, and many brilliant and educated community leaders were also arrested and held in 'protective custody' indefinitely. The days slipped into months and the months into years.

General *Ne Win*'s Burmese Way to Socialism was a combination of Soviet-style central planning and policy implementation based on superstitious beliefs. Faced with tumultuous uncertainties and self-imposed total isola-tion, Burma's military leaders now ran the country as they pleased without outside advice or know-how. General *Ne Win* controlled his inner circle by rewarding their loyalty with promotions and material benefits. If anyone became a threat, he was forced to retire or thrown into prison on fabricated charges. Even among the generals and officers of *Tatmadaw* there was deep mistrust and use of military intelligence to blackmail and intimidate. Polit-ical activists were interrogated and tortured until their spirit was broken and arbitrary confessions coerced. *Ne Win* and his generals kept military men under-educated and under-achieved in order to limit their job opportuni-ties and aspirations outside of the army. In such a climate of psychological and political stress, frustration, disappointment, and insecurity took a toll. Government could no longer make a positive contribution toward rebuilding the nation.

Where would Burma's future leaders come from, with universities closed for long periods? Young people were barred from studying abroad or leaving the country. Nations isolated and withdrawn from the rest of the world cannot prosper. *Ne Win* himself became not only isolated but out of touch with reality. Military culture also reinforced his isolation, as the generals and other subordinates were intimidated and reluctant to report bad news or express differing opinions and suggestions for fear of reprisals and retaliation from *Ne Win's* disapproval or dismissal from office. Only care-fully filtered, manipulated and selected news reached the top. He retained enormous personal power by purging rivals, betraying friends, and keeping followers constantly fearful, on guard, and off balance.

Ne Win consulted astrologers and fortune tellers for advice on how to prolong his rule. He ordered cars to be driven on the right side of the road, to stop threats of political attack from the right as warned by his soothsayers even though cars in Burma were built for driving in the left lane, since the British colonial era.

During *Ne Win's* era, the Burmese currency was demonetized three times, in 1964, 1985 and 1987, with the regime's stated goals to curb money supply, end profiteering and the black market, and redistribute wealth. However, demonetization ruined ordinary people and businesses and creating hyper-inflation while the black market shot up unabated.

In 1964 the authorities declared the demonetization of 50-*kyat* and 100-*kyat* notes to remove wealth from foreigners and 'evil capitalists'. Even after *Ne Win* nationalized the businesses of Chinese and Indian immigrants, in the name of the Burmese Way to Socialism, many of the businesses in Rangoon were still in the hands of the Chinese and Indians. Local resentment grew against them. In 1967, anti-Chinese riots broke out and both Beijing and Rangoon recalled their ambassadors. In 1985, *Ne Win* declared another demonetization with new 25, 35, and 75 *kyat* notes only to be devalued and replaced two years later in 1987 with 45 and 90 *kyat* notes because he believed 9 to be a lucky number. This time the demonetization accounted for an estimated 70–80% of the *kyat* banknotes in circulation and the government never offered any exchange or compensation. Hundreds of thousands foreigners, predominantly Chinese and Indians, who lost their life savings left the country in 1985.

As in the Great Depression in the US, some people went crazy and some committed suicide. However, the generals, having prior knowledge of the demonetization, profited by acquiring hard assets like land, houses, cars and jewelry. People had to pawn their possessions to buy basic necessities. With each round of demonetization, new notes were printed so fast that the money supply skyrocketed. The absence of a proper financial system and policies drove inflation into the stratosphere. The negative effects of demonetization are still remembered today and ingrained in the old generations with a deeply entrenched distrust of government. The devastating effects of demonetization were largely responsible for the 8.8.88 uprising which eventually brought about the fall of General *Ne Win*.

Fall of General Ne Win

As he advanced in years, *Ne Win's* temper and his attention span became even shorter. He was irritable, forgetful and often dozed off at meetings. His memory lapses, sleeplessness and depression clouded over his judgment and took over the aging general. Although *Ne Win* relinquished the presidency to *San Yu*, a retired general, in November 1981, he remained in control as chairman of the party. Even after his 'retirement' in 1988 he continued to wield power over the military for another decade. In his 80s, as his health deteriorated, *Ne Win* began to lose interest in politics and resigned himself to meditation to find comfort in a secluded world of his own. He began to blame himself for all the ills of the country. Once, he could do no wrong. Now, he felt he had done nothing right. He isolated himself even more and lived in seclusion at his Inya Lake villa.

Prior to his retirement, the largest demonstrations and riots broke out, now known as 8.8.88 uprising, due to worsening economic crisis and demand for regime change. Again the military violently crushed the unarmed demonstrators and massacred over 3,000 of them. Tens of thousands students fled into the jungles and border villages, or left the country. Martial law was declared by General *Saw Maung* who established the State Law and Order Restoration Council, SLORC, and ordered the army to suppress any ongoing public demonstrations. Intelligence agents penetrated student circles with constant surveillance, making any further mass gathering and political organizing difficult. *Insein* prison in Rangoon was full to capacity with arrested students, monks and activists. Many university classrooms were used as makeshift prison cells to accommodate the overflow from *Insein*.

This was the end of General *Ne Win*'s military career and almost three-decade reign of political, social and economic disaster. In the end *Ne Win* felt trapped, mired in the chaos he had created. He had refused to recognize the sound, impartial and rational recommendations of his closest confidant Brigadier General *Aung Gyi*. His paranoid fears also blinded him for decades.

After his retirement in 1988, General *New Win* became more spiritual and spent much of his time reading Buddhist scriptures. He admitted he had failed to achieve peace and prosperity through his Burmese Way to Socialism and self-reliance but declared that he had tried his best and always had the good of the people and country at heart. He died at his Inya Lake villa on December 5, 2002, and was quietly cremated in the presence of his family and a few friends, with no grandiose state funeral. His oldest friend and battle comrade, retired Brigadier General *Aung Gyi*, was among the few who attended the funeral and to pay last respect to the Old Man.

The 8.8.88 Uprising

Burma was a forgotten land, long hidden from the rest of the world until August 8, 1988, when a nationwide pro-democracy uprising known as 8.8.88 broke out in all major cities across the country. The pent up frustrations, grievances and bitter anger of the people of Burma had been growing and gathering steam for decades. People wanted an end to brutality and army dictatorship rule as they had completely lost trust and confidence in the autocratic military rule. The students felt hopeless as well with lack of future, job and career opportunities. The administration had promised change and promises had been conveniently broken at times of crisis or at elections. The people wanted the army to relinquish power and abandon the decades of failed socialist economy.

Students, Buddhist monks, and ordinary citizens called for an end to authoritarian rule and transition to democracy with mass protests and widespread demonstrations in Rangoon spreading swiftly to Mandalay and other major cities and came close to overthrowing the tyrannical government. Led by students carrying banners of fighting peacock, hundreds of thousands of people joined the protests — the *sangha* or the Buddhist clergy, businessmen, shop owners, scholars, peasants, farmers, doctors, nurses, housewives, factory workers, teachers, school kids, civil servants, actors, journalists, even soldiers – marched the streets for several days. The crowds grew bigger and bolder by the day, defying the regime's curfews and orders to disperse and demanding democracy and an end to decades of repressive one-party rule. People were lining both sides of the streets giving the marchers water, food and cigarettes, wishing them success. Monks carried their alms bowls upside down symbolizing refusal of alms from the regime and condemning them in both this life and the next. Even some soldiers were so moved by the demonstrations they laid down their weapons and joined the protesters. There were documented reports of defections from lower level police, army, navy and air force, many having complained of low pay and poor working conditions and felt trapped and hopeless in a brutal system.

Suddenly, the sound of machine guns reverberated into the crowd as the soldiers gunned them down. They opened fire, mercilessly killing and injuring thousands. Blood was everywhere. The army shot and killed an estimated 3,000 or more civilians and thousands more disappeared. The official death count was reported as only 350. Corpses were strewn in the streets, including those of many revered monks and school children with blood-stained uniforms. It is the ultimate sin for Buddhists to harm a monk, leave alone murdering one. Monks were beaten, shot, tortured, stripped of their robes in humiliation, and their faces smashed with rifle butts and bayonets. This was an act of blasphemy and a soldier could never atone for his sins tainted with such heinousness. Monasteries were raided, and monks, disrobed and beaten, were herded like cattle into trucks and taken to prison. Hundreds of other demonstrators were also carried away in army trucks never to be seen or heard again.

Rangoon General Hospital, RGH, was filled with injured students and monks screaming for help as they lay dying in the corridors and more wounded were rushed through the hospital by ambulances. The regime ordered the hospitals not to treat any of the demonstrators including injured monks. Soldiers were also ordered to shoot and kill doctors and nurses treating them. When medical staff lined up in front of RGH, begging the soldiers to stop firing at civilians, the nurses were gunned down. The Internet was shut down to prevent news coverage reaching the outside world but courageous students, activists and journalists risked their lives to record the army's acts of savagery and smuggled video footage of mass slaughtering and the bloodbath to Thailand and other neighboring countries. For days following the tragedy, chimneys billowed and smoke surged non-stop from the crematories while the world did nothing. The dead were cremated secretly without authorization and the names were not recorded, as Brigadier General *Aung Gyi* described to General *Ne Win* in a letter.[1] A spooked silence fell over Rangoon as martial law was declared.

The army justified the brutal massacre, claiming there were many communist agitators, terrorists and thugs who exploited the situation, who tried to seize government centers, utilities hubs, communication systems, ports, railroad stations, banks and businesses, plundering and looting, and provoking more violence.

Thousands of protesters fled to the borders on foot; many died of starvation and malaria and other tropical diseases. Others ended up in cramped refugee camps in Thailand and India. As the US Assistant Secretary of State for Democracy, Human Rights & Labor appropriately said, "[Burma] is one of the places in the world where it appears that pure good is at war with pure evil. The universe of other problems that the administration faces is far more morally ambiguous. Burma is refreshingly simple."

The brutal suppression of the protesters by General *Sein Lwin* won him the nickname, 'the butcher of Rangoon'. He was also responsible for the Red Bridge massacre killing 282 unarmed civilians when the armed security police under his order, chased the fleeing students and forced their heads into the lake until they drowned. Others were beaten or shot to death. The area was covered with corpses in pools of blood; thus the White Bridge became known as the Red Bridge. In a series of letters sent to *Ne Win* the retired Brigadier General criticized and exposed the corruption of the regime and its violation of basic human rights. Soon *Sein Lwin* arrested *Aung Gyi*, possibly seeking retribution against the retired General who had enough courage to oppose him. The arrest sent a shock wave throughout the international community, followed by a flood of letters expressing concern by world leadership including US Secretary of State George Shultz, Senators Patrick Moynihan and Ted Kennedy, Congressmen Thomas Foglietta and Stephen Solarz and others.[2] Under pressure from the international community, Brigadier General *Aung Gyi* was released after 27 days.

Where is the world? The people of Burma fought unarmed and were mercilessly massacred while the world remained silent. No foreign cameras were allowed into Burma. By the end of 1988, an estimated 10,000 people had been killed, and many more were missing. Although United States and other countries suspended bilateral aid, there was no international outcry and no

---

[1] *Aung Gyi's* letter to *Ne Win*. ‹http://asiapacific.anu.edu.au/newmandala/wp-content/uploads/2011/06/AungGyiLetters.pdf›

[2] July/August 1988 letters from the Committee for Restoration of Democracy in Burma to world leaders, in author's family archive.

urgent UN intervention or any substantial action taken by any international organization. Burma was so isolated that the regime's brutality was rarely reported outside of the country.

Following the 8.8.88 massacre, hardliner General *Sein Lwin* took over the government, briefly succeeding dictator General *Ne Win* as the chairman of the BSPP and ex-General *San Yu* as president. *Sein Lwin* lasted only 17 days as his ferocious methods instigated and provoked the mob and intensified the riots. He was replaced by a civilian lawyer, Dr. *Maung Maung,* who had studied at Netherland's Utrecht University and Yale University, but he too was unsuccessful at quelling the riots and lasted only 31 days. More protests and demonstrations erupted as hundreds of thousands marched in the streets carrying *Aung San's* portraits and crude weapons like sling shots and sticks. By mid-September, violence and lawlessness escalated and mass looting overran Rangoon and other major cities. Municipal government collapsed and the people took over local administration, threatening anarchy. General *Ne Win* ordered Generals *Saw Maung, Than Shwe,* and *Khin Nyunt* to organize a coup-like military to enforce calm and regain control of the country. On September 18, barely a month after the massacre, the armed forces led by General *Saw Maung* assumed all power in the nation to stabilize the country. As army commander-in-chief, he formed the 19 member military government, State Law and Order Restoration Council, SLORC, assuming total control.

General *Than Shwe* became deputy Commander-in-Chief and General *Khin Nyunt,* the spy chief in the Military Intelligence. General *Saw Maung* and his new government, SLORC, began more bloody crackdowns of protest. Troops were ordered to shoot to kill. Soldiers were strategically placed on roof tops. Without any warning they opened fire while ground troops emerged from side streets, firing machine guns as if they were fighting heavily armed enemy in a war zone. *Tamadaw* defeated the uprising but at a cost of thousands of lives and the creation of hundreds of thousands refugees.

Within a week, the revolt came to an end and power was ruthlessly secured by *Tatmadaw.* The soldiers picked up the corpses immediately and hosed down the streets to leave no evidence for the world to see. An estimated 2–300,000 ended up as refugees in the neighboring countries of Bangladesh, India and Thailand. Many ended up in the jungles where the armed ethnic armies operate. They joined the ethnic militia who trained them in guerrilla warfare in exchange for food and a promise to fight the central government alongside them. Many also died of disease or starvation. Students in Mon, Karen, Shan, Kachin and Chin States banded together and formed a student army called the All Burma Students' Democratic Front, ABSDF, based in various territories of armed ethnic nationalities.

The authorities shut down the internet and blocked phone lines and cell phone signals. Suddenly there was no more information, no images, fax, or phone communication emerging from Burma; and the horror of September dropped from international headlines. The regime controlled all forms of media to prevent news of events from leaking out. Universities were shut down again. Thousands of civilians and monks were held indefinitely in makeshift detention centers. Hospitals and clinics were prohibited from treating the injured.

Many monks were disrobed and forced to return to their villages as a way to disperse the once powerful monastic community of the *sangha*. The army hunted down ring leaders, protest organizers, and anyone who took photographs or filmed during the demonstrations.

The MI chief General *Khin Nyunt* viewed photographs and films of the demonstrations and crossed checked against registration lists to identify protesters. Under *Khin Nyunt* intelligence units harassed, intimidated and detained opposition activists. They also traced confiscated cell phones, and cameras were seized so images could be identified. Streets were thoroughly cleaned up from blood and corpses and all traces of demonstrations were erased. The world may never know what really happened in September 1988 in Burma.

The days following the uprisings, an eerie calm reigned over Burma. Martial law was instated and remained in effect until 1990. Curfews were enforced, and gatherings of five or more were forbidden. The constitution of 1974 was abolished. SLORC under General *Saw Maung* arrested thousands of people on arbitrary political grounds, some for simply distributing pro-democracy leaflets. Anyone who said anything considered to defame the government could be arrested. If your father or brother participated in anti-government demonstrations abroad, your mother and sisters would be arrested and sent to prison for no offense. In late 1988, the US cut off aid to Burma, followed by Europe and Japan.

General Ne Win's Legacy

The ruling military men of General *Ne Win's* era were trained as war fighters, not nation builders. In 1958 they cleaned up the country as a caretaker government, when needed, and they did a spectacular job in 18 months. However, when the army took over the country again in 1962, instead of handing over the helm to a civilian government after the caretaker period, corruption, power and greed overpowered the generals.

They seized all businesses and ruled as nation builders — a role for which they were grossly unqualified. The generals plundered the country's natural assets unchecked. Burma was stuck in a time warp for decades under military isolationism rule.

Even the capital, Rangoon, was frozen in time, a low-rise city with dilapidated buildings. Once a cosmopolitan hub and commercial center, Rangoon became a ghostly reminder of former glories; the British-built Victorian buildings from the colonial era fell into such decay that many have simply crumbled away. Many taxis and buses were World War II relics, and many airplanes in use were old propeller models left behind by the British. Bookshops continued selling books and magazines from the 1950s. Even today, in villages and rural areas, ox carts and bullock carts are still the only mode of transportation. Farmers use oxen to plow rice fields and about 73 percent of the population lack access to electricity. Water is hauled in from a river or public wells or captured in vats from rain. In key cities like Rangoon, running water and electricity are available but still unreliable and intermittent, frequently cut off without warning. General Ne Win's government has destroyed a prosperous country and drove its people to their knees. An agrarian nation with fertile soil and abundant sunshine, Burma was at one point the world's largest rice exporter. Under Ne Win, Burma's people now faced basic food shortages and rationed rice. General Ne Win's biggest and perhaps the only contribution to his country was the creation of solidarity within Tatmadaw, for he alone could have held the country together so intact for so long.

Chapter 5. The General *Than Shwe* Era 1992–2011

When General *Ne Win's* era ended after the massacre in 1988, General *Saw Maung* took over as chairman of SLORC for several years; he suffered a nervous breakdown and was removed in 1992.

Meanwhile, a power struggle between Generals *Than Shwe* and *Khin Nyunt*, the spy chief, intensified. *Khin Nyunt* was accused of corruption and insubordination; he was imprisoned with dozens of his aides by the opposition bloc within the inner circle of the establishment. General *Than Shwe* took over as the next iron-fisted dictator Chairman of SLORC. Over the next two decades General *Than Shwe* began a campaign of corrupt crony capitalism, opening trade with China, India and other Asian countries that did not impose sanctions on Burma. But the isolation from the Western world continued.

Oil and gas exports to China made *Than Shwe*, his families and other elite military officers extraordinarily rich while the rest of the country suffered in dire poverty. Roads were crumbling, the streets flooded during rainy season, disease was rampant, plumbing and electricity remained nonexistent outside of major cities, while the generals lived in gated mansions with swimming pools.

General *Than Shwe* was a reclusive army man trained in psychological warfare. He rose from a village boy to become the supreme ruler of *Tatmadaw* and would reign as 'emperor' for the next two decades. Under him, SLORC abandoned socialism in favor of a capitalist economy.

General *Than Shwe* 'Burmanized' all Anglo names of the British era. To erase any connection with the colonial past, names of cities, streets, parks, and places were changed to more nationalistic Burmese names. This was seen as a way to instill national pride and patriotism. Burma was renamed

Myanmar. The capital, Rangoon, became *Yangon*. Mail deliveries came to a complete standstill in the confusion; months of postal communication delays resulted in a chaotic mix up and permanent loss of mail in 1989.

Since independence, the name *Aung San* was not only magic but was the rallying cry for the people. *Bogyoke* (General) *Aung San* was the father of independence and creator of *Tatmadaw*, Burma's armed forces. In every government office, school, and public building General *Aung San's* portrait hangs. Every city, town, or village, regardless of size, has a street named after him. Over sixty years later, his daughter *Aung San Suu Kyi*, would lead the peaceful revolution against a tyrannical regime, just as her father did in 1945 against the foreign invasion and occupation of Burma.

Threatened, General *Than Shwe* took steps to counteract the *Aung San* name. The narcissistic dictator replaced *Bogyoke Aung San's* portraits at all public places with his own portraits. Burmese paper currency that depicted *Aung San's* image were removed from circulation and replaced with new banknotes bearing impersonal objects like the *chinthe*, the mythical lion insignia of the military reign. All museums dedicated to General *Aung San* were closed. Martyr's Day celebrations to honor his assassination, including lectures on his life at Rangoon University, were stopped.

General *Than Shwe* tried to open up tourism to attract revenue from foreign currency, but the campaign was unsuccessful. *Aung San Suu Kyi* boycotted the campaign, declaring tourism income would only benefit the generals and not the ordinary citizens.

Under General *Than Shwe*, *Tatmadaw* swelled in number from 180,000 to 400,000 soldiers, the largest armed forces in Southeast Asia. He also strengthened the military arsenal and bought weapons from China, North Korea and other countries.

In 1990, the authorities held an election, the first in 30 years and the main opposition party, National League for Democracy, led by *Aung San Suu Kyi*, won a landslide victory. However, *Than Shwe* refused to hand over power. Instead, he placed *Aung San Suu Kyi* under house arrest.

Under General *Ne Win*, *Tatmadaw* had consisted of men who patriotically fought for Burma independence. Under General *Than Shwe*, the soldiers were of a different generation. The younger soldiers had never been exposed to colonialism, global politics, or wars with global enemies. This generation was cut off from the world since birth. They grew up fighting civil wars against ethnic tribal groups and immersed in counter insurgency in jungle warfare.

General *Than Shwe's* regime spent only 2% of the national budget on healthcare, 4% on education and a whopping 40% on his army. Both *Ne*

Win's and *Than Shwe*'s regimes destroyed the country's once top quality higher education as Rangoon University was closed down for long periods to eliminate student activism and uprisings. *Than Shwe* created an elite class of military generals and officers who lived above the law and thrived on corruption, lining their pockets with money that could feed the poor, heal the sick and educate Burma's students.

The Ruthless Emperor

General *Than Shwe*, the supreme ruler, was also referred to as the 'Emperor' and the people feared him as he was cold and compassionless, cunning and calculating. For twenty-one years he was the supreme but shadowy ruler, shrouded in secrecy. Like many leaders and generals, *Than Shwe* came from a humble background. Born in *Kyaukse* in 1933, he started as a postal employee delivering mail after high school; he joined the army in 1958. He was trained in psychological warfare and graduated from the Officer Training School in *Hmawbi*. He rose through the ranks, becoming commander in 1983, and Vice Chief of Staff in 1985. *Than Shwe* was promoted to major general in 1986 and lieutenant general in 1987. He became Chairman of the BSPP in 1988, when pro-democracy protests broke out across the country.

During the mid-80s, General *Ne Win* started purging many high-ranking army officers out of *Tatmadaw* and filling top positions with loyal but non-threatening and lesser-known officers. *Than Shwe* was picked to be deputy commander-in-chief of the armed forces by General *Ne Win*, under commander-in-chief General *Saw Maung*. Neither was highly educated and neither had ever traveled outside of Burma, but they were *Ne Win*'s loyal puppets. *Saw Maung* became an alcoholic and later suffered a nervous breakdown; then *Than Shwe* replaced him.

From 1992 to 2011, *Than Shwe* held the reins as Chairman of the State Law and Order Restoration Council, SLORC, replacing General *Saw Maung* as Chief of Staff, Prime Minister, Minister of Defense, and Minister of Agriculture. It was a meteoric rise from uneducated village boy to be the country's No. 1 but he was relatively unknown to the outside world. He was best described as a pug faced man with glasses and teeth stained red from betel nut chewing. Fortunately, he rarely smiled.

> Betel Nut chewing is a popular custom with the working class. Many workers and farmers chew betel nut (areca nut), betel leaf and slaked lime mixture to stay awake through long hours of work. Almost every other corner of busy streets in Rangoon city center has a betel shop. This habit-forming custom causes many folks, like our driver and General Than Shwe, to have stained teeth. The driver claimed it not only kept him awake but acted as a breath freshener — more effective than Wriggly's gum. One

leaf wrap of the mixture gave him a buzz equivalent to five cups of strong coffee. But his smiles showed many missing teeth. The slaked lime (calcium hydroxide) mixture causes abrasion and wearing away teeth. The mixture creates a warm sensation in the body as the leaves have a spicy, pungent flavor, leaving a mild burning sensation in the tongue.

Although he came from a humble beginning as a lowly peasant, General *Than Shwe* had a lifelong yearning for power and wealth. He was humorless and lacked charisma or any personal charm and was fully loaded with egotistical self-regard. General *Than Shwe* was also ruthless, always ready and resolute at all cost to destroy anyone who challenged him. Over two decades of his rule, he eliminated his rivals one by one.

Than Shwe was also manipulative and very skillful dealing with the West and the UN; when the pressure was on, he made superficial concessions with minimal token steps to satisfy the international community. As time dragged on and the pressure eased, his promises were conveniently discarded. Like General *Ne Win* he also had a strong dislike for foreign intrusion and anything Western except US dollars.

He had a deep-seated distrust of intellectuals and didn't like having educated people around him. Like many military rulers, he did not like those who could think critically and independently. He craved insatiable adulation and used Buddhism as a political propaganda tool to make public displays of elaborate pagoda visits, generous meritorious work and extravagant donations.

King of Corruption

During General *Than Shwe's* rule, Burma was tied with Somalia as the most corrupt nation in the world. Burma has enough oil, gas, hardwoods and precious metals to be one of the richest countries in Southeast Asia, yet its people are among Asia's poorest. Prior to repressive army rule, Burma was one of the most educated and prosperous countries in the post-British Southeast Pacific region. Since King *Anawrahta* embraced Theravada Buddhism in the 11th century, education and religion had been inextricably linked; monasteries served as the main educational institutions. Monastic schools throughout the country provided basic education: reading, writing and arithmetic. According to UNESCO, at independence Burma had the highest literacy rate in its own language across the former British Empire largely due to the monastic schools that provided free education.[1] But shortly

---

[1] *Dictatorship, Disorder and Decline in Myanmar.* Monique Skidmore and Trevor Wilson: "Evolving Education in *Myanmar*: the interplay of state, business and the community", ANU Press, 2008, 132.

after the 1962 military coup, General *Ne Win* outlawed monastic schools, which remained banned from 1962 to 1988.

The Washington Post reported: "Sixty years ago, Burma was among the wealthiest countries in Southeast Asia, outshining its neighbors with higher standards of living and greater social mobility. Its universities attracted students from across the region".[1] Now people earned $1 a day while corrupt generals and friends of the military lived in luxury mansions. General *Than Shwe* and his junta plundered the country's rich deposits of oil, gas, minerals, and gemstones to line their pockets. They even stripped the country's cultural heritage and rare relics of Buddhist shrines and antiques. The generals, their families and their cronies amassed fortunes through monopolies over the country's lucrative businesses. Corruption was the key attribute of *Than Shwe's* era. The government's accounts were recorded using the official exchange rate of 6 *kyats* to the dollar while the bulk of the revenue, exchanged at the real rate of 12–1300 *kyats* per dollar, ended up in their pockets. As so much of the regime's energy was devoted to repressing its people rather than rebuilding a wardevastated nation, the marginalized population suffered.

During General *Than Shwe's* nearly two-decade reign the pervasive corruption continued to grow. Generals who had owned two to three mansions under General *Ne Win* now owned twenty or more. Patriotism within *Tatmadaw* was replaced by a passion to get rich quick. To maintain loyalty, *Than Shwe* allowed this corruption among his ruling circle.

All Burmese tycoons who were on international sanctions lists had close ties with the regime: *Tay Za* of the Htoo Group, *Zaw Zaw* of Max *Myanmar*, *Nay Aung* of IGE Group, *Chit Khaing* of the Eden Group, to name a few. General *Than Shwe* ensured financial security for himself and his family for generations.

He also secured his position as the unchallenged leader of the administration by promoting subordinates who were fiercely loyal to strategic command positions. He replaced high-ranking officers with younger officers to secure the military future of his establishment. He would not tolerate any challenge and would eliminate any opposition. His favorite tactic was 'divide and conquer,' creating division within any dissenting group or opposition party.

During his rule the authorities spent less than $0.40 per person per year on health[2], but his daughter's wedding cost an estimated $100 million

[1] *Facts and Details.* "*Myanmar*: Economics, Resources and Illegal Drugs". http://factsand-details.com/southeast-asia/Myanmar/sub5_5g/entry-3126.html.
[2] *BioMed Central Ltd.* Chris Beyrer and Thomas J. Lee: "Infectious diseases in Burma", March 14, 2008.

or more. General *Than Shwe* and his family were regarded with deep-seated contempt by millions of people of Burma.

The frontier regions of Kachin and Shan States are rich in deposits of gas, oil, minerals and jade, rubies, amber and gold. General *Than Shwe* and his allies suppressed the ethnic nationalities and exploited their ancestral land. According to US Congressional findings, in 2006 the regime earned over $300 million from the sale of rubies and jade, over $500 million from the sale of oil and gas, and over $2.16 billion from natural gas pipelines.[1] In these remote, hilly regions, the tropical rain forests yield some of the best hardwoods, like teak; the regime earned over $500 million from the sale of such wood.[2]

The mining and gemstone industry is controlled tightly by *Than Shwe*, his family and their crony business allies. Through a complicated network, they were deeply involved in the extraction, production, and trade of highly-prized jade worth billions of dollars. The minorities who owned these mines, located in their land, were displaced without compensation and received no financial benefit.

In the absence of law enforcement, government joint venture companies ignored the few mining regulations that existed at the time. Many areas surrounding the mines were unsafe and were prone to frequent collapses especially during the heavy rain monsoon season.

Under *Ne Win's* rule, all oil and gas resources were nationalized and renamed "People's Oil." Under *Than Shwe's* dictatorship, People's Oil was changed to *Myanmar* Oil and Gas Enterprise, MOGE. These companies became major focuses for laundering drug profits and other illicit funds hidden in offshore bank accounts for the generals.[3] Natural gas was one of the major sources of revenue that mysteriously disappeared from the official books. On rare occasion, when gas sold to neighboring countries was recorded, the rate of exchange used was outdated. These revenues benefited General *Than Shwe* and his generals handsomely but contributed nothing to improve the standard of living of the ordinary folks.

Construction of pipelines across Burma to transport oil and gas from the Middle East directly to Southern China via a seaport in western Burma was detrimental to the lives of the people who inhabited those regions. *Than*

---

[1] https://www.treasury.gov/resource-center/sanctions/Documents/pl110_286_jade_act. pdf, p3(7).

[2] *Than Shwe: Unmasking Burma's Tyrant.* Benedick Rogers; Silkworm Books: Chiang Mai, Thailand, 2010, 126.

[3] *The Burma Spring: Aung San Suu Kyi and the New Struggle for the Soul of a Nation.* Rena Pederson; New York: Pegasus, 2014, 456.

Shwe's soldiers confiscated land, displacing villagers, seizing their land, and burning their homes and villages.

Hydroelectric power was another major revenue source for General *Than Shwe*. More than 200 dams were built to generate electricity for sale to neighboring countries like China and Thailand. Again, villagers were displaced, and rivers were dammed indiscriminately, submerging surrounding homes and villages.

Illicit drugs became one of the most lucrative businesses of his reign. *Than Shwe's* cronies included drug lords; partnerships were formed to produce and launder money. At the local level there were alleged ties between local drug dealers and the junta's field commanders and soldiers. Extortion was commonplace.

General Than Shwe's Legacy

General *Than Shwe*, the bulldog, as he was often called due to his pug face, was General *Ne Win's* protégé and puppet. After *Ne Win* promoted him to chairman of State Law & Order Restoration Council, *Than Shwe* changed the name of SLORC to make it less intimidating. The name State Peace and Development Council, SPDC, was selected on the advice of an American PR firm hired in 1997.

During the 1990s General *Than Shwe* tried to generate foreign exchange revenue and revive Burma's economy by ending international isolation and encouraging foreign investment and tourism. He officially declared 1996 as the year of tourism, with colorful 'Visit *Myanmar*' posters with the hope of attracting half a million visitors. The economic liberalization was not intended to improve the people's well-being or standard of living but to enrich the elite and strengthen their control. A stronger *Tatmadaw* would be better able to keep down the minority ethnic forces with whom civil war had been simmering for five decades.

An English-language television channel was suddenly launched. Almost overnight, hotels, airports, roads, and rail systems were built with forced labor using thousands of people, including children. The majority of the hotels built for tourists were owned by the military, their families and their cronies. Towns and villages were bulldozed. People were forced to move, at gunpoint, to proposed but unfinished resettlement satellite sites with no water, electricity, toilets, clinics, schools, buses or food supplies. Many perished due to diseases in the punishing heat or from bites from venomous vipers in the barren, scorched ground.

Than Shwe harbored the most intense dislike for *Aung San's* daughter, *Suu Kyi*, whom he had confined to house arrest to prevent her from leading an uprising. As she continued to defy him and his administration, he rewrote the constitution, amending Article 50(f) to ban her from becoming president. *Aung San Suu Kyi* opposed the government's 'Visit *Myanmar*' program and supported a boycott of foreign aid and tourism, criticizing the construction of hotels and new infrastructure that did not benefit the populace. 'Visit *Myanmar*' year turned out disappointing. Meanwhile, Asia was hit by the financial crisis.

General *Than Shwe* negotiated multi-billion dollar trade and military deals with China and Russia. He imported weapons and military know-how from Russia and North Korea. He sold off Burma's oil and gas, teak, and precious stones. He granted licenses and construction contracts to build deep sea ports, pipelines, hydroelectric power plants and infrastructure projects and formed lucrative ventures with drug lords in the remote hills connected to the Golden Triangle. Earth Rights International reported the junta earned US$4.83 billion from gas sales alone, between 2000 and 2009, but this was never included in the national budget as the money ended up in offshore bank accounts of the junta's generals. With part of the revenues received, he more than doubled the size of *Tatmadaw* from 180,000 to 400,000.

In 2005 General *Than Shwe* poured $4 billion to move Rangoon, the capital since 1885, to the newly built concrete fortified city of *Naypyidaw*, or 'Abode of the Kings'. *Naypyidaw* is built as a Burmese-style fantasy, an extravaganza in a remote region in central Burma, approximately 200 miles north of Rangoon, backed by a protective mountain range. Living under constant paranoia of a potential attack from foreign powers, *Than Shwe* felt *Naypyidaw* was less vulnerable to invasion by sea. The move further isolated the government from the public and international community as foreign embassies and consulates were still located in Rangoon, the commercial and financial capital.

Naypyidaw was built in great secrecy and unveiled in a surprise public announcement by the military in 2006. The new capital, complete with North Korean-designed underground bunkers and escape tunnels, was built with 20-lane highways, 8-lane avenues, spotless clean pavement and multiple golf courses, but few planes were seen on the tarmac. Several gilded buildings with elaborate steeples, supposedly to house various ministries and departments, remained empty except for occasional political summits and meetings. Communication with government officials at *Naypyidaw* became more cumbersome and access to ministers more limited. General *Than Shwe* was profoundly paranoid about a foreign invasion to restore democracy to Burma, especially from the US.

The sprawling new capital also fed his vanity as an 'emperor'. During the Burmese monarchy, the establishment of a new capital coincided with the founding of a new dynasty. Did *Than Shwe* believe he was a reincarnated king of Burma? In the new capital he also built the *Uppatasanti* Pagoda to replicate the *Shwedagon*, a huge new zoo with AC-equipped penguin house, an Olympic-size soccer stadium, five golf courses, and a jewelry museum displaying Burma's gems. A profound waste of time and money as the locals and villagers could not afford the price of admission nor understand or appreciate what is there. A million soldiers and bureaucrats were relocated to *Naypyidaw*, four times the size of Singapore, leaving their families behind until schools, recreation facilities, hospitals, and other related essential facilities could be built.

The surreal capital, built with multi-lane highways and manicured roundabouts remain mostly empty and devoid of traffic. Luxury villas in the surrounding hills of *Pobbathiri* township, dubbed the 'row of six' mansions, including a fortified villa for General *Than Shwe*, were built for the ruling elite while concrete block housing were assigned to the soldiers and low ranking government employees. The six mansions are reserved for *Than Shwe* and his five inner circle SPDC top brass, General *Thura Shwe Mann*, Vice Senior General *Maung Aye*, former President General *Thein Sein*, Lieutenant General *Thiha Thura Tin Aung Myint Oo* and Lieutenant General *Tin Aye*.

In 2008, *Than Shwe* rewrote the constitution, the country's third and current constitution, giving *Tatmadaw* key control of the government with 25% of seats in parliament reserved for military officers and the ministries of home, border affairs and defense to be headed by the military. The new constitution also contains provisions to stop any attempt to prosecute the ruling generals for crimes committed while the administration was in power. Hence, no *Tatmadaw* soldier or officer can be prosecuted for human rights violations, atrocities committed, irresponsible exploitation of resources, and the untold cost of damage caused by illegal trade, epidemics, drug addiction, deforestation, and destruction of ecosystems. Rule of law meant nothing over the last half century.

Human Rights Violations

General *Than Shwe*'s reign of terror consisted of two decades of indiscriminate killing and torture of non *Bamar* ethnic nationalities of Burma. He was guilty of crimes against students, monks, minorities, ordinary people and anyone with anti-government sentiment. The barbaric acts were not only widespread but repeated and consistent, as if in a written policy of his administration. *Than Shwe* would not tolerate dissent in any shape.

General *Than Shwe* thrived in a system based on inequality and exploitation. His soldiers killed and tortured, burned homes, confiscated land and property, forced the displacement of citizens, and made arbitrary arrests. The army employed helicopter gunships, military artillery and anti-tank rockets. Villages were razed to the ground for lucrative government projects that benefited the military generals and their families. In these predominantly Christian villages, soldiers destroyed churches and ordered the villagers to build Buddhist pagodas or temples. Burmese soldiers frequently demanded forced labor, food, shelter, ox-carts, bicycles, and sexual services from the local tribal people. Young girls and women were kidnapped, raped, tortured, and sold as sex slaves and mail-order brides while boys and young men were taken to be trained as child soldiers and used as human mine sweepers. Often, army field commanders used forced labor to dig trenches, build army camp fences, and to carry soldiers supplies in dangerous mine strewn terrain.

Than Shwe authorized the use of landmines in conflict regions around ethnic villages and unsuspecting villagers were severely injured or killed by accidentally stepping on them as the ground was littered with landmines. The military has been known to contact the bereaved family to ask for compensation for the lost mine. Villagers were kidnapped to be used as slaves, human shields, human minesweepers or unpaid coolies (porters) using threats and violence if their orders and commands were disobeyed. Thousands of ethnic villagers fled on bare foot through impenetrable jungles to neighboring countries ending up in refugee camps while others died of injuries inflicted by poisonous scorpions, snakes, and crocodiles. Many died in crossfire between the military and the armed ethnic fighters. Forced to survive in harsh jungle conditions without any medical care, many died from mosquito-borne disease like malaria or bacteria and parasitic infections such as cholera, dysentery and severe diarrhea, others died of malnutrition and starvation. Human rights abuses took place in jungles and remote regions of bordering states and were largely hidden from the international view rarely seen or heard.

Rape is a common war weapon and minority girls and women were abducted to be used as sex slaves and prostitutes while others were gang-raped and killed afterwards. Those who escaped to refugee camps told of heinous acts by *Tatmadaw* soldiers: the rape of a 12-year-old girl in front of her mother, a gang rape of a woman while her husband was held and made to watch, the rape of a disabled and helpless woman, just to cite a few. Some reported that the army cut off women's breasts and gouged out their eyes.

Sexual violence and torture were almost never reported because of fear of stigma and reprisals; if they were reported, investigations were rare and no soldier has ever been convicted or jailed for his crime.

Military attacks on tribal villages displaced almost a million people, forcing them to flee to refugee camps across the border, mostly to Thailand. The UN and other international human rights groups were denied access to the regions and their investigation were obstructed. The United Nations never prosecuted *Than Shwe* for crimes against humanity due to China voting against the ballot before the UN Security Council. China always protected the Burmese military establishment, as Beijing holds a formidable economic stake in Burma's gas and oil, timber and gemstones, and hydroelectric power. The corrupt generals negotiated deals and formed joint ventures giving China unlimited access to mineral deposits and lined their own pockets with profits from the sale.

Than Shwe's subordinates were required to kneel down before him and his family, stooping in self-abnegation, with total disregard for human dignity. In 2002 he accused *Ne Win*'s close relatives of plotting to take over the country; he placed his old boss and his daughter, *Sanda Win*, under house arrest at their Inya Lake villa. *Ne Win*'s son-in-law, *Sanda*'s husband and three grandsons were also arrested for allegedly plotting a coup and imprisoned on charges of high treason.

Torture and Imprisonment

The Buddhist clergy, the *sangha*, has always been regarded with respect and superstitious veneration by the people of Burma; and General *Than Shwe*'s regime wanted to reduce the influence and political voice of powerful saffron-robed monks. Over decades, the monks and the university students courageously staged protests but each time, they were brutally suppressed. There were so many arrests — students, monks, civilians, democracy activists, political dissidents, social workers, civic leaders, journalists, and veteran politicians — the number of prisoners grew to hundreds of thousands and the jails were overflowing, necessitating the use of university classrooms as temporary makeshift prison cells. Confessions were extorted from political prisoners whose only crime was expressing anti government sentiment driven by a burning desire for freedom. Torture included physical, psychological and sexual abuses.

According to Human Rights Yearbook of the exiled National Coalition Government of the Union of Burma all methods of torture were used in Burmese prisons that defied international standards. Prisoners were viciously beaten, suffocated, sleep- and light- deprived, stabbed and starved. Other prison tortures include shackling of necks, legs and arms for prolong periods, burning body parts with cigarettes and lighters, applying repeated electric shocks to genitals, walking or crawling on sharp stones, metal and glass, being suspended from the ceiling and then spun around, solitary confinement, and forms of mental torture. *Tatmadaw* soldiers also mutilated people grotesquely, gouging out eyes, cutting off fingers, and chopping off heads.

Even monks were beaten to death or shot and killed. The s*angha*, esti-mated at around 400,000 monks, is the second largest institution in the country next to *Tatmadaw*. The relationship between the two has been rocky under the dictatorship. Like the university students, the monks have been politically active and pose a threat due to their potential opposition to the ruling generals. Military intelligence agents infiltrated the monasteries long ago; they defrocked, beat and killed hundreds of monks who resisted and defied their rule. If one monk engaged in anti-government activities, the rest of the monastery was given communal punishment. Some soldiers also looted the gemstones donated by the Buddhist community and buried in Buddhist shrines.

Over decades of *Ne Win's* and *Than Shwe's* autocratic regimes the practice of Buddhism seemed to have declined among the uniformed men of *Tatmadaw*, as both dictators placed more trust in numerology and astrology. The generals also curried favor with senior monks and abbots, showering them lavish gifts like automobiles, cash donations, merit accumulating ceremonies offering *suhn* (prepared food offering for monks), and financially supporting religious restoration projects. But the younger monks were angered by the suffering of the people and the army's brutality. The divisions between senior abbots and young monks, and between the s*angha* and *Tatmadaw* widened over the years with the rise of militarism.

Cut Off from the World

Like his predecessor, General *Than Shwe* also imposed total seclusion and detachment from the world. With the economy stagnant and isolated from the world, technological advances were almost non-existent. Facto-ries stopped operating due to lack of raw materials and spare parts. Elec-tricity was intermittent at best. Workers sat all day reading magazines or engaging in gossip. Radio and television stations were state-owned and aired only government propaganda. All books, magazines, newspaper, and media were censored and controlled by the authorities. There was no TV in

Burma until the mid-80s, when it became available on a strictly limited basis to air government propaganda. Modern conveniences like smart phones and credit cards were non-existent for decades while they flourished in neighboring countries. Even when they became available, few people could afford cell phones. Land phones were tapped, and telexes and postal mail were routinely censored and read. When the internet came along, access was controlled. There were no private email providers and unauthorized ownership of modems or fax machine was punishable by 15 years of imprisonment. Not only were the generals of *Tatmadaw* isolated from international life, the seclusion from the world community was passed down to the people of the following generations.

The Saffron Revolution

Over the decades of tyranny there were many failed uprisings; the army's tanks were no match for unarmed students, monks and civilians. In 2007 unannounced and without warning, *Than Shwe's* regime removed the state fuel subsidies, causing a dramatic rise in fuel prices to unaffordable levels. Natural gas increased by 500%, oil prices rose almost 66%, and bus and train tickets doubled. Other commodities, food and basic necessities also shot up due to the administration's mismanagement, irresponsibility and corruption. People could not afford to go to work or buy food as increased transportation costs pushed food prices even higher. People had enough as their living conditions deteriorated rapidly.

Mass protests began with the support and collaboration of the *sangha*. At first protests were led primarily by students and democratic activists, some carrying the flag of the fighting peacock, democratic symbol of National League of Democracy. As the protest rapidly gained momentum, tens of thousands of monks peacefully joined the protesters. The monks have prior confirmation with *Aung San Suu Kyi* of their unity and mutual support of the *sangha* and the pro-democratic movement for each other. The participation of the Buddhist clergy gained and energized the support of ordinary citizens throughout the country and the demonstrations grew swiftly, with increased participation of the general public. Many people joined hands forming a human chain to protect the monks. Thousands of bystanders applauded and offered water to the marchers. People thought the authorities would not use violence as in the 8.8.88 crackdown on the students, due to the presence of the Buddhist clergy. However, this proved wrong and it became one of the bloodiest crackdowns in Burma's history.

On September 26, 2007, the military junta fired on the protests killing, beating and arbitrarily detaining thousands. The next day, the army barricaded the *Shwedagon* and gunned down more unarmed protesters in a massacre dubbed 'Saffron Revolution' by the international press. In the midst of chaos, a Japanese journalist was shot point blank and killed, in broad daylight, by a *Tatmadaw* soldier.

In Buddhist countries like Burma, the killing of monks constitutes an unforgivable sin. It is unimaginable for a Buddhist soldier to attack, let alone kill, a *hpongyi* (monk). The number of fatalities was kept hidden but it was believed to be in the hundreds. Buddhist monks responded to this violence with more marches, spread across the country, with hundreds of thousands of people peacefully protesting in the streets. In retribution, more monks were beaten and arrested, others were disrobed, and monasteries throughout the country were raided, ransacked, and closed. Hundreds of monks were arrested and hauled away in army trucks like common criminals instead of venerable Buddhist holy men. To the Buddhist population such disrespect and attack is an act of sacrilege, an unfathomable sin which can never be atoned. The authorities produced fake Buddhist monks by planting soldiers with shaven heads in monasteries as informants to learn of any anti-government plans.

Among the thousands arrested, imprisoned and/or tortured were student activists like the famed *Min Ko Naing*. Even the country's famous comic, *Zaganar*, was jailed for making anti-government jokes and comments. Thousands of people were imprisoned and tortured. Those that survived went in hiding, some went underground while others escaped across the border to Thailand. A strict curfew was imposed by the army throughout Rangoon and other major cities.

Unlike the 8.8.88 revolt, this time the world could see the bloody massacre live on their TV screens as the events unfolded. In 1988, all camera footage taken by journalists and tourists was confiscated at the airport, but in 2007 many folks had digital cameras and were able to email the footage and images abroad. Real time coverage of bloody scenes reached the global community and hit the headlines of every major television network and newspaper.

Radio broadcasts blasted the news on BBC, VOA, Radio Free Asia and DVA. The world watched in horror and disbelief. The junta desperately shut down the internet to cut off international phone calls and access to the media. General *Than Shwe* immediately ordered the army to hide the evidence. Blood stained streets were hosed down and corpses picked up and carried away in army trucks. *Than Shwe* was secured and secluded in a concrete-fortified residential fortress in *Naypyidaw* while his wife and family fled the country.

Meanwhile, *Than Shwe* and his MIs began mass arrests of ordinary civilians in the thousands, not just the protesters and monks. They scanned photo-graphs and video footage and arrested civilian bystanders who supported the demonstration by cheering, applauding, and offering water and ciga-rettes to the marchers.

Following the Saffron Revolution, public gatherings were banned. Although soldiers heavily guarded the streets, pagodas, and monasteries scattered small demonstrations by the people continued in the days that followed the Revolution. The *sangha* refused to accept alms from the generals and their families. The monks walked the streets with the alms bowls upside down known as *thabeik hmauk*, as an act of defiance against the military. The streets of Burma may have quieted down but the sense of dissatisfaction, alienation, and anger against the ruling junta remained visibly strong.

International Reaction and Sanctions

The US, EU, Canada, and Australia tightened economic sanctions against Burma and black listed its top officials for the mass killing of unarmed protesters. Unfortunately, punitive action and threats by Western countries had little or no impact on the administration as it continued to trade with other Asian countries.

Decades of trade embargo with the West resulted in little change as Burma continued to do business as usual with its major trading partners. The US banned imports of Burmese products and banned investment in Burma. Washington also prohibited financial transactions with Burmese organiza-tions and imposed visa bans on high-ranking Burmese government officers, their families, and business cronies. The UN sent a special envoy to Burma, and the UN secretary general, Ban Ki-moon, condemned the crackdown as 'abhorrent and unacceptable'. Although China called on the Burmese leaders to restrain from violence, it maintained its traditional reluctance to partici-pate in sanctions of any kind, under the banner of non-interfere in Burma's domestic affairs.

For decades the West imposed economic sanctions and other punitive measures to punish the military regime but the Burmese government just kept expanding and growing stronger. Sanctions did not alter the admin-istration's attitude or its policies. Instead, they made the government more xenophobic, resenting any external interference from the West and inten-sifying the junta's bunker mentality. Western sanctions also heightened its isolation as the authorities restricted tourists and journalists.

Life for the ordinary people became even more difficult as basic necessities became unavailable and shortages widespread. The regime recognized
Burma's geo-strategic position and used it to its advantage by playing one
country against another. At the same time the junta accepted military, political and financial aid from China, India and Pakistan, and whoever offered
aid in exchange for the rights to exploit Burma's natural deposits. Eventually, increased trade with Asian countries flooded neighboring countries
with Burmese heroin and other drugs, causing epidemic addiction among
their population.

History Distorted

The administration rewrote Burmese history, falsifying the facts on a
grand scale. Decades of isolation kept the ruling generals inscrutable and
shrouded in secrecy. State archives were inaccessible to outsiders. Every
photograph, manuscript, document or film that did not meet censorship
was destroyed. Ordinary citizens have no rights or justice and no freedom
of speech; the military regime defied the rights of people and the views of
the international community. Past uprisings were portrayed as mere 'distur-
bances' instigated by terrorists and political dissidents. No one has been held
responsible to this day for the savage suppression of demonstrators.

Cyclone Nargis

In early May 2008, Cyclone Nargis, the worst natural disaster in Burmese
history, ripped through the Irrawaddy Delta region and devastated Southern
Burma, leaving over 200,000 dead and over 2.5 million injured and homeless.
Other estimates suggest the death toll may be as high as 500,000. The
official toll was reported at 138,000. Fishermen and farmers of the delta
region were most affected, as their homes and livelihoods were swept away
overnight. Most of the livestock was killed, fishing vessels destroyed or sank,
and million acres of rice paddies in the Irrawaddy delta flooded and ruined
by seawater. *Than Shwe's* junta shockingly closed doors to international relief
aid, downplayed the damage and dragged its feet in callousness. Despite
foreknowledge from meteorological reports from India, the authorities did
nothing to warn the people or to prepare them for the disaster. Tens of thousands died due to the natural disaster but many more died after the cyclone
due to the regime's criminal negligence. The willful indifference and neglect
of General *Than Shwe's* regime toward its people before, during, and after the
cyclone were more shocking than the storm itself.

Cyclone Nargis cost an estimated loss of $4 billion. The authorities refused international aid and denied foreign relief groups access to the Delta regions. All aid from the UN, US, UK, France and others was adamantly turned down. Foreign aid workers and disaster relief specialists were denied entry. The government also delayed the entry of UN planes delivering medicine, food and other needed supplies.

Cameras, videos and related equipment were seized from people's homes to prevent filming cyclone victims. Soldiers were sent to blockade the roads, preventing news media and journalists from seeing the devastation. Eventually the neighboring Asian countries that sent rescue teams and relief supplies were allowed access, but for weeks, US, British, and France naval vessels and aircraft with hundreds of thousands pounds of emergency relief supplies, water purification tablets, food, tents, mosquito nets and life-saving medicines circled Burma coastal waters waiting for permission from the junta to dock. They had to leave with the aid undelivered. Consequently, thousands more died due to starvation, untreated injuries and infectious diseases.

When the military government failed to respond to the humanitarian crisis, ordinary Burmese folks from local communities and other Delta regions across the country emerged in droves and undertook emergency rescues, providing food, water, supplies and shelter to the affected region. Rich and poor, Buddhists and non Buddhists, banded together.

No effort was made to collect the corpses or identify them. They were left to rot, floating in rivers and surrounding villages in the heat of the tropical sun. Following the cyclone, when billions worth of donations from abroad started to pour into the country, the generals diverted the funds to themselves. They also changed the foreign relief supplies and had the *Tatmadaw* generals' names written over the names of the actual donors from abroad.[1] A truly contemptuous way to use aid for propaganda purpose.

Further, the administration enriched itself by selling donated food and other relief supplies on the black market. Loads of rice and other supplies donated by relief teams were stolen by the pariah regime and sold at inflated price in black market to line their pockets. Even Western-made donated nutritional food bars were taken by the army and used for their soldiers. Container loads of supplies received by air, marked with labels such as US AID, were taken to government warehouses and some showed up at regime's army camps or were sold on the black market.

---

[1] *The Burma Spring: Aung San Suu Kyi and the New Struggle for the Soul of a Nation.* Rena Pederson; New York: Pegasus, 2014, 395.

The authorities had the gall to request almost $12 billion in cash dona-tions for reconstruction from the international community while providing so little of its own and stealing supplies that were delivered. Even in times of catastrophic tragedy *Than Shwe*'s junta profited from donations by distorting exchange rates, giving themselves a profit of 250 times. The UN also reported a loss of $10 million aid intended for cyclone victims that was skimmed off by military banks using manipulated exchange rates.[1]

According to the New York Times, the total donation from the inter-national community was $240 million or about $100 for every person who survived the cyclone, but the military did not pass it all along.[2] After one week of foot dragging the junta, under global pressure, finally gave permis-sion to land plane loads of relief aid which were loaded into military trucks and disappeared. Other aid in terms of supplies ended up with the junta with no accountability, transparency or ability to track the delivery of the goods. In his book, Benedict Rogers reported another insolent regime manipulation to produce distorted images to the world for propaganda purposes.[3] Two weeks after the cyclone, *Than Shwe* and his generals were filmed visiting the devastated area and handing out relief supplies to the displaced locals living in tents. As soon as the TV crew and the generals left, the displaced villagers had to hand back the aid supplies, the tents were dismantled, and they were sent away without food, water, medicine or shelter.

In the midst of the fiasco, the junta was busy planning to stage a new constitution to guarantee that no government officials would be held liable for their actions, i.e. protection from prosecution for all acts of brutality from international tribunal. Despite the cyclone tragedy and devastation and subsequent chaos, the junta proceeded with a national referendum rigged to achieve a desired result by intimidating voters to vote 'yes' with threats of prison, loss of job, cut off water or electricity supply, or be beaten. Students were harassed to vote 'yes' or fail to graduate.

The regime introduced a sham constitution in 2008 and declared a bogus 97% turnout and 99% 'yes' vote. The same year the name of the country was changed from the Union of *Myanmar* to the Republic of the Union of *Myanmar*. The regime also changed country's flag and its national anthem.

The following year a conflict between the government and ethnic minorities broke out in Shan state in eastern Burma, forcing 10,000 civilians to flee into Yunnan province in southern China. In anticipation of a new election in 2010,

---

[1] *Reuters*. Louis Charbonneau and Megan Davies: "UN admits 'significant' *Myanmar* exchange rate loss", Jul 28, 2008.

[2] *The Burma Spring: Aung San Suu Kyi and the New Struggle for the Soul of a Nation.* Rena Pederson; New York: Pegasus, 2014, 456.398-9.

[3] *Burma A Nation at the Crossroads.* Benedict Rogers; London: Rider, 2012, 193.

many top echelons of the military resigned their positions to become candidates for the military-backed Union Solidarity and Development Party, USDP.

Than Shwe's government passed the election laws with provisions for an electoral commission hand-picked by the junta. To no one's surprise, USDP claimed resounding victory in the first election in 20 years. Not surprising, widespread fraud was rumored and the election was widely condemned as a sham.

Nonetheless, the regime declared a transition from military rule to a civilian democracy, and *Aung San Suu Kyi* was released from house arrest. General *Than Shwe* is said to have 'retired' in 2011 (although no one thinks he has stood down entirely), and is living in a heavily guarded compound in a concrete fortified fortress in *Naypyidaw*.

Ex General *Thein Sein* was elected President. The new government under President *Thein Sein* began the opening of the country to the outside world.

Chapter 6. Pro-Democratic Leaders

After the 1962 coup, as we've seen, Brigadier General *Aung Gyi* headed multiple key ministries under General *Ne Win* and he became the second most powerful man in the nation. Brigadier General *Aung Gyi* was a person with depth and expertise in national affairs including Burma's economy, and he represented the government of Burma to the West and the outside world.

Brigadier General Aung Gyi (1919–2012)

Aung Gyi was born in *Paungde* on Feb 16, 1919, to middle class textile merchants, *U Tint* and *Daw Lay*. After high school, he attended the British Imperial Staff College in Rangoon and received training in military structure, organization and strategy implementation. He worked at the British Secretariat office for the Burma Revolutionary Party, collecting vital information about the British. He was hand-picked by *Bogyoke* (General) *Aung San*, the national hero of Burma and father of independence, as an honest, smart and hard-working recruit.

General *Aung San* recruited *Aung Gyi* from *Ne Win*'s 4th battalion as he saw him as an astute but decent young politician. *Aung Gyi* was nominated to run for the Constituent Assembly and became Secretary of Defense. He drafted the Burmese constitution with other members of the Committee. As a member of the Constituent Assembly *Aung Gyi* was politically senior to *Ne Win*, who was only a colonel at that time. Prior to independence *Aung Gyi* was appointed a member of General *Aung San*'s cabinet by the British Governor of the time, and as such, *Aung Gyi* was also politically senior to *Ne Win*.

At General *Aung San's* wedding to *Daw Khin Kyi, Aung Gyi* stood as his best man. He was not only loved and respected by the common folks but by *Tatmadaw* as he was a man of principle, integrity and no pretension. Despite his high position *Aung Gyi* was always readily accessible to his subordinates and colleagues. People valued his ideas and opinions.

In 1944, *Aung Gyi* together with *Maung Maung* (later Brigadier *Maung Maung*) and several young officers,[1] built foundation to educate and train recruits to fight for freedom. They organized the various rickety and crumbling groups of freedom fighters into one cohesive team and planned how to throw off foreign dominion; they shaped Burmese history and got its independence. They created an educational and training institution modeled after West Point US Military Academy which became the Defense Services Academy, DSI, the best structured professional organization of the country. This provided world-class military reform and professional training to Burma's armed forces. He was largely responsible for building the foundation that is today's military, *Tatmadaw.* New recruits, high school graduates, studied science, math, engineering, economics, history, geography, and military related subjects. In affiliation with Rangoon University they were trained to be sophisticated military leaders. *Aung Gyi* and *Maung Maung* also created the Officer Training School, OTS to train front line soldiers and field commanders of the armed forces.

Aung Gyi did not drink, smoke or gamble; he meditated and lived a clean uncomplicated life guided by Buddhist principles. He believed politicians must be spotless, free from corruption, and honorable and loyal to their country. He lived a plain, simple life with his wife and daughter. *Aung Gyi* was known as a compassionate person, benevolent leader and the country's economic guru. He was entrusted with the entire national economic planning and international trade policy of the country. During *Ne Win's* frequent trips abroad to London and Europe, which could extend to months, Brigadier General *Aung Gyi* was left in charge of the military, the economy and the entire country.

But Brigadier General *Aung Gyi* resigned from the military government in February 1963. His resignation might have averted a potential civil war, but it jolted the nation and shocked the international community. Several senior army officers of the Revolutionary Council resigned, too. Some were Japanese-trained and had fought under General *Aung San* for independence; now they had fallen out of favor with General *Ne Win,* and they opposed his

---

[1] *Aung Gyi, Tin Pe, Chit Khine, Aye Maung, Ye Htut,* served in the field while *Bo Khin Maung Gale, Bo Win, Maung Maung* served at the War Office.

principles and mission for the country. Two decades later, together with Brigadier General *Aung Gyi*, they would join hands with General *Aung San's* daughter to form an opposition party against the military dictatorship, known as National League of Democracy.

Foreign dignitaries visited the retired Brigadier General in his home, voicing concerns over Burma's break with the rest of the world, especially with respect to non-payment of interest on loans from foreign banks, rice export commitments, and other obligations. Reports of this nature, sent to *Ne Win* via official channels, generally got lost or their original meaning distorted by the time they reached the top.

Aung Gyi was informed by overseas buyers that the rice exported from Burma were infested with insects and not fit for human consumption. He reported in his letter to General *Ne Win* that quality inspections were needed before shipments, or Burma would lose world's major market share. Rice mills and storage facilities had been run down or closed, and rising transportation costs prevented adequate distribution. *Aung Gyi* also reported mistreatment of farmers by soldiers, including the use of torture if they were unable to meet government demanded quotas of rice production.

Since the mid-1960s during Red Brigadier *Tin Pe's* tenure as trade minister, many farmers had given up growing rice, causing steadily declining production and threatening rice shortages and domestic famine. Once, en route to Australia for medical treatment for his wife, retired *Bogyoke* (General) *Aung Gyi* stopped over in Bangkok. He saw how Thailand's economy was booming and had progressed decades ahead of Burma. He was shocked to see the varieties of premium-quality rice unseen in Burma. Even the split rice which was used for animal feed was superior to the rice used for human consumption in his country. He sent many written communication to *Ne Win* criticizing corruption, mismanagement and incompetence and advised his old boss of the situations at grass root levels and repeatedly suggested urgent reforms.

When *Ne Win* continued to ignore his advice, *Aung Gyi* began to make speeches of protest against the government. The retired Brigadier General openly criticized the mismanagement and the human rights abuses by the army and the junta. Support for *Aung Gyi* spread throughout the country, among students, the *sangha*, and ordinary citizens. Despite his loyalty to his long-time colleague General *Ne Win* and the *Tatmadaw* he cofounded and nurtured, *Aung Gyi* was critical of the Burmese Way to Socialism. It had failed the country and impoverished its people.

He knew the risks of criticizing *Ne Win's* rule and understood the consequences of making public the army's crimes. As General *Ne Win's* regime became more ruthless and corrupt, *Aung Gyi's* continued blunt criticisms resulted in his arrest and imprisonment four times. From 1965–68 he was imprisoned in Mandalay in solitary confinement for four years and eight months, with no contact with the outside, not even his family. He not only suffered total isolation during this prison confinement, he lost his voice due to vocal cord atrophy and damage resulting from prolonged disuse. Although he regained his voice through meditation and therapy, it was permanently changed, with a loss of volume and the need for increased speaking effort. The soft-spoken man spoke even softer.

People's aspirations turned into rumors that strengthened by the day, suggesting that former Brigadier General *Aung Gyi* would soon return and save the people. Many former prominent political leaders including *Bo Let Ya, Bo Setkya, U Kyaw Nyein, U Ba Swe, Thakin Tha Khin, Bo Khin Maung Galay*, Brigadier Tommy Clift and *Bomhu Aung* had joined former Prime Minister *U Nu* to form an anti-*Ne Win* opposition group.

U Nu also unsuccessfully tried to recruit the retired Brigadier General to stage a rebellion against *Ne Win*. *Aung Gyi* knew how *Ne Win's* inner circle worked and tried to discourage *U Nu*, explaining the army's staunch loyalty and devotion to *Ne Win* meant that his effort would be futile. *U Nu* was unconvinced and proceeded anyway; he failed, as predicted. *U Nu* fled to Thailand and was later exiled in India. He remained an opposition leader in exile but returned to Burma in 1980 as a proponent of democracy for the nation until his death in 1995 at the age of 88.

Ne Win felt increasingly threatened as rumors spread throughout the country that former Brigadier General *Aung Gyi* would rise again to lead the people. *Ne Win* wanted to suppress people's support of the increasingly popular Brigadier General *Aung Gyi*. General *Ne Win* imprisoned Brigadier General *Aung Gyi* again, this time for eighteen months from 1972–74. *Aung Gyi* was detained in political custody with former prime minister *U Nu* and hundreds of other political opponents of the administration. So many brilliant, educated men and distinguished scholars, many were Western educated from the colonial days, including financial, intellectual and political elites, were taken into 'protective custody' indefinitely, without a trial. At the same time ill trained and misguided officers ran the country, digging Burma into deeper economic chaos. Burma had achieved a great leap backward just as the rest of Asia was enjoying record growth.

After the 8.8.88 uprising and barbaric crackdown by the regime, *Aung Gyi* was the first senior military man brave enough to attack *Ne Win's* policies openly. His letters to General *Ne Win* called for drastic reforms, and they were widely distributed and circulated throughout the nation by students and civilians and even reached foreign embassies and the international media.

Aung Gyi gained increasing support of the people as his predictions proved correct. The retired General warned *Ne Win* that news of army violence and abuses had spread worldwide; news of how protesting students were trapped and beaten to death; and women students were dragged by their long hair, raped and kicked into nearby Inya Lake to drown. Those still alive but injured were crammed into trucks, many suffocating to death. Some were taken to jail and massacred. There were so many bodies — on the streets, Inya Lake embankment, trucks, jail, hospitals — they were cremated without family notification, identification or record. University professors, doctors and hospital staff, and ordinary people were eyewitnesses to these brutal events.

Photographs of these incidents were taken by some foreigners, smuggled out of the country and sent to human rights organizations outside the country. *Aung Gyi* wrote a 41-page letter to General *Ne Win* describing what he had seen, criticism for the devastated economy, and the violence, brutality, and human rights abuses. Once more he was arrested and imprisoned for 27 days in 1988. In 1992 under General *Than Shwe*'s rule *Aung Gyi* was arrested for the fourth time and imprisoned for six months by Military Intelligence chief General *Khin Nyunt*, who fabricated allegations in a desperate attempt to assassinate his character and bring down his business success as an ordinary civilian owner of a tea house.

When Uncle Aung Gyi was placed under house arrest, Military Intelligent informers and soldiers were placed around his house and in his compound 24/7 to spy and follow him. Once the soldiers were so engrossed in a card game they didn't see Uncle Aung Gyi leave the compound with his driver for an appointment. A few minutes later Uncle returned and reprimanded the soldiers for neglecting their duty and for failure to 'spy' on him. He was looking out for their best interest, as they could get fired or court martialed for disobeying orders. Our family watched this scene unfold with great respect and amusement. The soldiers grinned sheepishly with heads bowed for the Bogyoke they honored, and they thanked him for his unconventional consideration for their well-being. The retired general left again, this time with the 'spies' trailing behind his car.

Brigadier General *Aung Gyi* emerged again as a prominent opposition leader when he and *Aung San Suu Kyi*, the daughter of General *Aung San*, co-founded the National League of Democracy, NLD , in 1988. Brigadier General *Aung Gyi* became Chairman, former retired Brigadier *Tin Oo*, Vice Chairman, and *Aung San Suu Kyi*, General Secretary.

NLD membership consisted of many varied factions who would like to end the five decade old military dictatorship but each group maintained different and often conflicting political views and agendas. They included members and communist sympathizers of BCP (Burma Communist Party), AFPFL (Anti-Fascist People's Freedom League), BIA (Burma Independence Army), BSPP (Burma Socialist Program Party), NUP (National Unity Party) and other leftist factions, pro *U Nu* party members, ex army officers, former prominent political leaders and student activists. As *Aung Gyi* raised concerns over increasing communist infiltration within NLD he was soon forced out of NLD by *Aung San Suu Kyi*. Some speculated she forced *Aung Gyi* to resign, acting perhaps in respect to her mother *Daw Khin Kyi*, whose sister, *Daw Khin Gyi*, was married to *Thakin Than Tun*, leader of Burma Communist Party. *Tin Oo* supported the expelling of *Aung Gyi*, his former army colleague, boss and friend. A dozen years later, in 2011 a remorseful *Tin Oo* visited *Aung Gyi* at his home and *shikoed*[1] him, asking for forgiveness. In 1990, when general elections were held for the first time in decades NLD won with a landslide victory. By then General *Ne Win* has retired and General *Than Shwe* refused to turn over the power to NLD. Instead, he put *Aung San Suu Kyi* under house arrest at her home adjacent to Inya Lake.

The following year, in 1998, *Aung Gyi* visited the United States at the invitation of his friend Allen Dulles, former CIA chief. The two had met four decades prior, in 1958, when Brigadier General *Aung Gyi* first visited the US. This time, in an extensive interview for the CIA broadcast operation Radio Free Asia, retired Brigadier General *Aung Gyi* spoke of how the people of Burma had lost faith in *Tatmadaw* and described the pervasive corruption of General *Than Shwe's* inner circle. He also expressed concern for *Aung San Suu Kyi* being surrounded by left wingers within her party, the NLD.

A Unique Relationship

Aung Gyi and *Ne Win* had been together for decades and had been comrades since the days of the underground movement. *Aung Gyi* respected *Ne Win* as a political colleague, but he firmly disagreed with *Ne Win* on matters of economic policies and other national interests. *Aung Gyi* and *Ne Win* never hated each other personally. *Aung Gyi* told his boss on more than one occasion, "I left the army because I just didn't agree with your politics. My definition of Socialism that fits Burma and your definition are not the same."

Over several decades *Aung Gyi* wrote many times to *Ne Win* complaining about the crumbling economy, the regime's human rights violations, and armed insurgencies, and suggested action necessary to stop the suffering

---

[1] To '*shiko*' is to kneel down on the floor with both hands joined in prayer position, and head bowed before a superior or an elder as a gesture of respect.

of the people. In times of turbulence *Aung Gyi* was the lone voice to tell *Ne Win* the blunt truth regardless of personal risk of reprisal and imprisonment. *Aung Gyi* was accused wrongly by General *Ne Win* and other jealous and threatened generals. During his retirement the army, led by these insecure generals seized his property and tried to damage his reputation and assassinate his character. Although Brigadier General *Aung Gyi* was indiscriminately imprisoned four times, the man never held a grudge. He stood for forgiveness without anger or ill will against his perpetrators. On 25 October 2012, Brigadier General *Aung Gyi* died peacefully at age 93, at his home, surrounded by his children and grandchildren. He had lived a full and productive life as a statesman and a generous and devoted practicing Buddhist. Among the hundreds of people who came to pay respect were *Sanda Win*, General *Ne Win's* daughter, and *U Tin Oo*, Vice Chairman of NLD.

Shwe La Min (Golden Moon)

As a man of principle, retired Brigadier General *Aung Gyi* rejected General *Ne Win's* many offers to be the US Ambassador. He would rather find a way to make an honest living and pursue his private life as a civilian. Power and material wealth were never his mission in life. As a civilian, he did not feel that running a tea shop to provide for his family was beneath his dignity. Former military colleagues were amazed at such humility in *Ne Win's* No. 2 man and the co-founder of Burma's armed forces. *Aung Gyi* never became wealthy while in military service like the other generals. He resigned with nothing, not even ownership in a house or a car. The family home on *U Wizara* Road was returned to the government upon his resignation and Dagon House became the government's official guest house when he left. As an ordinary citizen, he began a new life. In 1976 *Aung Gyi* opened a tea shop named *Shwe La Min*, translated, Golden Moon tea house.

Tea houses are the center of Burmese culture. Here, people gather, exchange news, gossip, watch people or just hang out. There is a tea house on almost every block; very little food is served but there is a great deal of tea and conversation. Political and social gossip spread throughout the country as social activity in tea shops. Most Burmese families live in tight quarters, hence communal places like tea shops are popular. Retired *Bogyoke Aung Gyi* believed that opening a tea house would not only provide an honest living for his family but would create employment opportunity for former soldiers who had served the country during and after independence. Profit was never a key motive. He envisioned potential work opportunities for his followers and former subordinates as ingredient suppliers, food brokers and wholesalers and tea shop employees. He was also a dedicated Buddhist and donated generously and routinely, providing *suhn* (prepared food offerings) to monasteries to feed 100–200 *hpongyis* at a time. He continued this practice throughout his life.

The Golden Moon tea house was an instant success. The name *Aung Gyi* carried enormous weight, as many people still believed and hoped he would be the one to restore the country one day. His reputation as an honest and decent person was well known. Soon, *Shwe La Min* tea house was the thriving 'Tea Circle' forum with customers exchanging political dialogues or setting up rendezvous to share the political perspectives over a cup of tea.[1]

Many supporters and well-wishers would leave large 'tips' or donations to wish *Shwe La Min* success. Within three months, '*Aung Gyi* cakes' became a phenomenon and there was not enough to go round in Rangoon. Some people waited in line for hours to purchase *Aung Gyi* cakes and leave big 'tips'. The cake was so popular the bakery side expanded quickly and soon *Shwe La Min* became a franchise chain with over 800 bakeries producing and supplying '*Aung Gyi* cakes' in other major cities. To help local entrepreneurs, the retired general granted personal loans and extended credit to enable new franchise owners to buy supplies.

Meanwhile the dictator General *Ne Win* retired and General *Than Shwe* began to see *Aung Gyi's* burgeoning popularity and *Shwe La Min's* financial success as a threat to his establishment. With *Aung San Suu Kyi* still under arrest, *Aung Gyi* was perceived as the regime's No. 1 threat and enemy of the state. The retired general was the only one with political clout, people's support, leadership and experience, and, now with *Shwe La Min's* phenomenal success, financial resources, potentially capable of overthrowing the military dictatorship. The MI head Lieutenant General *Khin Nyunt*, the powerful spy chief, was tasked with destroying this perceived threat.

First, *Khin Nyunt* banned the use of *Aung Gyi's* name in his cakes, destroying the brand and goodwill. Then he revoked license to operate *Shwe La Min*, levied outrageous and inordinate taxes on fabricated past revenues to create excessive financial burden and strain to end *Shwe La Min's* enterprise. *Khin Nyunt* also destroyed *Aung Gyi's* support network by arresting and jailing his supporters, employees, suppliers and business associates. *Khin Nyunt* trumped up an incident to frame *Aung Gyi* on charges of theft and tax evasion. *Aung Gyi* was arrested and imprisoned.

This was a classic case of character assassination to end someone's political career, as the Burmese constitution forbids anyone with a criminal charge

---

[1] *Tea Circle Oxford.* Daw Htay Htay Win: "Unfolding Scenes Behind the Curtain", August 8, 2018.

to hold any political position. This was also the beginning of the demise of the *Shwe La Min* bakery chain. *Aung Gyi* was imprisoned for six months but was later freed under an amnesty. As a free man he continued to support Buddhist monks and monasteries with donations and *suhns* and lived his last years peacefully and in excellent health, surrounded by his loving children and grandchildren. As a fundamental doctrine of Buddhism, supporters of Brigadier General *Aung Gyi* believed *karma* would inflict consequences on spymaster *Khin Nyunt* for such injustice. Indeed in 2003 Lieutenant General *Khin Nyunt* fell from grace, was demoted, and a year later he was accused of corruption by dictator General *Than Shwe* himself. He was placed under house arrest for seven years, totally cut off from family and friends.

Daw Khin Kyi

After the assassination of *Bogyoke Aung San*, the father of independence, *Suu Kyi* and her two brothers were raised by their widowed mother, who was appointed ambassador to India in 1960 by General *Ne Win*. Upon retirement from that post, *Daw Khin Kyi* returned home to Burma and lived alone at 25 University Avenue in Rangoon by the Inya Lake. She stayed in touch with Brigadier General *Aung Gyi*, who provided *Bogyoke's* widow friendship, help and support whenever she needed. He addressed her as *Ma Ma Kyi* or Big Sister *Kyi*, out of respect. Once when she was hospitalized at Rangoon General Hospital, the hospital staff failed to accommodate her adequately until *Aung Gyi* wrote to then President *San Yu* (president from November 1981 to July 1988). He complained to the President lack of adequate medical care and proper treatment for the widow of *Bogyoke Aung San*, the national hero of Burma. At *Aung Gyi's* intercession, not only was the needed care provided, the Minister of Health personally came to ensure *Daw Khin Kyi* was moved to the VIP corner room at RGH. When *Ma Ma Kyi* needed cataract surgery Brigadier General *Aung Gyi* requested, via a letter to the President, that the government honor and assist the widow of the *Bogyoke*. Again, his request was obliged and *Daw Khin Kyi* was flown to London for eye surgery at government expense. Even *Daw Khin Kyi's* son, *Aung San Oo*, the estranged brother of *Suu Kyi* (who was a US citizen living in California at the time), sought Brigadier General *Aung Gyi's* help in personal matters. *Aung San Oo* asked the long-time family friend to intercede and present his relationship with *Lei Lei*, the woman he wanted to marry, to his mother. Much to the young couples delight *Daw Khin Kyi* granted consent with her blessings and the two were married. Might this goodwill gesture from *Aung Gyi* upset daughter *Suu Kyi*? She and her alienated brother had been fighting a 12-year legal battle over ownership of their family house on University Avenue. She must have felt antagonized that anyone was helping her own brother in this case.

Shinpyu Ceremony

When boys come of age, it is Buddhist tradition and a rite of passage to initiate them as young Buddhist novices. The ritual and celebration is called *Shinpyu*, or coming of age novitiation ceremony. Young boys spend time in the monastery as novice monks to learn the teachings of Buddha for a period of time ranging from a week to several months, when they are on school break. The tradition dates back some 2,500 years to when Siddhartha Gautama, who was a prince, gave up a life of royal splendor to live as a holy man after witnessing sickness and death outside the palace. *Daw Khin Kyi* wanted her two grandchildren, *Aung San Suu Kyi*'s two sons (in England), to experience *shinpyu*. She sought Brigadier General *Aung Gyi*'s help to gain an entry visa. At that time, due to General *Ne Win*'s isolationist rule and hostility toward foreigners, security was heightened and foreigners were not welcome. No one could come in and no one could leave. At *Aung Gyi*'s request directly to General *Ne Win*, entry visas were granted to *Suu Kyi*, her British husband and their two sons for a one-month stay, which was later extended with *Aung Gyi*'s second request to *Ne Win*. In addition, *Aung Gyi* was able to approach a well-known *sayadaw*, the monastery abbot in Rangoon, to perform the *shinpyu* ceremony at his monastery. *Suu Kyi*'s family arrived Rangoon in 1986 and the boys performed the *shinpyu* ceremony with all expenses paid by Brigadier General *Aung Gyi*. He was a steadfast friend to *Daw Khin Kyi* and her family. A photograph of Bogyoke *Aung Gyi* with *Aung San Suu Kyi* and her two sons, Alexander and Kim, at the *shinpyu* novitiation ceremony, can be seen at Tea Circle, Oxford, courtesy of Daw *Htay Htay Win* [1].

Aung San Suu Kyi (1945–)

Suu Kyi is the assertive Oxford-educated daughter of General *Aung San*, Burma's national hero who fought the British to gain Burma its independence. General *Aung San* was assassinated a year before independence was granted. She was two when her father was killed; she and her two brothers were raised by their widowed mother, who worked in the diplomatic corps. During her early years in Burma, *Suu Kyi* attended Methodist English High School, MEHS, the elite private school in Rangoon. At 15, *Suu Kyi* left Burma

---

[1] *Tea Circle Oxford.* Daw Htay Htay Win: "Unfolding Scenes Behind the Curtain", August 8, 2018.

with her mother for New Delhi when *Daw Khin Kyi* was appointed the ambassador to India after independence.

For the next 40-plus years, *Suu Kyi* lived outside of Burma with no involvement in Burmese politics or national affairs. After high school *Suu Kyi* went to England for further education. She attended Oxford University where she met and married an Englishman named Michael Aris, a scholar specializing in Tibetan studies. Although she returned to Burma for many visits with her mother, she was settled in England and lived as a homemaker with little interest in the affairs of her motherland while she and her husband were raising their two sons.

In 1988 *Suu Kyi* returned to Burma to nurse her sick mother *Daw Khin Kyi*, who had suffered a stroke, and she was completely caught up in the democracy movement uprising. The biggest national revolt in Burma's modern history is now known as the 8.8.88 massacre. At that time, she was an unknown both inside and outside of Burma. She had very little name recognition and no political experience.

Unlike the Western custom, there is no last name (surname) in Burmese tradition, and Burmese women do not take their husband's name after marriage. *Suu Kyi* was unknown, even though she was the daughter of Burma's independence hero. But that was rectified in 1988 by a politically astute plan of action. When her father's name was added to hers, *Aung San Suu Kyi* became an overnight idol, embodying the hopes and dreams that her father didn't have the chance to fulfill. *Aung San Suu Kyi* became the symbol of the country's fight for freedom and democracy. She and retired Brigadier General *Aung Gyi* created the National League of Democracy and she continued to lead the party as a non-violent democratic movement; she became an international icon of peace. She was now shaped by her father's legacy, with a sense of duty to her country.

The Lady, or Aunty, as she was fondly called, was also revered because she was the daughter of Burma's founding father who had led the country to independence from the British. The name *Aung San* and her heritage gave her an overwhelming advantage over her political rivals and the generals of *Tatmadaw*.[1] She was not only educated but her familiarity with the outside world and especially the West, her fluent command of English, and her ease at communicating with foreigners gave her a phenomenal advantage. She would visit the British ambassador at his residence and meet with foreign presidents, heads of states and dignitaries of the world including United Nations with ease, charm and grace.

---

[1] *The Economist.* Richard Cockett: "Special Report *Myanmar*: A Burmese Spring", May 25, 2013.

Following the 1988 massacre, *Aung San Suu Kyi* made her first political speech at the *Shwedagon* and drew an estimated one million demonstrators calling for an end to the authoritarian regime and demanding democracy. She dazzled the crowd with her speech. She rose to become a world-class inspiring international icon. This was her entry into politics.

Drawing on both Western democratic practice and Buddhist ideology, *Aung San Suu Kyi* articulated what was wrong with authoritarian rule and called for unity and a second non-violent struggle for independence. She also had her father's great name. *Aung San*'s daughter now would lead the struggle for independence from homegrown tyrants. Tens of thousands followed her showing their solidarity to her and their hostility to the tyrannical establishment. It was a culmination of peaceful defiance to half a century of incompetence and brutality, with the military bent to kill as many unarmed people as it took to stay in power.

When General *Ne Win*'s era ended, General *Than Shwe* became Burma's new supreme leader. *Aung San Suu Kyi* had antagonized him and defied the authorities repeatedly since 1988. He therefore banned public display of her photos, posters, and souvenirs bearing her image. The authorities tried to break her spirit by not allowing her to see her husband and children; they tried to destroy her morale using emotional blackmail, forcing her to choose between her family and her fight for democracy. Her husband was diagnosed with terminal cancer; the state-controlled media insisted she should, as a dutiful wife, leave and return to England to be with him. She knew that if she left the country, she would never be allowed to return. The authorities also denied an entry visa to her dying husband. The government even cut her home phone line. She remained unbreakable and would not leave Burma. Her husband died of prostate cancer in March 1999 and her sons grew up motherless. *Aung San Suu Kyi* refused to leave Burma and continued her democracy movement from her family house on University Avenue. Her older son lost touch with her as he was distraught by her choosing a political career over family. But she was determined to see democracy materialize in Burma, the mission she now lived and hoped to achieve, whatever might be the cost or consequences.

National Democracy League, NLD

Following the 8.8.88 uprisings, the abominable acts of the military rule became exposed to the world. The West began to enforce economic sanctions on Burma. Many activists fled to the jungles in remote bordering regions while others joined forces with the ethnic militia that had been fighting for their rights since Burma's independence from the British in 1948.

The brutality and killing of unarmed civilians angered and alarmed past prominent democratic leaders and politicians. Retired Brigadier General *Aung Gyi* and former Prime Minister *U Nu* met with the people and both spoke up for reprieve from punishment, prison, or death of the imprisoned protesters. This was the context in which *Aung San Suu Kyi* was launched as a new democracy leader. Three years later, in 1991, she became a Nobel Peace Prize laureate and international icon of peace. She spoke to an estimated one million people who gathered during the pro-democracy demonstration. She also defied General *Than Shwe's* military reign for years to come, calling for an end to his repressive rule.

One important event precipitated from the 8.8.88 uprisings and changed the course of history. That was the founding of a democratic organization by three prominent leaders who formed *Aung Suu Tin*, a united front against the one-party rule. *Aung Suu Tin* was created by former Brigadier General *Aung Gyi*, retired General *Tin Oo*, a trusted friend of *Suu Kyi*, and the Lady, *Aung San Suu Kyi*. It was later renamed the National League of Democracy, NLD.

Retired Brigadier General *Aung Gyi*, with his depth and expertise in politics and military government, became Chairman, *Tin Oo* became Vice Chairman, and *Aung San Suu Kyi*, the general secretary. As a newly founded organization NLD lacked funds so *Aung Gyi* sold his personal assets earned from the spectacular success of the *Shwe La Min* bakery, including land, buildings, and vehicles, to cover printing, operating and travel expenses for the NLD. He ventured out to cities outside of Rangoon and remote villages to promote democracy and what the NLD stood for. People cheered enthusiastically everywhere he went as they were euphoric and energized to see the familiar pro democratic former military general who fearlessly defied the army regime for decades with speeches and letters. Now he has come in person to lead them in their struggle for freedom and against the tyrannical army rule. Everywhere he went he was surrounded by people with hope and jubilation and speech was demanded of their beloved leader whom they trusted and respected for decades. *Aung Gyi* believed in bottom up strategy encouraging local people to form satellite groups to support democracy and the NLD. He stopped at every city, town and village distributing NLD pamphlets and giving encouraging speeches until he reached Mandalay, almost collapsed with exhaustion. The six-hour journey took fourteen days punctuated by multiple stops at villages and towns along the way to meet the village elders and greet crowds of people waiting to hear him speak.

Contrary to his bottom up strategy encouraging local NLD supporters to form and expand NLD groups at the grass root level, *Aung San Suu Kyi* favored a top down strategy with central control, selecting and placing desired NLD people in the field satellite offices. Disagreement and internal conflict began to build between the two leaders. Other dissensions and political infighting also developed among the NLD groups with conflicting agendas; and communist insurgency had always been a looming threat within parties and organizations since independence. NLD welcomed many groups, including reformed communists, into its membership. Besides communist sympathizers there were the BSPP faction; the army faction of *Tin Oo*; elite politicians and members of CEC (Central Executive Committee); and ex high-ranking army officers and other political groups who wanted to control NLD. *Suu Kyi*'s mother *Daw Khin Kyi* was sympathetic to the communists as her sister was married to *Thakin Than Tun*, the communist leader.[1] Political disagreements regarding communist infiltration within NLD began to emerge. *Aung Gyi* was fully aware of the left wing orientation within the organization and had previously proposed purging them, however he did not get the support of the other two NLD leaders.

Aung San Suu Kyi might have inherited her father's great name but she was a political neophyte; and *Aung Gyi* was the only one who dared challenge her. *Aung Gyi* also discouraged direct negative campaigning against the military junta and had advised NLD members against a direct confrontation with *Tatmadaw* and personal attacks of General *Ne Win* or other regime leaders. He knew that *Tatmadaw* was strong and well-trained to be unified, with stalwart loyalty to General *Ne Win*. The leftists began stirring up internal dissent, accusing *Aung Gyi* of being a spy for *Ne Win*'s establishment.

After 8.8.88, General *Saw Maung* took charge as commander-in-chief. He had promised an election which NLD could win, being the strongest political party in the country. But the left wing feared they would diminish as a group should NLD win the election with *Aung Gyi* as Chairman. They felt their position would be stronger with Vice Chairman *Tin Oo*, who had served previously under *Aung Gyi* and later became Chief of Staff of *Tatmadaw*. *Tin Oo* was imprisoned by General *Ne Win* for alleged involvement in a coup attempt in 1976 and later released in a general amnesty. The communists and left wing factions wanted to remove Brigadier General *Aung Gyi* as Chairman prior to the 1990 election promised by General *Saw Maung*.

---

[1] While he was Minister of Defense in 1942, *Aung San* met and married *Daw Khin Kyi*, and around the same time her sister *Daw Khin Gyi*, met and married *Thakin Than Tun*, the communist leader.

The three NLD leaders met at *Aung Gyi's* house to discuss the left wing and how and when best to purge the group, but disagreement resulted. Chairman *Aung Gyi* reminded Secretary *Aung San Suu Kyi* that without any depth of experience in government or intimate involvement in Burmese politics for over five decades, she could not grasp the complexities of the inner workings of the government, fundamentals of policy making and how the regime used to think. Lacking a deep understanding of the administration's inner circle, *Aung San Suu Kyi* was easily swayed, even manipulated by the various factions of NLD. *Aung Gyi* reprimanded her for sheltering and supporting the communists, the same leftists her father General *Aung San* had fought against. *Aung San Suu Kyi* might have harbored a personal revulsion for political opponents and anyone who challenged her, but her decisions and actions were a reflection of strict discipline and intractable determination, as confirmed by NLD insiders. Those who worked closely with her knew she could be unrelenting and would try to eliminate any opposition. Armed with a rock hard determination and guided by her unyielding beliefs, she was often perceived as stubborn. She could be dogmatic, inflexible and often seemed incapable of compromising. She was reluctant to accept defeat with *Aung Gyi*, who was the first and only person that ever criticized and challenged her. They failed to find a win–win solution. Heated argument ensued and *Aung Gyi* ended the meeting, asking her to leave his house.

As for *Tin Oo*, he knew he could never be chairman as long as *Aung Gyi* was the head of the party. With support from communist elements, a hate campaign was started, separating NLD leadership into two fractions. *Aung Gyi* was accused of being *Ne Win's* spy and a regime sympathizer. To accuse a man who had been sent to prison by *Ne Win* of being a spy for him seemed preposterous. However, *Aung San Suu Kyi* and *Tin Oo* joined hands with the communist faction against *Aung Gyi* and expelled him from NLD.

The worst part of *Aung Gyi's* expulsion from the party was the heavy price NLD paid: they won the election but lost the seat of power. Even the military was shocked at such a rash decision, dismissing their chairman only a few months after the inception of the NLD. The military under General *Saw Maung* had intended to hand over the power to civilian rule via NLD in 1990 after its overwhelming victory. But the split in the NLD upon the expulsion of *Aung Gyi* would have meant giving the state control to a group comprised of communists and ousted army factions, which the military would never do. The price of disunity and infighting within the party was indeed high. Although NLD won the elections with a landslide, it lost the political power and control of the country. The military establishment refused to hand over the helm. Instead *Aung San Suu Kyi* was put under house arrest and military rule resumed for another quarter of century.

Prior to General *Saw Maung's* promised election in 1990, the authorities welcomed new political organizations as a strategy to 'divide and conquer' or 'divide and rule,' to weaken any one strong opposition party, as NLD has become the biggest opposition force in the nation. The election was held as promised in 1990, and 93 political parties participated. NLD won an astounding victory. Although NLD lost its leadership unity and effectiveness with General *Aung Gyi's* discharge, the whole country was intact as one strong unified force in support of the democratic party of '*Bogyoke's* daughter'.

More than 80% of the people voted for NLD, giving the party 392 out of 485 seats in the parliament. The military-backed opposition National Unity Party, the proxy party of the military's Burma Socialist Program Party, secured only ten seats in the assembly. Unfortunately NLD under *Aung San Suu Kyi's* nascent leadership did not act expediently in the formation of a new democratic government, an administration that would have gained immediate recognition and support by the people of Burma and the international community. They waited two months before making any tactical decision, giving the military sufficient time to step in and take control again.

Tatmadaw seized the opportunity, took charge and began purging the opposition. They put *Aung San Suu Kyi* under house arrest. NLD members were also arrested, imprisoned, and tortured. Many died behind bars while others fled the country. The election became the regime's excuse to purge its biggest opposition. Had *Aung San Suu Kyi* and General *Aung Gyi* been able to work together, the country would have taken a whole different path. Opposition leaders of the establishment like *U Nu, Aung Gyi, Aung San Suu Kyi, Tin Oo* and others did not emerge as a cohesive group with a common plan of action. *Aung Gyi* and his colleagues of former army officers left NLD and founded a new party, the Union National Democracy Party. Meanwhile at NLD, *Tin Oo* replaced *Aung Gyi* as chairman and *Aung San Suu Kyi* was confined for five years. She was released in 1995 but was put under house arrest again from 2000–2002 and 2003–2010 under *General Than Shwe's* rule. Fortunately she was never imprisoned in the overcrowded unsanitary conditions of Burmese jails nor subjected to inhumane tortures like many other political prisoners. She was detained in the comfort of her own home, in a gated compound on University Avenue, with two female helpers. To isolate her from the outside world, the authorities cut her phone line frequently, preventing her from conducting phone interviews with journalists. This went on for the next 25 years. This was the beginning of Western sanctions toward the pariah government. Washington also withdrew its ambassador to Burma in 1990. Soon the world lost contact with Burma.

Back at the home front, *Daw Khin Kyi*'s condition took a grave turn and she was moved from the hospital to be cared for in her own home for the remaining days of her life. *Daw Khin Kyi* expressed her desire to see her son before dying, and she again asked *Aung Gyi* for help with obtaining an entry visa for *Aung San Oo* (who had given up Burmese citizenship and was living in San Diego). Brigadier General *Aung Gyi* wrote again, this time to President (General) *Saw Maung*, and the visa was granted. Before *Daw Khin Kyi* passed away, Brigadier General *Aung Gyi* asked to see her once more, to pay his last tribute to a long-time friend and widow of the *Bogyoke*, but the message was never delivered to the dying woman. *Daw Khin Kyi* passed away on December 27, 1988, and her body lay in state at her home. Thousands of people came to pay last respects. Among them was her life-long friend Brigadier General *Aung Gyi*, but he was refused admission. The Lady's harshness toward a steadfast family friend is difficult to explain.

In 1991 after continued persistence by her British husband with various international peace committees and human rights organizations, *Aung San Suu Kyi* was awarded the Nobel peace prize for standing up for non-violent democracy against a military regime.

She was also awarded the Sakharov Prize and the United States Presidential Medal of Freedom. The Nobel not only earned her $1.3 million but further raised her stature as an international icon, and conferred a guaranteed lifetime security of lucrative speaking lecture circuits and writing bestseller books.

When *Aung San Suu Kyi* was released from her first house arrest in 1995, foreign journalists poured into the country to interview her. They were captivated by her education, Western and Eastern insights, and enigma, personal charm and charisma. The regime underestimated her power to draw international attention. Her gated residence became a political center with frequent visits from foreign governments and dignitaries, goodwill ambassadors, political leaders and journalists. *Aung San Suu Kyi* was seen as the best hope, if not the only hope, for democracy in the country. People loved her as *Bogyoke's* daughter but they also despised the military regime with at least the same passion, having suffered under its autocratic rule for half a century.

In reality what was perceived of NLD on the surface and what actually lay beneath were quite different. The NLD culture was authoritarian and undemocratic because it was *Aung San Suu Kyi*'s NLD. People joined the party and served her with blind obedience and loyalty. By wielding her iron rule within her party, she prevented any younger generation of leaders from rising through the ranks. Power centered on *Bogyoke's* daughter and she was not willing to delegate decision making to other NLD members, including trusted senior members. No one dared question her. *Aung San Suu Kyi* and her inner leaders were in their 70s and 80s, and yet they did not develop or promote the younger members.

NLD was synonymous with *Aung San Suu Kyi*. There were other educated, younger members, who were strong supporters of democracy and qualified to be groomed to carry on her work. Given leadership guidance and support for professional development, NLD could have harnessed their skills for the country's rebuilding and economic success. NLD must be able to carry on as a democratic organization, not *Aung San Suu Kyi's* autocratic institution.

Chapter 7. The Transition

It's 2010 and Burma is about to experience a major overhaul in men's fashion: Tatmadaw generals ditched their medal-decorated uniforms and donned civilian clothes. Army generals traded in their green combat uniforms for a kaleidoscope of colorful civilian longyis (sarongs) and exotic gaung baungs (headwear) in preparation for a transition to a quasi civilian government.

Most people in the country, including Grandma, aunts and uncles, and Papa wore traditional Burmese longyi. However, it was difficult for Mommy to wear a wrap-around due to their tendency to unravel. She had custom tailored longyis sewn to accentuate the waistline. Men's longyis are also called peso. It is a cylindrical skirt that allows for good air circulation in hot tropical weather. Men wear them by tying a knot in the front, women wear them by wrapping around the waist and tucking to the side. In villages they wear their longyi high around the knee to give better mobility when working in the fields. In the cities, longyis are worn down to the feet. Men's longyis or pesos are usually woven, striped or checkered, and women's are striped with more elaborate intricate designs of mixed colors. For everyday wear, women's longyis are made of factory-produced fabric with colorful floral patterns topped with casual blouses. For business and formal occasions, men generally wear a white shirt with a short front-buttoned jacket. The official dress code for men also includes a fitted silk hat called gaung baung that looks like a turban with a loose wing on the right side. Women's dressy attire includes a short (usually sheer or lace) front-buttoned blouse called aingi, revealing a lace trimmed bodice and a short lace shawl or pewah, which hangs down from the neck to just below the waist.

Everyday footwear consists of thong slippers made of leather or plastic and for important functions, formal events and special occasions, the slippers are made of velvet. Women's formal footwear is raised platform velvet slippers. As Burmese fashion evolved over the decades it is common today to see men and women wearing longyis with Western style blouses, shirts, and T-shirts. Western influence is particularly significant in ladies fashion as the longyi may have skirt-like waistband with hooks, zipper or buttons like Mommy's designs of the 60s. The traditional Burmese aingyi or top has also lengthened just below the waist and resembles any Western style tightly fitted blouse with various sleeve lengths. Longyis are quite versatile and can double up as swimsuits. If you come across a river or pond and have an urge to swim but don't have swimwear at hand, all you have to do is pull up your longyi from the waist and wrap around your upper chest and you're ready for a cool splash.

The Generals Become Civilian Cabinet Members

Beginning in 2010, the generals of *Tatmadaw* began to shed their service uniforms in favor of traditional *longyis or pesos* and colorful silk hats. After a bogus election they formed a new nominally civilian administration. This was the transition from a military authoritarian regime to a semi army controlled government. The nation had been a military dictatorship since 1962 when General *Ne Win* staged a coup against the civilian government of *U Nu*, the Prime Minister. Since that time, outside of North Korea, Burma has been the most isolated country on the planet.

In 2010, the Burmese government ended its one-party system and held a general election for the first time since 1990, when National League for Democracy led by *Aung San Suu Kyi* won a stunning and unexpected victory. But the military junta, the State Law and Order Restoration Council, SLORC, refused to hand over the reins and instead they arrested *Aung San Suu Kyi* and imprisoned many of the opposition leaders. This time, in 2010, NLD and several other leading opposition parties decided not to register. They boycotted the election, which led to a party split, creating another opposition group, National Democratic Force, NDF. The year prior to the transition to the quasi civilian administration, all active-duty cabinet ministers of the previous military regime resigned from their army posts in preparation to participate in the elections.

In preparation, dictator General *Than Shwe* and his generals began dumping hard-asset possessions in a fire sale. They sold hospitals, schools, buildings, factories, warehouses, movie theaters, mines, dams, and other infrastructure for undisclosed but hefty prices to foreign companies and pocketed the immense profits. These generals, with uniforms removed, would occupy positions in the new civilian cabinet, filling in the 25% seats guaranteed by the constitution for the military. General *Than Shwe* dissolved the State Peace and Development Council, SPDC, and appointed a younger military chief, General *Min Aung Hlaing,* to lead the armed forces. A new partially-civilian government was formed under a retired army general, *Thein Sein*, as President, and Burma suddenly opened its doors to the global community for the first time in five decades.

The election won by the new army-controlled 'civilian' administration was reported to be rigged, as expected, with massive polling violations and vote-count manipulations. Many unaccounted early votes were included in favor of the regime, thus ensuring continuity of *Tatmadaw*. NLD asserted the government used fraud to achieve an outcome favorable to the regime. People were intimidated and coerced at polls to vote for the new government and the regime's political party, Union Solidarity and Development Party, USDP. USDP won over three-quarters of elective parliamentary seats while the military appointees filled one-quarter, as stated in the army's 2008 constitution. General *Thein Sein* became President *Thein Sein* while other high ranking military officers, now 'retired', were appointed key cabinet positions. Dictator General *Than Shwe* retired and dropped out of sight but was believed to be still pulling strings behind the scene from his heavily guarded luxurious residential fortress in the new capital *Naypyidaw*.

The military government was officially 'ended' and former General *Thein Sein* was now to lead the new administration toward a Burmese-style democracy. Former army generals and officers, many involved in past atrocities, were now Members of Parliament, MPs, in the new USDP dominated government. As the outside world watched, President *Thein Sein's* new government acted quickly to draw positive reaction by freeing two hundred political prisoners as part of a general amnesty. Although *Thein Sein* had been a general, his approach seemed different from his predecessors. He might have recognized that the past regime's mismanagement and brutality had impoverished the country; he began by taking a softer stand toward the international community.

Nevertheless during the transition years, he still had to deal with hard-liners who opposed major changes. There was massive corruption in the government and generals who feared exposure restrained him from pushing too hard, too fast toward reforms. The generals, their families and their crony allies had, for decades, illegally amassed wealth and huge piles of cash had been deposited in offshore bank accounts in Switzerland, Dubai, England, and Singapore. Many bought prime real estate outside of Burma. *Thein Sein* was not totally free to express views or propose policy changes that might incriminate them. Meanwhile, battles with ethnic armies in the hills and jungles of Burma and ethno-religious conflict in Arakan state continued nonstop. Rising expectations of the ethnic nationalities demanded autonomous rule, self-determination, economic improvement and complete political freedom from the central government in their respective areas of Shan and Kachin states and other ethnic regions of the nation.

Reactions from Global Community

President *Thein Sein*'s quasi civilian administration was welcomed by the international community. In December 2011, Hillary Clinton, US Secretary of State, visited Burma, to encourage further progress toward democracy and to improve relations. The European Union suspended all non-military sanctions against Burma for a year and the European Commission offered Burma more than $100MM in development aid. The ASEAN members approved Burma's bid to chair ASEAN, Association of South East Asian Nations, to be held in 2014. In April 2012, US President Barack Obama visited Burma. The following year President *Thein Sein* visited Washington and London. Although President Obama praised political and economic progress, he criticized violence against the Muslim minority in Arakan state in western Burma. (The multi decade long violence against the minority Muslim population will be discussed in Chapter 11.)

Although Burma was armed by Russia, China, North Korea and India, China is the real force fueling the junta economically, even more so since US trade sanctions. Burma's rich deposits of oil and gas help meet China's growing need for energy. Burma's monsoon forests yield prized tropical hardwoods and the Irrawaddy delta is ideal for rice production. China also has an interest in Burma's jade and other gemstone extraction. To increase trade with China, the military junta has relocated whole towns and villages to make way for wider roads. The growing trade along the eastern border of Burma benefits China and extends to other parts of Asia. On the western border the PRC is building infrastructure, pipelines, seaports and improved roads to access Burma's western seaboard on the Bay of Bengal, linking interior China to the Middle East and beyond. Despite improved communication and increased trade, local Burmese remain poor. They are still denied an outlet for their grievances while the resources are being sold with huge profits for the military.

Reforms under President Thein Sein

President *Thein Sein*'s government began to initiate a series of major political, economic, and social reforms, as it unraveled from five decades of isolation, xenophobia, army abuses and mismanagement. He reiterated the need for economic reform, political reconciliation, ending of ethnic conflict, elimination of corruption, establishment of democratic principles, and improvement in education, health, and environmental protection. The once remote and obscure country was now becoming a new geopolitical center and a rising potential megalopolis of Asia.

A fast track transition with its open door reforms was transforming the country to a more open democracy, at least superficially. Former Brigadier General *Aung Gyi's* proposed market-oriented economy was finally becoming a reality. In response to the new government's interest to build a modern market-based economy, major reforms immediately took place. Signs of the fifty years of dictatorship began to disappear fast. Attitudes toward foreigners were changing. The retired generals started overhauling Burma's economy, lowering export taxes, easing restrictions on its financial sector, relaxing media censorship, legalizing trade unions and protests, freeing political prisoners and agreeing to cease-fires with ethnic minority rebels in bordering provinces.

President *Thein Sein* freed political prisoners, including the high profile student leaders and activists of 8.8.88 who were arrested and imprisoned for over twenty years. The National Human Rights Commission was established, allowing the formation of labor unions and granting the right to strike. *Aung San Suu Kyi* was not only released from her latest house arrest, she was given a seat in the new parliament, where some open debate was now permitted.

The new administration also initiated preliminary cease fire agreements and negotiated peace treaties with Shan, Kachin and Karen armed ethnic nationalities, referred to as EAO's, ethnic armed organizations. *Thein Sein* signed laws allowing peaceful demonstrations for the first time in decades. Media and print censorship were relaxed and reporters no longer subjected to state censorship. He lifted website bans and publicly invited exiles and expatriates to return home and help rebuild the country. For the first time in almost five decades the *New Light of Burma*, the regime's mouthpiece was no longer the sole monopoly as private daily newspapers began to appear. Newspapers were publishing real news and even mild criticism of the government. The once isolated regime was now welcoming assistance and advice from the world including the West.

Sanctions and investment bans by the US and EU countries were being eased as the oppressive military government dissolved itself and transitioned to a nominal civilian government in 2011. The new government embarked on ambitious high speed economic and political reforms directed to stimulate foreign investments as its primary goal. As Western sanctions were partially lifted, Burma was reconnecting socially, economically, and politically with the rest of the world. As political reforms kicked in, the US, European Union, and Australia dropped most economic sanctions, and many especially Asian firms, began to invest heavily in the Golden Land. Eventually, EU granted Burma wholesale lifting of sanctions. Obama, Clinton, David Cameron and other world leaders began first time visits in decades to the new open Burma. The country was experiencing unprecedented change for business returning to the global marketplace, including the West for the first time in decades. Its emergence from half a century of isolation made it one of the most exciting places for exploration and investment opportunities. A fixed exchange rate was abandoned in favor of a managed currency float. To encourage more foreign investment and trade a new Foreign Investment Law was approved and trade license requirements on the import and export of many products were removed.

Burma was now open for business, trade and investment after fifty years of isolationism and anti foreign sentiment. It was fast becoming known as the last frontier and a new center of commercial activities in the region. Scores of optimistic Asian and Western businessmen were flooding into the city intoxicated by the opportunities and ready to exploit its riches. The bright red billboards once filled with government propaganda were now replaced with colorful commercial billboards advertising Western products and high tech gadgets. Genuine Western brand products were replacing pirated versions in shops. Fortune seekers from around the globe began rushing in to tap the rich resources of Asia's last frontier. Foreign investors sought to enter a market that has been largely untapped due to decades of isolation from the world economy. Trade with outside world soared as foreign investment began to flood in. Analysts and experts agreed there were vast opportunities for foreign companies across the industrial and commercial landscape, from energy, mining, manufacturing and construction to agriculture, finance, tourism, health, education and service sectors. Burma was now getting global attention offering unprecedented investment opportunities and a virgin market of 55+ million potential consumers with growing appetite for imported products and services. All sectors of business were burgeoning industries scrambling to catch up to the rest of the world. Many observers believed Burma could become Asia's next economic tiger if it could successfully leverage its rich natural endowments.

Changes were everywhere but most pronounced in Rangoon, previous capital and now the financial center. The old capital has seen several transformations, from *Ne Win's* socialist isolationism to several corrupt and brutal military dictatorships, and now to *Thein Sein's* semi-civilian government. Unlike other cities or satellite towns Rangoon was not only the commercial center but a cultural and political hub of the time. It had the flavor of a quaint city with relics of World War II and post-colonial charm with many historical remnants of the era. Unlike most cities in other Southeast Asian countries that have replaced their colonial heritage with modern high rises, Rangoon was still intact with Victorian architecture of the British era. Rangoon has more colonial buildings built during the British rule than any other Asian cities, although many of these charming Victorian buildings of colonial grandeur were crumbling and decaying due to decades of neglect and lack of proper maintenance and repairs. In the city multi-level buildings were no higher than five stories with few exceptions and elevators were not included. Old buses still ran the streets of Rangoon so did 3-wheel orange car taxis and trishaws (taxis with 3 bicycle wheels). The city hall and the railway station were two famous landmarks with British colonial style buildings mixed with Burmese architectural ornamental roofs. The city was always buzzing with all sorts of street vendors, produce sellers, saffron clad monks, and ordinary commuters traveling by buses and trains which passed through many villages that surrounded Rangoon. The glistening golden shrines provided balanced insight from the hustle bustle into the serene majesty and tranquility of Buddhism. The scenery changed from urban to rural quite dramatically as the train left Rangoon passing through villages with thatched roof huts and kids playing bare feet in ponds. Cows, pigs, and chickens and stray dogs roamed the grounds and farmers with coned bamboo woven hats and women with *thanaka* on their faces worked in the rice fields. Outside the big city of Rangoon are these idyllic towns and small gem cities across Burma that have been hidden and unknown to the world for centuries. They offer distinct charm and uniqueness without tourist crowds and commercialism.

Rapid Urbanization of Rangoon

As Burma opened to the world, like other major cities it could not escape modern development and civilization. Fast-forward to 2011 when Rangoon experienced the inevitability of high speed urbanization. Although the city has retained much of its faded colonial charm, dramatic changes are taking place with new five star hotels, posh restaurants, Western style supermarkets, air conditioned shopping malls, ATMs, and car showrooms. Public spaces are being converted to shopping malls in a hurry and seemingly with no master urban development plans. Signs of modern Western consumerism are creeping in everywhere with burgeoning car ownership and ubiquitous mobile phone use. This is Burma's entry to 21st century Asian life.

Internet connectivity has improved immensely across Burma and cell phone use is becoming widespread with over fifteen million users and growing steadily with explosive speed. Prior to 2010 less than 1% of the population (roughly 302,500) had internet access. By 2018 over fourteen million have online capability and are actively using social media, with Facebook becoming their primary source of news and information, or misinformation.[1] Just a few years ago less than 5% of the estimated 55-59 million people in Burma had cell (mobile) phones. The number of cell phone users continues to explode and by 2017 the majority of the people have access to smartphones. New construction work is taking place all around Rangoon and other major cities and more air flight routes are now being introduced. Much of farmland is being converted for industrial development as the population swells to 5.2 million in Rangoon alone with two thirds of the population uneducated who migrated from villages looking for low skilled work. Telecommunications towers are being erected, garment factories and other plants are going up, new roads and ports are being built and special economic zones are established. Construction cranes, wrecking balls, and bulldozers are everywhere building condominiums with lightning speed and without proper construction guidelines and zoning ordinances. Hotels are sprouting up to accommodate new visitors and fortune seekers and hotel room rates skyrocket as international visitors and tourists arrive in droves. Rangoon expanded to satellite regions as population grew by leaps and bounds. Traffic in major cities like Rangoon choke with daily gridlock and dramatic increase in commute time. Added to this is the congestion in internal and external networks which threatens normal function as the urban sprawl surged to over five million changing the lives of its people forever.

Rangoon was far different from even a few years ago with new high rise buildings, tall residential apartments and condominiums, and Western-style restaurants popping up everywhere. Real estate prices have tripled, quadrupled and in some locations, escalated six times since 2010–11. Much of the increases were attributed to speculation exacerbating housing shortage for the average working class of locals. Burma's supply of hotel accommodations could not meet the flood of business and tourist travelers with room rates equaling those of industrialized nations. Hotel rates, apartment and house rentals, and retail and commercial premises rental rates in Rangoon have surpassed those in high rent districts of Bangkok, Kuala Lumpur or Jakarta. In a country where people earn $2 a day rents in Rangoon climbed to US$10 per sq ft. per month in 2013. Population in Rangoon swelled as job seekers from rural areas flooded the city. For the average citizen home ownership in these new developments is out of reach. The banking system is undeveloped and under capitalized with little possibility of establishing a mortgage system. Many Burmese lack trust in banks preferring to stash their cash in their homes instead of in bank accounts. A high end condo cost

---

[1] *The Guardian.* "Revealed: Facebook hate speech exploded in *Myanmar* during *Rohingya* crisis", April 3, 2018.

US$ 350–400,000 and with no mortgage payment plan it is economically prohibitive for the majority of the population except the super wealthy and the military elite.

When the government relaxed import regulations and taxation on imported cars, thousands of used cars — primarily from Japan — entered the country, and most ended up on the streets of Rangoon. The Ministry of Transportation reported over half a million cars had entered the country since 2011. Roads now became choked with gridlock, creating pollution and traffic snarls never seen before. The Government had spent millions on the army but lacked funds to resolve traffic congestion and improve infrastructure. Efficient mass transport systems like in neighboring Bangkok were non-existent and all public transport systems including rail were outdated and overburdened. Commute times doubled, tripled, quadrupled and more. During the rainy seasons many roads were flooded and near impassable.

As foreign investors and tourists surged into Burma offering new businesses and employment opportunities, Rangoon became flooded with a wave of low skilled workers from villages hoping to escape rural poverty and to fulfill material goals and dreams. Overcrowding, the growth of squatter districts and unsanitary living conditions placed an enormous strain on resources as cities like Rangoon became a magnet for rural migrants.

According to census estimates 5–6 million people called Rangoon region home with at least 80,000 families living as squatters around the garment factories in various satellite townships like *Hlaing Tharyar* and its peripheral area. Trash was everywhere in the fringes of the city around these industrial zones, with squatters' shacks built of sticks, bamboo, tin and plastic. Functional waste and sewage disposal systems were absent in these makeshift structures as poverty and desperation stripped people of human dignity and respect. Almost 90% of families in poor communities in satellite towns of North *Okkalapa, Shwepyithar* and *Seikgyikanaungto* earned less than $1–$2 a day. Malnutrition, lack of clean drinking water and sanitation facilities created health problems and diseases such as tuberculosis, coronary diseases, diabetes and respiratory and gastrointestinal diseases. In Rangoon city center, there were over 6,000 hawkers and street vendors selling food and miscellaneous items by the roadsides cluttering the sidewalks with products and trash and further compounding traffic congestion and endangering human lives. Rangoon was now plagued with robberies, stabbings, theft, drugs and addiction, prostitution, kidnapping, even explosions and many more afflictions typical of rapid urbanization, the necessary evil that terrified its residents. According to UN forecasts, Rangoon's population would double to more than 11 million by 2040. The City Development Committee has made plans to extend Rangoon by creating seven more satellite towns around the city region that would accommodate 10 million people over the next 25 years.

Booming Tourism

Many changes to accommodate the new Burma were apparent in daily life. The opposition leader *Aung San Suu Kyi* went from house prison to a position in parliament. Once forbidden, souvenir shops now proudly display and sell souvenirs and other items decorated with *Aung San Suu Kyi's* portrait. Her pictures were also hung conspicuously in coffee and tea houses and retail stores. Local coffee shops and tea houses were buzzing with discussions on sensitive topics previously forbidden for public dialog. Former activists exchanged information about other political dissidents still in jail and could freely joke about the government and their corrupt ministers without the threat of harassment. People were allowed to gather in public places to engage in open conversation without the fear of being watched and retaliated by the regime's plain clothed spies and secret informants. Tourism under authoritarian rule was almost nonexistent as the xenophobic regime granted limited visas only to select mostly Asian diplomats and regime connected tycoons.

As tourism, trade and investment opened up Burma is becoming a tourist destination offering unspoiled sights and sounds, and well preserved exotic culture. Few other countries offer such vast and varied range of cultural sites with local ethnic tribal customs, rituals, ceremonies and festivals, untouched by modern development. Much of the country is still undeveloped, unexploited, and unspoiled. The countless awe-inspiring ancient Buddhist temples merge with the colonial charm of Victorian architecture from the British era which has all but disappeared in other parts of the world. Now open to tourists is the spectacular *Mergui* Archipelago with more than 800 pristine islands scattered throughout the Andaman Sea. Indeed Burma is blessed with its wealth of stunning scenery, glistening and mesmerizing golden pagodas built by Burmese monarchs and the Buddhist communities over centuries, idyllic ethnic tribal villages, beautiful snow-capped mountainous, and miles of pristine beaches.

Foreign Investment

One of the least developed and most isolated countries in Asia, Burma now was offering market opportunities in every sector imaginable. Believing this might be the last frontier for capitalism, foreign investors flooded in.

They formed joint ventures and partnerships with the new government and major local enterprises owned by former generals and their friends. Anxious to beef up the economy, President *Thein Sein's* new nominally-civilian government encouraged gigantic foreign investment in extraction, infrastructure, transportation and telecommunications. US corporations — GE, Coca-Cola, Pepsico, Chevron, GM, Caterpillar, Ford, Marriott Hotel, Hilton, Best Western, Microsoft, HP, Intel, Google, Unilever, P&G, DuPont, and Visa — were piling into the Golden Land to create a corporate presence and set up liaison offices.

Investment potential reached feverish levels and real estate soared steeply. Not surprising, corruption was rampant and widespread as profit seekers from all over the world arrived to invest in the frontier land. The landscape outside the big cities was also changing rapidly. Mining towns were booming with land grabbing by the government in order to extract metals, minerals, gems, gold and silver. Over 140 oil and gas JVs were underway. Major companies also started infrastructure projects, building roads, bridges, ports and rail lines. Manufacturing of apparel and other consumer products flourished as companies exploited cheap labor. Amid these new economic activities and speedy urbanization, the *Thein Sein* government still controlled many lucrative sectors including banking, insurance, timber, staple crop farming and mining of jade and other gemstones. Former 'retired' generals, now cabinet ministers, and their families, deeply involved in these businesses, were reluctant to relinquish control of industries to protect their ownership interests.

Neighboring countries including China and India were eyeing infrastructure deals with road and port building projects to reconnect with Burma. China accounted for a third of total investment and exerted an overbearing influence in the region with mega investment in a massive highway, railroad and pipelines across Burma. Mines to extract copper and precious stones threatened the villages with landslides, toxic waste and pollution.

On the west is India, who recognized Burma was a land bridge to Southeast Asia, and India's booming economy desperately needed Burma's rich natural deposits too. India has built infrastructure across the Himalayas to connect with Burma and China. Neighboring Thailand was developing a seaport to connect with Burma and access some of its rich resources as well. Japan has started the development of a giant economic zone including a deep sea port, a thermal power plant, factories and gigantic housing projects. Other overseas investors from Hong Kong, Jakarta, Manila, Kuala Lumpur, and Singapore were now in Rangoon ready with cash to propel Burma into the global economy. At this rate of development this last great frontier may vanish quickly as superhighways and high-speed trains connect billions of people from the two economic giants and the rest of Asia.

Many foreign businessmen speaking multiple languages could be seen with calculators already counting the money to be made. Airlines began offering direct flights to Rangoon, Bagan, Mandalay, *Naypyidaw* and other tourist destinations. Factories, shopping malls, condominiums and high rise hotels were springing up in the Rangoon landscape. Luxury river cruises went up and down the Irrawaddy River. GM, Suzuki, Thai Auto, Yamaha Auto and others have opened car dealerships and sales offices in Rangoon and high end showrooms displaying new models of Mercedes, BMWs, and other luxury cars.

The Asian Development Bank and the World Bank have opened branches; so have other lending institutions from Singapore, China, Japan, Malaysia, Thailand, Cambodia, Brunei, Bangladesh, Vietnam, South Korea, Netherlands, France, the United States and the United Kingdom. So far nine Asia Pacific banks have been granted licenses to operate in Burma, making loans to foreign business. However, retail banking was rudimentary or still not available, and at least 90% of the population (approximately 50 million) did not have a bank account. The cash dominated economy was transitioning to digital economy at high speed with operational ATMs and MasterCard, Visa, and other bank cards. Visa opened its first ATM in 2012, and by 2016 it has over 3,500 outlets in Burma. With Japan's help Burma's central bank was developing a capital market with the opening of *Yangon* Stock Exchange, YSX, in December 2015 but trading was not expected till spring 2016. Japan was also extending over 50 billion yen in loans to Burma, and the World Bank planned to write off Burma's old debts.

Investment in health was also pouring in with pharmaceutical distributorships in drugs and medical equipment. In education, higher learning institutions like Johns Hopkins, SAIS and the Bloomberg Schools were renewing ties and educational exchanges with Rangoon University. University of Southern California was offering scholarships to Burma's talented mid-career business professionals to develop international business skills. Other US universities were establishing financial aid programs to Burmese students. New Zealand was also offering scholarships through their aid program and other learning institutions from Europe were establishing various educational opportunities in Rangoon.

Due to past government restrictions the digital population in the country remained below global level low but that would change as telecommunication, TV, and other media firms began to eye Burma as a new frontier ripe for development. Two telecom service providers were granted licenses to operate in 2014 and two more in 2016, and local enterprises began forming with Japan, Norway, Qatar, and Vietnam. A high speed internet exchange was in the works to connect to international networks and Singapore planned to increase network connectivity with Burma.

Foreign Relations

For decades Burma was shunned by the US and EU, who imposed trade sanctions on the country further secluding it from the West. In reality most sanctions were not only ineffective but had a negative impact on small and medium businesses, creating unemployment and unintended hardships for the working class.

Nearly 90,000 factory workers were laid off as factories and warehouses closed down during the embargo of the military regime with the West. The regime viewed sanctions as a bullying tactic and defied the West by selling off natural deposits to China and Thailand. The generals and the army did not suffer, only the low wage earners and ordinary working folks. For the regime, funding for major projects was much easier and accessible from China and other neighboring countries than from the West. Burma turned to its immediate neighbors and thrived by cutting trade deals in gas, oil, gemstones, timber and other natural extraction with China, India, Thailand and other SE Asian countries. Western companies stayed away while Burma's economy flourished dominated by Asian corporations. As sanctions relaxed after 2011 by President *Thein Sein's* quasi civilian administration, the West began to show presence with the British and the French topping the list of Western investments. Today Burma's major trading partners are still Asian countries - China, Thailand, Singapore, India, Malaysia, Vietnam, Japan, and South Korea with slow but steady increase from the West.

With China's increasing dominance in the region, the US wants to refocus its attention in Asia Pacific and assert a more aggressive position. A new, improved relationship with Burma not only counters China's uncontested access but it also lets China know it has to deal with all of SE Asia in a way that's going to be respectful of each country.[1]

Shortly after Hillary Clinton's visit in 2012, the US restored full diplomatic relations and appointed an ambassador to Burma. President Barack Obama became the first American President to visit the country the following year. The US has eased its sanctions, allowing Burmese products to be imported

---

[1] *Wall Street Journal.* Laura Meckler: "Obama's Asia Trip Comes amid Tug of War with China", November 17-18, 2012.

to the US and to encourage continued political and economic reform. The EU and Australia have lifted their sanctions completely. However, in the foreseeable future, US influence in Burma is unlikely to outweigh that of increasingly prosperous and powerful Asian neighbors.

Burma does not appear to rank very high on the list of US foreign policy priorities in the near future, so resources to address US goals in Burma will be limited. The Trump administration's withdrawal from the Trans-Pacific Partnership, TPP, makes that clear. Burma has good economic relations with neighboring countries. With continued economic, social, and political improvements, and with foreign investment, Burma can rebuild itself. There is hope that one day in the future Burma will be able to lift its people out of poverty, hunger and disease.

Transition Challenges

The new government under President *Thein Sein* was faced with the monumental task of rebuilding the country, with deep-seated problems, half a century old, to be resolved. There was a flood of foreign investment, but was Burma ready for such a change? Burma was devoid of any functioning legal, social, financial, telecommunication, or transportation infrastructure and services at international levels. The lifting of US and EU sanctions and a sudden rush of capital will not immediately rectify decades of mismanagement or lift millions of people out of poverty.

Burma still ranks bottom in global measures on health, human rights, poverty, economic development, transparency, and basic political freedom. Any flight leaving neighboring Bangkok and landing at *Mingaladon* Airport in Rangoon seems to move backward in time, arriving at a third-world city of the 1960s. Dilapidated buses and cars from that period still run, with steering wheels on the left, tell-tale remnants of the British era. Most hotels and airlines use hand written paper registration and tickets. Financial sector was rudimentary in this cash economy making transition to digital economy difficult as merchants do not accept credit cards and only accept new, crispy US$ bills of $10, $20, and $100 for payment. ATMs are beginning to appear but most fail to work due to lack of reliable electricity or power strong enough to access international banking systems.

Infrastructure and Basic Amenities

Burma's infrastructure was in dire need of reform as the country was not connected by road or rail to any of its neighbors. Investments in infrastructure including water supply, electricity, telecommunications and transportation are imperative to support and propel future growth. Poor infra-structure was a major impediment to distribution of goods and services. Telecommunications and internet access was one of the lowest in the world with <2% internet users. International roaming service and cell phones were useless until recently and mostly in internet cafes where it's often irregular, intermittent or snail pace. Internet access in private homes was financially prohibitive. Electricity was unavailable, rationed, or intermittent and frequent blackouts are common occurrences even at the few existing four star hotels in Rangoon. Fewer than 30% of the 55 million people have access to electricity. In rural areas more than two-thirds people lack access to reli-able electricity. In satellite towns and rural regions people must still rely on candles to do work and for students to study and do homework at night. Factories often have to stop operation due to power outages.

Burma's poor human rights history and widespread drug trade prevented the country from obtaining any multilateral financial assistance. The govern-ment limited permits and imposed 120% tax on imported cars making auto-mobiles unaffordable except for the elite generals, their families, and the well connected inner circle crony friends. A standard used economy Japanese car would cost over $100,000 considering a black market permit, import taxes, custom fees, shipping and other related expenses, until recent modification of import taxation regulations. Public transportation is inefficient as buses are overloaded and rail travel is crowded, slow, tedious and seldom on time. Most recent development has been focused on the larger cities.

Nothing seems to change in rural Burma. Outside of big cities and in rural regions, village life consisting of manual labor, farming in paddy fields and tending to animals remains the same for hundreds of years. Trav-eling in oxcarts is still the primary mode of transportation and electricity and running water nonexistent. Villagers do not have cell phones or land phones for that matter. Access to drinking water is limited, and refrigerators, washing machines and television sets remain luxury items and unaffordable to majority. Fifty years of authoritarian rule has resulted in a great leap back-ward for Burma just as the rest of Asia is enjoying unprecedented growth and prosperity for their people.

Vague Regulations

The absence of written, consistent rule of law in Burma propagates abuse of power and corruption by the military regime as it views itself above the law. Thein Sein's new administration has introduced new regulations but many financial and legal policies are arbitrary. Unpredictable legal and regulatory systems rely on government discretion and interpretation rather than written laws. Overt intimidation of the past is being replaced by overly vague guidelines that can be used as authorities see fit.[1]

Legal and financial systems are still rudimentary and inadequate for large scale investments or for international transactions. Although the government has made significant macroeconomic reforms, new regulations are unclear and still subject to interpretation. Legal system is unpredictable and regulations are inconsistent with frequent unwritten policy changes and up to the minister's discretion of each situation rather than concrete written laws with definitive interpretation. Government ministers and their staff not only lack experience but are overwhelmed due to the sudden spike in interest and requests for information from foreign governments, UN agencies, NGOs, international financial institutions, foreign donors, and multinational companies. Bribery and corruption in the court system still prevails among judges, lawyers, prosecutors, court clerks, police, and all levels of the legal system. Payment of bribes can drop charges or release of accused party without proper investigation. Lack of legal certainty on property rights and intellectual property laws and government inexperience in commercial litigation and arbitration plague the corrupt and incompetent legal system in the country. Market information is not available and official sources of information are unreliable, inadequate or incorrect. Government statistics and data are largely guesses or intentionally skewed and manipulated to support past regime's propaganda. Uncertain and fast changing rules and regulations and a bloated bureaucracy stifled with corruption and incompetent officials are many of the impediments to foreign investment. Additionally, lack of cooperation among government departments and ministries hinder development progress.

Corruption and Cronyism

Under President *Thein Sein's* quasi civilian administration reforms are taking place but are recent and fragile and anti-reform elements and attitudes of the past within the new government still prevail. The generals of the past authoritarian regime deeply mired in half a century of corruption and graft problems are finding it difficult to let go of the iron clad fist and inducement of corrupt money under the table. They may have shed their military uniforms but a culture of top-down decision making and central control still thrives and corruption is pervasive and remains endemic at all levels. Reforms are volatile and many including foreign investors, fear government can easily

---

[1] *Los Angeles Times.* Mark Magnier: "Media's Old Fears Return in *Myanmar*", March 17, 2013.

revert back to army dictatorship. Two military owned economic institutions UMEHL, Union of *Myanmar* Economic Holdings Limited and MEC, *Myanmar* Economic Corporation still own and control large commercial activities and many profitable projects are still owned by the generals, now cabinet ministers. Crony capitalism still dominates in the new market economy with privatized assets remaining in the hands of the same elite individuals with high level connections in the regime. Military families and their business allies have tentacles extended into every industry and every sector of the economy. They use anonymous companies or secret ownership structures to hide illegal transactions and activities, for tax evasion, and money laundering. Former army generals who are now MPs, still enjoy business monopolies and formed bogus companies for their families with ownership in every sector ranging from hotels to airlines, chicken farms to jade mines, casting doubts about the sincerity of the reforms or the commitment to improve the lives of its poverty stricken people.

Corruption is widespread and punitive actions are rarely taken. Bribes and kickbacks occur at every ministry including the judiciary. Judges who were hired and trained under the authoritative military rule were conditioned to favor the regime, and the army's constitution of 2008 guarantees them their position until 70 years of age. *Tatmadaw* still controls major resources in the country and many lucrative business sectors. The elite continue to profit. The ruling generals exchange gold-plated pistols or boast of real estate holdings in Singapore, Malaysia, Dubai and elsewhere.

Unskilled Workforce

The frequent closures of colleges and universities and the lack of government funding eroded the quality of education, leaving generations of youth uneducated and ill prepared. The government spent 40% of the total annual budget on the military and only one tenth of the budget on education. The lack of basic education and low skill levels mean the workforce will not be globally competitive any time soon. The people are intelligent but uneducated. They are courageous yet live in fear.

Unlike the ordinary folks, officials and their cronies were able to send their children abroad for education and technical training. The broken education system will take decades to turn around. A severe shortage of skilled workers is apparent in all fields and qualified professionals of every kind — doctors, engineers, architects, business managers, and teachers — are in short supply.

The dictatorship and the destruction of the education system contributed to a brain drain; millions of Burma's most educated and talented citizens fled the country since the coup of 1962. When wholesale nationalization brought a halt to all private commercial activity, many experienced business people and professionals left the country. The devaluation of the currency also stripped Chinese and Indian residents of their wealth, and resulted in the mass exit of hundreds of thousands. Anti-Chinese sentiment fueled riots in the 1960s, causing mass expulsion of Chinese merchants and professionals, further stripping the country of business and technical expertise. At least a generation of British-era educated and trained professionals and intellectuals also left the country to seek opportunities elsewhere. Even fresh graduates of Burmese universities and technical institutes left to seek work in factories, restaurants and shops in Thailand, Singapore and Malaysia, and they remitted money home to support their families. In many communities whole generations of working men and women were absent from their homes while their children were left in the care of grandparents or other relatives.

Roadblocks for Foreign Investors

Foreign investors entering the emerging Burmese market find that nothing is straightforward and the bloated Burmese bureaucracy is difficult to navigate. The directness of Western business communication and practice is replaced with ambiguity and obscurity. They also face competition from many Asian companies that established a presence and strong business relationships during the years of Western sanctions. Hard data is scarce and statistics are unreliable and difficult to substantiate. Every foreigner rushing into Burma with capital needs to know there is no legal protection for his investment.

There were no stock or bond markets until 2015, and four years later the Rangoon (*Yangon*) Stock Exchange had only five companies listed. The rudimentary banking system limited the ability of investors to cash out through the local markets; and infrastructure, legal and financial systems were lacking for conducting international trade and commerce. Even basic accounting standards had to be developed from scratch.

Roads were prone to flooding and often became impassable during the monsoon season. Most foreign cell phone plans didn't work. Transactions were still predominantly cash based, even for large assets. Visa and MC have recently arrived but were not accepted, at first, at retail levels. ATMs didn't work or did not function properly, in part due to intermittent electricity and internet connections required to link cards back to the user's bank in his home country.

Industrial parks and zones have been developed but decades of Western sanctions and economic mismanagement have left factories abandoned or demolished. Other risk factors also weighed on President *Thein Sein's* ambition to fast-track economic development. Decreasing global energy demand and falling energy prices slow down many oil and gas exploration projects with foreign joint venture companies. The falling value of the Burmese currency, the *kyat*, and fast increases in domestic demand caused a widening trade deficit. There was a general lack of reliable data to enable due diligence as accurate and relevant market and financial data were not available. Government statistics for Burma's economy were difficult to verify, making it difficult to accurately forecast or predict future performance of new investment ventures.

Poorly Diversified Economy

Prior to the 1962 military coup, Burma was exporting around 2 million tons of rice annually. The rice exports steadily declined due to incompetence, mismanagement and corruption. Lack of funds to buy equipment and machinery further reduced output, and finally rice had to be rationed at one point.

Burma's economy was predominantly based on agricultural, with two thirds of the people engaged in subsistence farming, rendering a per capita income of just over $400. Agriculture, livestock, fisheries, and forestry accounted for almost half of GDP, primarily exporting rice, beans and pulses, marine products and timber. Major improvement is needed in all aspects of rice cultivation and production, including higher quality seeds, mechanization, modern agricultural technology, adequate storage to eliminate crop spoilage, rice milling and easier access via reliable transportation to the marketplace.

The government still controlled the extractive and energy sectors as they provided significant export revenues, but the numbers were unavailable and kept non transparent. The manufacturing and service sectors also remained undeveloped. The informal economy was very large and included activities from currency trading to education to commodity trade. Unrecorded border trade and black market flourished along all of Burma's borders trading illicit narcotics, gems and jade, religious relics, rubber and timber for consumer goods, medicines, vehicles and vehicle parts, electronics, fertilizer, and diesel fuel. Many products like Chinese-made household appliances and apparel,

Thai toothpaste and American sunglasses were smuggled over the opium trails on horseback or on foot.

The Golden Triangle, the confluence of Burma, Laos and Thailand, is well known for large production of opium, Ecstasy, and other amphetamine-type stimulants. Decades of civil war have stimulated drug production and consumption, especially in marginalized ethnic communities. Most of the opium is turned into heroin and exported to Europe and the US. With the increasing wealth of Asian urbanites, demand for illegal drugs was also rising rapidly in the region with increasing use in China, Indonesia, Malaysia, Singapore, Thailand and Viet Nam.[1] Improved connectivity throughout the region offered by the India–Burma–Thailand Trilateral Highway and the Tran-Asian Railway is speeding up both legal and illicit trade among Asian countries like never before. Most Asian governments, Burma included, have given economic development a top priority and less attention is devoted to illicit trade and organized crime.

Conflict with Ethnic Minority Nationalities

The Burmese people are made up of many different ethnic nationalities, each with customs, language and traditions of their own, and with their own sense of ownership of the mineral deposits found in their territories. The hilly border regions are easily stirred to a sense of conflict with the central authorities, and unrest has simmered in these frontier areas for almost seven decades.

Instead of protecting the people along its borders with neighboring countries, the military regime positioned its troops to extract resources from the remote ethnic regions. *Tatmadaw* controlled the mining, timber, and other industries. The army confiscated land to build pipelines to transport petroleum and other extractives out of the ethnic regions, frequently involving vicious acts committed against the local people and villagers. The locals have no choice but to take up arms and defend their ancestral land and dwindling natural wealth.

Since independence, the Karens, Kachins, Chins, Karrenni, Shans and other minority groups all wanted equality and the autonomy of self governance but this desire was never honored by the central government. With total disregard for environmental destruction, toxins from metal and gemstone extraction poured into rivers and lakes, and forests were depleted for hardwood smuggled into China. HIV/AIDS from drug use has become

---

[1] UNDC. Report/TOCTA-EA-Pacific: "Ch 5 Trafficking of Opiates from *Myanmar* and Afghanistan from East Asia and the Pacific", 51.

rampant in bordering states as the regime turned a blind eye to production and distribution of opium, heroin and amphetamines, debilitating local population.

Since the Chinese have a large economic interest at stake, especially with jade mining in Kachin state, they too were less than interested in ending conflict in that region. In fact, China has always protected the military regimes of Burma from international retribution and diplomatically shielded the Burmese army from global scrutiny and justice voted at the UN Security Council. This intervention and support at UNSC has embolden *Tatmadaw* and the soldiers attacked the ethnic minorities who fought back through their jungle militia or ethnic armed organizations, armed with Chinese weaponry which they purchased with profits from heroin, opium and meth produced in the region. Peace talks and political dialog between the *Bamar* central government and EAOs have been ineffective. Even within a specific armed nationality group, the dynamics, goals, tactics and processes are highly complex.

Another longstanding challenge for President *Thein Sein's* government was the conflict between the minority Muslims and the majority Buddhists living in Arakan state in western Burma. Known to the world as the *Rohingya*, they are referred to by the Burmese government as the *Bengalis*.

In 1982 the regime passed a law stipulating that to be considered an ethnic minority, immigrants must have lived in Burma before the first Anglo–Burmese war of 1824–26. The government claimed these Muslim immigrants were brought in as slaves from Bangladesh by the colonialists, and therefore they are classified as *Bangalis*, not a local ethnic minority, and thus are denied Burmese citizenship regardless of how long they have lived in the country.

Muslim historians and leaders in Arakan have disputed this view and asserted that their roots in Arakan state date back before the British era. They say they were a stateless group living in Burma for centuries. The hostility toward the minority Muslims dates back to British colonial era when the immigrants began to occupy land in the luscious valley of Arakan and prospered at the expense of the local Arakanese people, who are primarily Buddhists. Mistrust, dislike and grievances brewed among the local Arakanese Buddhists who regarded the minority Muslims as less than human, calling them *kalar*, a derogatory term similar to 'nigger'. This prejudice was so prevalent that even the militant Buddhist monks have inveighed against the minority Muslims.

Since 2012 anti-Muslim sentiment among leading radical Buddhist monks was spread with fiery rhetoric and inflammatory speeches in Arakan. They branded their Buddhist campaign and nationalist movement '969' with the mission to protect Burma from an Islamic invasion. The three digits 969 refer to the nine virtues of Buddha, the six attributes of his teachings or *dhamma*, and the nine attributes of the *sangha*. The conflict between the Muslim minority and Buddhist majority in Arakan represents one of Burma's most complex and challenging issues facing the new government.

Chapter 8. 2015 Democratic Government

President Thein Sein's Legacy

Although the *Thein Sein* government released political prisoners, legalized trade unions, improved labor standards, and initiated peace and ceasefire negotiations with armed ethnic groups, the country still lacked significant legislative, institutional and constitutional reform.

There was superficial diplomacy and a transition to a modern-style authoritarian regime rather than direct military rule. Hundreds of activists were still in jail without trial and many were arrested for merely expressing opinions against the regime. There were recent arrests of journalists; one journalist was killed in custody, indicating a resurgence of media repression. Even as some political prisoners were released, new arrests, some on bogus charges, were being made. Anyone could be jailed for 20 years or more for sending a single email criticizing the regime or just simply because it contained an anti-government sentiment.

Most imprisoned activists and political dissidents were convicted in closed-door hearings of 'unlawful association, illegally distributing print and video media, or generally destabilizing public security and the security of the state', and were given arbitrary lengthy sentences of 50, 60, or 70 years. President *Thein Sein* has broken his promise to release all political prisoners by the end of 2013, and the people of Burma continued to face threats of arrest and lived in intimidation.

Since General *Ne Win's* era, a censorship board was established to ban anything that would vilify, disgrace, or dishonor the military regime. The few state-owned newspapers only printed government propaganda, lacking in content of any substance or truth. President *Thein Sein* relaxed restrictions on travel and trade, media and censorship, but laws and regulations that restricted genuine freedom remained in force. Publication of corruption activities of high ranking officials or their cronies was still prohibited. Direct criticism of the government was also banned and subject to arrest and harassment. Firewalls on the internet were still a barrier especially on sites deemed sensitive by the government. The new government still has the power to revoke publishing licenses or to reverse any new censorship relaxation. President *Thein Sein's* administration does not appear to be fully committed to true democracy with regard to freedom of speech and press, as the laws are broad and flexible, allowing the authorities to interpret them as they see fit.

Military attacks on ethnic nationalities continued full force and the old regime's tactics were still evident. The army continued to commit human rights abuses against the ethnic minority peoples, including the Muslims in the west. Systematic discrimination, sexual violence and rape, severe persecution, arbitrary arrests, torture, discrimination, restrictions on religious freedom, and denial of citizenship and access to health, education and jobs continue today.

The old racism against the Muslims has erupted in new waves of crime in the absence of government intervention. Soldiers often participated with the mobs in the attacks, burning mosques and houses, driving people from their homes, and preventing people from helping the injured and dying. Acts of savagery and destruction of villages in Arakan drove thousands Muslim villagers across the Naf river where they ended up in no man's land or squalid makeshift camps. Violent clashes with *Tatmadaw* in the ethnic regions of Shan and Kachin states destroyed entire towns and villages, killing and displacing hundreds of thousands of villagers. Soldiers who committed hideous acts were never punished.

Burma has been mired for decades in injustice and corruption permeating every aspect of business and government. Major corporations of *Tatmadaw*, UMEHL and MEC, continued to control many segments of the economy with little transparency and accountability in *Thein Sein's* new government. They operated above the law and without regard for environmental requirements or labor rights. Many large businesses were still in the hands of the regime's families and inner circle connected crony friends who were involved in everything from toothpaste to taxis, supermarkets to shopping malls, and garment manufacturing to gemstone mining. The ministers of the new parliament played down on human rights violations and focused on promoting trade and investment, which were still in the hands of the military elite; and military dominance of the economy continued to contribute to corruption. The military elites have a strong vested interest in economic development as that will in turn increase the value of their holdings.

Burma has become dangerously dependent on China as a major ally and trading partner with whom it shares a 12,000 mile border. China was seeking energy stability through mining, extraction, manufacture and infrastructure, building mega projects, roads, dams, and pipelines in Burma. India, too, was doing business with the regime, especially in information technology and financial services.

Burma needed to balance ties with Beijing and Delhi as the two giant powers strive for supremacy in the Pacific Asia region. Billions of dollars in jade were mined in the hills of Kachin state and smuggled out without taxation or benefit to the state and its people. Thousands of tons of teak were shipped into Yunnan province, depleting the forests belonging to their ancestors. The highly profitable drug and sex traffic from the Golden Triangle were controlled by Chinese drug lords and heavily armed drug militias who were trained in jungle warfare. China has invested in numerous hydroelectric power plants, many of them having negative environmental and social implications and affecting the rights of local villagers. Some projects, like the *Myitsone* dam, were not only designed but are being built by Chinese workers, which aggravates anti-Chinese sentiment among the locals. The generals of *Tatmadaw* wanted to reduce dependency on their powerful neighbor and to improve relations with the West as a counterbalance. To rebuild its economy from a centrally-controlled to a market-oriented economy, Burma also needed an end to Western sanctions. However, *Thein Sein's* government might also have been trying to shed Burma's reputation as a pariah state while taking purely token measures. As indicated by Emma Larkin,[1] the generals have a tried and tested strategy dealing with the West. Promise them what they want to hear and get a 6–9 months window before the international community realizes you haven't delivered. By then the urgency diminishes and outrage subsides.

The outside world began to question the real reasons for the sudden open door policy of 2011 and subsequent speedy reforms. Was this transition to democracy only a charade, a clever strategy to entice foreign investments? Was it a just a new form of authoritarian rule with the same people in charge? What if the regime only wanted to get Western sanctions lifted? No one could be certain if their priority was only to build prosperity, not democracy.

---

[1] *Everything is Broken.* Emma Larkin: New York, Penguin Books, 2010.

Retired dictator General *Than Shwe*, who had ruled the country with an iron fist for the past two decades, still exerted considerable influence over *Thein Sein's* government. He had been handpicked by *Than Shwe* to lead the new 2011 administration as he was soft spoken and politically less threat-ening. Meanwhile, the generals and their cronies continued to live lavish lifestyles.

Under *Thein Sein*, National League of Democracy was no longer outlawed; it was permitted to register as a political party for the first time. As a free citizen and leader of the opposition party, *Aung San Suu Kyi* was now allowed to participate in the political process. NLD registered to take part in the April 2012 by-election and entered parliament. NLD won most of the allotted seats in the parliament with *Aung San Suu Kyi* elected as Member of Parliament.

President *Thein Sein* replaced the hardline Information Minister with a moderate to improve communication and relation with *Aung San Suu Kyi*. He also told the BBC he would accept *Aung San Suu Kyi* as president if she was elected, knowing full well she was barred from the presidency as stated in the 2008 constitution (written by the military). Meanwhile, *Aung San Suu Kyi's* role seemed to be transforming into that of a symbolic figure head, a non-violent human rights advocate and democracy fighter, while President *Thein Sein* was becoming more prominent with world leaders as the head of the quasi civilian Burmese government since 2011.

President *Thein Sein's* government planned to hold free elections in November 2015, the first free elections in almost fifty years. Just prior to the elections, an internal reshuffling occurred, in August 2015, when Speaker *Shwe Mann*, chairman of the ruling Union Solidarity and Development Party, was removed by force due to his close relationship with *Aung San Suu Kyi*.

U *Shwe Mann*, also known as *Thura Shwe Mann*, a retired army general, also supported constitutional change that would reduce the power of *Tatmadaw*. He was once the third-highest-ranking official in SPDC and was regarded as one of the most powerful men in the military regime. When General *Than Shwe* chose the politically less ambitious U *Thein Sein* to be president in 2010, *Shwe Mann* was elected to the much less powerful position of Lower House Speaker. He forged a political alliance with *Aung San Suu Kyi*, foreseeing her imminent victory in 2015. This resulted in strained relations with many top party leaders of USDP and generals including General *Min Aung Hlaing*, the army chief; and *Shwe Mann* was ousted as chairman of USDP. After NLD won the elections, *Aung San Suu Kyi* appointed him head the Legal Affairs and Special Cases Assessment Commission within the parliament, which was abolished three years later when he formed a political party, the Union Betterment Party, to re-enter the political environment.

In the current constitution, written by the military and imposed by past regimes, the army was guaranteed a quarter of the seats in parliament and local assemblies and had veto power over any constitutional amendment. *Tatmadaw* also controlled the ministries of defense, home affairs, and border affairs, and its own budget.

Tatmadaw also controlled how the president was selected, giving it ultimate power to dissolve the constitutional government and reestablish military rule anytime in the future. Thus, the constitution of 2008 ensured they would retain ultimate control over the country, regardless of who won the election in 2015.

Could NLD win the elections, come into power, and end half a century of military control? To win NLD needed to secure two thirds of the seats in parliament, but the opposition USDP, crammed with military cronies, only needed one third since 25% was already allotted by the constitution of 2008. Thus the 2015 elections might be free but the constitution was undemocratic, guarantying *Tatmadaw*'s grip on the government.

Clause 59(f) of the current constitution also barred *Aung San Suu Kyi* from the presidency as her two sons were British citizens. Nevertheless, the elections took place and people voted to change a military dictatorship to a parliamentary democracy.

As president *Thein Sein* retired and faded from the scene, credit should be given for his achievements during his five-year presidency 2011–2015. President *Thein Sein*'s legacy included an election and the formation of a new parliament where *Aung San Suu Kyi* was invited to participate. *Thein Sein*'s government began reforms by releasing thousands of political prisoners and easing press censorship. Another highlight of his achievement was the opening of the economy to the global community for trade and investment, encouraging foreign investment to grow at record rates and freely allowing imports of foreign made basic and luxury products, including cars and cell phones. But his most significant political decision was his suspension of the controversial Chinese hydroelectric-power installation on the Irrawaddy, the *Myitsone* dam. By supporting the local people who opposed the project, he sent a powerful message to China to be more equitable and to comply with Burmese law. *Thein Sein* was the first Burmese head of state to visit the United States in 46 years. The retired general was awarded the Asian Cosmopolitan Grand Prize in 2016 for his leadership and accomplishments during this transitional period by the Economic Research Institute for ASEAN and East Asia (ERIA) in Japan.

Euphoria

To ensure the 2015 elections were free and fair, a few reputable international observers were present to monitor and track the polling and election results. According to the Union Election Commission, 23 million or 69% of the population voted and the results were overwhelmingly pro-democracy, with National League of Democracy winning against the army-backed USDP in a landslide.

Burma now has a democratically accountable administration with a leader who is not a former general. *Aung San Suu Kyi* was released from house arrest and became head of the civilian government. Among those who voted, aspiration for democracy was high with an overwhelming 79% voting for democracy; 60% of the voters preferred civilian government while only 8% voted for military government. A resounding 94% also voted for freedom of religion.

As expected, the election results caused exhilaration among the people of Burma. NLD won 80.5% of elected parliament seats. The nation was overcome with exuberance. Euphoria was in the air. This was the first election based on a democratic platform where ordinary folks were empowered to vote freely as citizens. People basked in the newfound freedoms during the honeymoon period. The military dominated party USDP was crushed and faced humiliating losses nationwide. *Aung San Sui Kyi* might not be president, but she would definitely lead the new administration. Whatever her title, the Lady would be seen as the head of the newly-elected administration.

There would be many challenges for *Aung San Sui Kyi* and her new government, as the army included many clauses in the constitution to limit the power of the winning party, and the military would most likely continue to exert majority control over every level of government and every aspect of life and economy regardless who was elected the new government.

The Lady and the President

As the people voted strongly in favor of a democratic party, former generals and military party members of USDP woke up to realize they had more to gain by working with *Aung San Sui Kyi* and that to continue on the path of isolation and autocratic control was unsustainable. As an international icon, she joined the global ranks of Nelson Mandela, Mahatma Gandhi, and the Dalai Lama. Together with the Lady, opening and welcoming the West spelled economic improvements which the army elite believed would benefit them the most. *Aung San Sui Kyi* also recognized her role had changed from that of an international icon to a politician, and with fluency in both English and Burmese, she was the Western-educated voice of Burma.

Aung San Sui Kyi had also made considerable concessions to President *Thein Sein* and his government by downplaying the need to punish past military abuses; she allowed generals to feel secure against retribution for war crimes and confiscation of property and other assets. Instead, she emphasized, in accordance with Buddhist principles, the need for forgiveness for their crimes, including those perpetrated against her and NLD members. That was truly admirable even if it was politically motivated.

Former General *Thein Sein*, on the other hand, did not come from privilege, as he was the son of a poor farmer, received training more as an army bureaucrat than a combat soldier, and never traveled outside of Burma until middle age. He was born April 20, 1945, in *Kyonku*, a small village in the Irrawaddy delta. Many army officers of his time came from a humble background. His father earned a living carrying cargo at the river jetty and weaving bamboo mats, while his mother worked in a tea shop to help support the family. After completing village school he joined the army, *Tatmadaw*, embarking on a 40-year career. He attended the prestigious Defense Services Academy, graduating in 1968 with an art degree, and rose steadily through the ranks. He became a general and served under the brutal dictator General *Than Shwe*.

Thein Sein was quiet and soft spoken, non-threatening and loyal, posing no threat to the junta leader *Than Shwe* who orchestrated his rise to prime minister in 2007 during the Saffron Revolution. After serving four years as PM, he was chosen by the 'emperor' General *Than Shwe* to lead the quasi-civilian government as president in 2011. He was serious and cautious, and not too charismatic, and spoke only through translators, repeating well-rehearsed statements.

After Cyclone Nargis hit, as chairman of the country's disaster preparedness committee and leader of the military junta's emergency response efforts, he was criticized for the gross mishandling of the relief effort. Over 200,000 people died in the disaster. During his career as a general, the military was responsible for horrific human rights abuses and war crimes. Like most of the generals, he was reported to be involved in and benefited from the trafficking of drugs such as methamphetamine and opium; but as the first civilian president in almost fifty years, *Thein Sein* led the country from dictatorship to semi democracy and opened Burma to the outside world, pushing for the sanctions to be lifted by the EU and the US. He freed 6,300 political prisoners, made peace deals with ethnic minorities and relaxed media censorship. His releases of political prisoners were generally tied to prominent visits by foreign heads of states as bargaining chips. Under his semi civilian rule, Burma's economy began its upward climb and doors began to open to the outside world.

The Deified Leader

The international community reacted most favorably to the NLD victory, as Burma now had a democratically-elected government. On one hand, the NLD government would be confronting daunting issues to negotiate legal, financial and social accountability with the military elite. On the other there was vast opportunity to improve the quality of life for the people.

In 2015 both *Thein Sein* and *Aung San Suu Kyi* were 75 years old, with no plan of succession or second-tier leadership strong enough to take over after the Lady. The next election was only five years away. For now, the Lady was at least the head of the civilian side of the administration. Although changes were taking place quickly, the new administration had no master plan for economic reform and no government funding allocated to education, health-care or development programs.

Within NLD's inner circle, it was reported that *Aung San Suu Kyi's* followers were fiercely loyal but were not as well-educated, politically strong, or talented as their leader. She had a pedigree as *Bogyoke Aung San's* daughter, an Oxford educated, Nobel laureate, world democracy icon; and she had the language, charisma and charm to command a world class audience. As a democracy and human rights icon *Aung San Suu Kyi* was beyond criticism. Her followers were so in awe that whatever she said was taken as law. This, plus her autocratic style of leadership prevented new blood and new ideas into the organization. She had also been described as haughty and rigid occasionally displaying her stubbornness and flashes of temper. Not only was there a lack of new leadership, new ideas, and unity, but the first tier leadership was aging and becoming less effective for rebuilding the country.

Since 2012 when she became a Member of Parliament, *Aung San Suu Kyi* seemed to have made political and moral concessions to build bridges with the crony capitalists, some of whom were now her political donors.[1] She was reported as having accepted large donations from pro regime entities including Sky Net. The Lady herself admitted in an interview that it was better to accept donations from cronies which could be used for the needy than for the money to be used by the cronies to buy another private jet. Some claimed she also accepted free flights for life and a generous budget for wardrobe expenditures from allies of the regime.

---

[1] *WSJ*. Bret Stephens: *"Aung San Suu Kyi's Narrow Road"*, June 11, 2014.

After the 2015 victory, she began limiting contact with foreign press and seldom granted interviews to foreign journalists. Most obvious to the international community, she had remained silent about the government's heinous acts against the Muslim minority in Arakan state. She had also not spoken forcefully about equal rights and self-determination for the minorities of Shan, Kachin, Karen and Chin. Her support for minorities seemed to be eroding rapidly. For now, the biggest priority for *Aung San Suu Kyi* and NLD was to change the constitution rather than to negotiate peace with ethnic groups.

As the press reported, the halo around *Aung San Suu Kyi* as the nation's moral authority and global peace icon might have slightly dimmed, but she was still the only symbol of hope and freedom for the country. *Aung San Suu Kyi* had already changed the course of history for her country. She had brought the world's attention to Burma. Her personal residence at 54 University Avenue in Rangoon, a crumbling old Victorian home, had been the heart of NLD, her pro-democracy party, where members, politicians, academics, scholars, activists, exiles, journalists, diplomats and supporters would meet, organize, and plan strategies and tactics. Although she was put under house arrest for 17 years, she remained strong and resolute. She was not only the woman but the *only* person who had ever defied the Burmese regime. But her role and arena in 2015 had changed. As head of the newly-elected civilian government, she had to learn to work with the army generals who were determined to control and retain power. And now the world's attention was focused on her, with expectations that she would end the atrocities and corruption and bring peace, justice and equality to all the people of Burma. This would be the most significant test of *Aung San Suu Kyi's* leadership.

Democratic Civilian Government

Burma now had a democratically elected civilian government led by a true civilian and not a retired general. Although the military remained strong, their control over the new parliament was shared. The new political system also included non-*Bamar* ethnic representatives.

Perhaps the military regime has been planning the transition process for a long time. As Brigadier General *Aung Gyi* indicated in 1990, the military under General *Saw Maung* had fully intended handing over the helm to civilian rule when NLD won the elections with a landslide. However, when the party expelled *Aung Gyi*, the most honored and respected retired general, handing control to NLD would have meant giving the country to an organization infiltrated with communists and ousted army officers who opposed the regime. This the military would not do, so *Tatmadaw* resumed the seat of power for another two and a half decades.

This time, in 2015, when NLD won another resounding victory, the generals were prepared and ready to open Burma to a series of unprecedented changes. They cleverly allowed the transfer of responsibilities they were not interested in — such as health and education — to the civilian government. However, the army did not relinquish control of strategic and critical matters such as defense, law or politics.

Tatmadaw's priority has always been for its sovereignty, territorial integrity of central control, and safeguarding the regime's interests. Regardless who was elected, the military would continue to exert majority control over every level of government, politics and many aspects of economy. As the most powerful institution in the country with power to veto any major constitutional change, the military held the key to any reform in Burma's political, legal and power structures controlling the three most important ministries. Military matters such as the ethnic insurgencies in war zones of bordering regions, the entire police force, and all levels of government — central, state, region, district and township, were under *Tatmadaw's* jurisdiction. It has been a long thought out, planned, designed, and implemented political system of *Tatmadaw* to preserve its power and control.

General *Than Shwe* had been contemplating ways to reduce China's geopolitical and economic influence. The generals began to seek international aid and turned to the West. By relinquishing responsibilities they were not interested in, and retaining key ministries, they protected their position while pressuring the NLD to work with them; this made the NLD part of the status quo political system. They executed a plan to manifest their deep-rooted military ideology within a democratic establishment. They transferred civilian responsibilities to a homegrown democratic government with carefully selected non-strategic sectors of governance like agriculture modernization, fisheries and aquaculture expansion, health and education overhaul, improved transportation, increased access to electricity, and tourism development.

As in the past *Tatmadaw* could have intervened at any stage of the process to manipulate the elections to give a different outcome, or they could have simply not handed over the controls, as before. But General *Than Shwe* and his inner circle decided that a Burma open to the international community would become more prosperous and better serve their interests. *Than Shwe* even hired a PR firm, Podesta Group, to improve their image. Rather than genuine transformation to democracy, the regime paid Washington lobbyists to pretend they were doing that. Indeed, *Tatmadaw* loosened the reins just enough to incorporate democratic principles without giving up control.

After the electoral win in 2015, *Aung San Suu Kyi* stated clearly during a BBC interview that she had plans to create a position for herself that would be even 'higher than the President'.[1] For the new cabinet she appointed *U Htin Kyaw* as president, a trusted buddy from the NLD. This choice was a testament to her absolute control of power of the civilian side of the new establishment; all she needed was a trustworthy ceremonial mouthpiece.

For vice president she and her NLD party selected an ethnic Kachin named Henry *Van Thio*. They created a separate ministry for ethnic affairs, hoping to emphasize the importance of ethnic minority nationalities and the civil-war related issues. A year later, a new position of state counselor, not included in the 2008 constitution, was specially created for the Lady by the legislature and signed into law by her loyal president, *U Htin Kyaw*. She declared, as the state counselor, a position 'above the president', that she would "make all the decisions, because I am the leader of the winning party." The military disagreed and refrained from voting on the bill. In case the 'super-president' position of state counselor was insufficient, *Aung San Suu Kyi* also decided to take on four ministerial positions. It seemed the Lady wanted to be the minister of everything.

President *U Htin Kyaw*'s service lasted less than three years as he resigned in March 2018 for health reasons. He was replaced by *U Win Myint*, a lawyer and another trusted friend of the Lady, as the new president with no significant change in the government's policy.

The military selected Lieutenant General *Myint Swe* to be vice president in the new parliament to safeguard military control and to ensure *Tatmadaw's* presence in the civilian government. As mentioned above, the 2008 constitution also created a divided government, in which the *Tatmadaw* chief appoints a quarter of Parliament's members and three powerful cabinet members report directly to him and not to any civilian president. Therefore, control of police force and the administration of justice remain under the military. In addition to the three crucial ministries the army also oversees the National Defense and Security Council, a body which can seize power in times of national emergency. As an old style army hardliner, Lieutenant General *Myint Swe* resisted reforms and transparency during his service with *Tatmadaw* and was on the US sanctions blacklist. It is believed *Tatmadaw* selected him as a confrontational move and challenge to the NLD government. He is believed to be General *Than Shwe*'s personal choice.

---

[1] *Forbes.* Doug Bandow: "A Brighter Dawn In Burma: *Myanmar* Not Yet A Democracy But No Longer A Dictatorship", Mar 31, 2016.

Many generals and military families wanted to cling to the status quo. Another provision of the constitution allows the vice president to replace the president in case of illness, disability, resignation or death of the president.

The Lady and the General

Winning the election was just the beginning. In view of a powerful army who still worked independently and who did not report to the president, what could NLD do to implement democratic reforms and resolve Burma's myriad problems? The constitution secured the role of the military in politics, safeguarded the men in uniform from prosecution and guaranteed *Tatmadaw's* control in national affairs. There were issues of land rights, ethnic fighting in bordering states, violent attacks in Arakan state; corruption, the drug trade, colossal projects of China; relationship between NLD and *Tatmadaw* and issues facing farmers, students, workers, women, the environment and much more.

Most critical of all was the relationship between *Aung San Suu Kyi* and Senior General *Min Aung Hlaing,* the army chief. *Aung San Suu Kyi* knew she must get along with the 54-year-old commander-in-chief of *Tatmadaw, Min Aung Hlaing* who succeeded Senior General *Than Shwe* in 2011.

Her success would depend largely on how well she got along with the army chief and how she worked with the military. She would have to shift the focus from power and control of the parliament to building a democratic government that genuinely addressed issues of national interest and the economic well being of the country. Sooner or later she would have to accept *Tatmadaw's* position on banning her from the presidency. The military saw itself as the guardian of the constitution and hence, the bar on *Aung San Suu Kyi* could not and would not be lifted.

Senior General *Min Aung Hlaing,* the supreme commander-in-chief of *Tatmadaw* with more than 450,000 troops, the police force, and other special security forces, nominated a vice president for the new cabinet and controlled three key ministries and National Defense and Security Council. The 11 members of NDSC included the president, the two vice presidents (one appointed by the military), the two parliamentary Speakers of the houses, the foreign minister, the commander-in-chief and his deputy, and the three key ministers for defense, home affairs and border affairs. These three ministers were selected and named by the commander-in-chief giving the military appointed members of NDSC a majority six to five advantage over the civilian government. Like his predecessor Senior General *Than Shwe, Min*

Aung Hlaing enjoyed a position of power reserved for the president in most countries in the world.

Aung San Suu Kyi did not get everything she wanted even after three meetings with the army chief *Min Aung Hlaing*. Rather than create a confrontation, she was finally resigned to not being eligible for the presidency, at least for now, and named her long-time friend and loyal confidant, *U Htin Kyaw*, to the top position. Instead, as state counselor, a position 'above the president', she could advise him on matters of national interests as her spokesman. To move forward, both sides seemed willing to set aside some of their differences at least for the time being.

The NLD Party and the NLD-led New Cabinet

Since *Aung San Suu Kyi* had become the leader of the democratic government of 2015, she could no longer participate in NLD party activities, as specified in section 64 of the constitution, and the party continued under the leadership of another of her trusted senior confidants. Before the election, when *Aung San Suu Kyi* was the authoritative leader of the NLD party, many members of her organization were devoted to her with adoration and blind obedience. Consequently NLD never groomed anyone to succeed her, although there were qualified men and women in the organization.

While a truly remarkable democracy icon, the Lady never took the opportunity to practice the principles of democracy herself. There was never interest to empower or mentor capable younger people. Gender inequality was manifested within the organization as educated and capable female members were never recognized for advancement or promoted to senior positions. There were many university educated professionals within the party. There were lawyers who were politically astute and physicians and engineers who were not only technically savvy but had insights into health problems, ethnic conflicts and infrastructure issues. Businessmen and entrepreneurs knew ways to improve Burma's economy and political activists knew and understood the issues facing ethnic nationalities, farmers, the environment, workers, women, and students.

There were also professors holding advanced graduate degrees who could offer advice on many areas that were of vital importance to the successful rebuilding of the country. Other NLD members included savvy politicians, educated intellectuals and scholars, dedicated journalists and veteran activists. However, it seemed that NLD was used as a personal vehicle to promote only one woman and to campaign for top cabinet positions for her alone.

To date, *Aung San Suu Kyi* has remained the only female minister in the central government of Burma. A leader who loves her country also needs to mentor, teach and guide younger supporters so the baton can be passed on when the time comes. The time has come.

As the only woman among the 18-member cabinet, *Aung San Suu Kyi* took on *four* ministerial positions. As Minister of Foreign Affairs, Minister of Electric Power and Energy, Minister of Education, and Minister of the President's Office, *Aung San Suu Kyi* would have majority power in parliament and control over the president. As Minister of Foreign Affairs she also had a seat on the 11-member National Defense and Security Council which is controlled by the military. She would address critical issues of national reconciliation, peace, development, rule of law and other national issues and the relationship with Burma's key political and economic ally and formidable neighbor, China.

Cooperating with the military was critical and already tension was apparent in the new cabinet. She knew she must compromise, and she decided to focus on national reconciliation instead of constitutional reform to remove the ban on her presidency. Disagreement with the generals on how best to resolve armed ethnic conflict was a looming challenge as both sides held steadfast on how peace and national reconciliation could be achieved.

Challenges for the Democratic Civilian Government

For decades the Burmese government had been mired in corruption, and the military regime not only tolerated but encouraged it. In the legal system, police, lawyers, witnesses and judges took bribes and frequently demanded payment to effect favorable outcomes or lenient sentences. Since the new democratic civilian government took office, corruption in the form of misuse of public funds by former ruling party USDP had been uncovered and was being investigated, as over seven billion *kyats* were found missing.[1]

Most large business conglomerates were owned by the military or by its officers, and controlled by *Tatmadaw* under its two institutions, UMEHL, later renamed, the *Myanmar* Economic Holdings Public Company Limited, MEHPCL and MEC, to serve *Tatmadaw's* interests. However, the new civilian government's policy was not to dig up the past, and therefore they would not take any retroactive action against the perpetrators.

As NLD assumed control, the new parliamentarians and cabinet ministers were subjected to the same system of corruption. How would they function and with what guidelines? *Aung San Suu Kyi* boasted of her cabinet

---

[1] *The Irrawaddy.* "Magwe Chief Justice: Misuse of Public Funds Could Finish USDP", April 26, 2017.

members being corruption-free but she tolerated their incompetence and lack of clear vision, clear economic policies and clear sense of what they were trying to achieve and how. Her appointment of ministers based on personal loyalty instead of competence backfired.

Already there were complaints about the ineffectiveness of her parliamentarians; many were out of touch with issues in the field. Numerous high ranking officers of the NLD government had displayed politically immature conduct and administrative naiveté. They could not make decisions independently without her approval, were not allowed to attend civil society events without her permission, were not to ask tough questions during parliamentary sessions, and were banned from speaking to the media. It seemed the country could not move an inch forward without her involvement and consent. The system of governance was paralyzed by her lack of trust and need for control.

Libel laws were so unclear that it was difficult to distinguish between defamation and legitimate reporting and criticism. The distinction was cloudy even in the minds of those running the country, resulting in arrests and punishment of journalists and activists. The telecommunications law pertaining to media and press freedom was so vague and broadly worded that it was subject to a wide range of interpretation and imposed fear of intimidation, prosecution, arrest and punishment. The Government used Article 66(d) of the Telecommunication Law as a retaliatory tool to curb freedom of speech as people in powerful positions used it to harass, intimidate, threaten and punish those who criticized or complained against them. Due to a total misunderstanding or deliberate misinterpretation of the law, the military intimidated journalists from covering sensitive issues that could lead to criticism of the armed forces, further damaging press freedom and a fundamental concept of democracy.

Freedom of expression was not only stifled by the 'unlawful association' clause, it prevented accurate reporting and hands-on coverage of the ethnic armed nationalities and peace negotiations in conflict regions, as human rights abuses and violent conflicts with EAOs continue in bordering states. Some NLD ministers were told not to talk to the media on sensitive issues.

Press freedom became worse under *Aung San Suu Kyi*'s government and her promise with regard to press freedom indicated a mismatch between the words and deeds. Business and investor confidence was low in the face of rising prices for basic commodities and essential goods.

Another challenge facing the NLD government concerned disputes over farmland which had been seized by the army in preceding decades. NLD committee members set up to handle these matters were inexperienced and too weak to confront the military over land seizures. Outside help was needed.

There were International resources available to assist the new administration achieve smoother internal functioning. Both the US and the EU organized workshops and set up training centers providing support to Burmese ministers and parliamentarians.[1] Since 2017, support for *Aung San Suu Kyi* and the NLD government from the US might be less, due to its policy of reduced engagement in Asia. The *Rohingya* crisis has strained her relations with the international community and her silence concerning the crisis has weakened her global support. Her relationship with the army chief is tense, and new challenges are emerging with increasing threat of militant monks and terrorism. Under her leadership progress has been slow, the peace process has stalled, the economy tanked, ethnic violence has increased, ethnic goodwill has faded, and confidence in the Lady has fallen. Looking ahead, what happens after *Aung San Suu Kyi*? Will there be other new parties organized by prominent political activists and leaders of the past to run in the November 2020 election? Observers believe the army chief *Min Aung Hlaing* may be aiming to be the next president, given his voluntary postponement of retirement. As for the younger generation, there is no other leader of any stature within the NLD, who has been groomed to take over. The younger members have not been permitted to take on material responsibility. *Aung San Suu Kyi's* confidants like *U Tin Oo* are retiring, in their 80s. The military's political dominance continues while the constitution remains unchanged. When *Aung San Suu Kyi's* era ends, will there be another military coup?

China's Dominance

As Burma's most dominant investor and powerful neighbor, China continues to seek opportunities to influence policy decisions. China is interested in Burma's reserves of oil, gas and hydro electric power, strategically located ports, hardwood, gemstone and a market of 55 million consumers. When economic reforms began in 2011, Burma had been enjoying 7–9% annual growth with China investing billions of dollars.

The single largest Chinese investment was the $3.6 billion *Myitsone* hydro electric power project in Kachin state, intended to produce 6,000 MW of electricity, the bulk of the energy generated to be exported to China. The dam would flood an area the size of Singapore, displacing 10,000 locals and resulting in irreparable damages and loss of people's life support and heri-

---

[1] *Caretaking Democratization, The Military and Political Change in Myanmar.* Renaud Ergreteau; New York: Oxford University Press, Oxford, 2016, 76.

tage. Catastrophic flooding of the Irrawaddy would cause monumental irreversible destruction and mass displacement of people who depended on the river for livelihood. The *Myitsone* project faced growing public opposition and was suspended by *Thein Sein's* government due to protests by the locals.

In 2013, President *Xi Jinping* of China proposed a massive, ambitious infrastructure development profgram, the Belt and Road Initiative (BRI). Involving over 60 countries and linking China to broader Asia, Africa, the Middle East and Europe, the BRI seeks to expand China's economic access and, inevitably, political influence and geo-strategic dominance across the continents. In this US$1 trillion grand strategy, *Kyaukpyu* on Burma's west coast is a crucial connector due to its unique strategic location: the city would provide China direct access to the Indian Ocean. *Kyaukpyu* sits on the Bay of Bengal and provides the shortest route to sea by connecting the land route from China's landlocked southwestern Yunnan province to Burma's western seaboard and the sea route from the Bay of Bengal to the Indian Ocean. According to Bertil Lintner, a prominent journalist on Burma, over sixty percent of the world's oil shipments pass through the Indian Ocean, from the oil fields of Middle East to China, Japan and emerging economies in the Pacific region. Seventy percent of container ship traffic uses the ocean route between Asia and the rest of the world.[1] A part of this trade involves China: 60% of the country's GDP is based on trade, with much of that trade being seaborne.

Much faster access to the Middle East and Europe is possible by cutting across Burma to the Bay of Bengal, eliminating thousands of miles that would otherwise have to be transported by sea through the Strait of Malacca, a route currently used by the Chinese to transport 80% of its energy imports. This shortcut land route not only bypassed the Malacca Strait, beset by pirates, but shortened the distance the oil and gas would have to travel by sea to reach China by 700 miles. The pipeline route also cut 30% in travel time.[2] The existing sea route is also vulnerable to blockade by US Navy ships if the Americans decide to take such action.

China's $7.5 billion maritime infrastructure development plan in *Kyaukphyu* includes a deep sea port to accommodate large oil tankers, an industrial park and a Special Economic Zone. In 2013–14, the PRC completed part of this project: the construction of a $2.5 billion, 1,500 mile long crude oil and natural gas pipelines across Burma. An estimated 260,000 barrels per day of imported oil will be transported through the oil pipeline while the parallel

---

[1] *The People's Republic of China and Burma: Not Only Pauk-Phaw.* Bertil Lintner; Project 2049 Institute, May 9, 2017.

[2] *Forbes Asia.* Eric Meyer: "With Oil And Gas Pipelines, China Takes A Shortcut Through *Myanmar*", February 9, 2015.

gas pipeline has already transported billions of cubic meter of methane from both Burmese and Middle Eastern (Qatari) sources.[1] Some 10% of the gas is supposed to stay in Burma, but none of the oil, as the refining facility will be built at the end of the line in Kunming, with a capacity for 10 million of tons of oil. The cash-strapped Burmese government has scaled down the project, spending only an additional $1.3 billion over fear of heavy indebtedness (a debt trap) to China and the nation's economic sovereignty in the event of default.

The gas and oil pipelines across Burma to Yunnan are critical to China. Therefore, Beijing would support or fight either the Burmese army or ethnic armed groups to gain influence with whichever was the winning side at the border. The Burmese military believed Yunnan provincial authorities were helping and arming the ethnic armies such as the *Wa* and the *Kokang* to fight the Burmese army along the border. Neither all-out war nor total peace at the 1,200 mile Sino-Burma border would be optimal for China as Beijing has varying motives — security risks, stability concerns, economic interests, and a desire for political influence in Burma. As reported by the US Institute of Peace, "Continued friction between central authorities and border populations provides Beijing a major source of influence over *Naypyidaw*. That leverage may be used, among other things, to prevent 'unwelcome' influence of the United States in the country and thus the region. Genuine sustained peace also would weaken China's influence over ethnic nationalities, particularly along the border. That includes the *Wa* people, who speak Chinese, trade in Chinese currency, and receive substantial support from China to maintain the thirty-thousand-person *Wa* army and political autonomy. As a result, Chinese business actors provide revenue to conflict actors on both sides and help sustain Burma's civil war."[2]

Community leaders and activists also said the construction project lacked transparency and put locals at risk of losing their homes and livelihoods. Destruction of the environment was another consideration. The Chinese would bring their own engineers and builders which did not contribute to local employment and operating companies employ mostly Chinese workers. The new NLD government must review the scope of the project to determine if it served the interests of the local communities. After negotiation with the Chinese state-owned oil company which funded the project, an agreement was reached that the Chinese would pay $53 billion in royalties over 30 years

---

[1] *Forbes Asia.* Eric Meyer: "With Oil And Gas Pipelines, China Takes A Shortcut Through *Myanmar*", February 9, 2015.

[2] *USIP.* "China's Role in *Myanmar*'s Internal Conflicts", September 14, 2018.

to the Burmese government and $25 million to the local communities to fund schools and other development projects.[1]

Although the Chinese had almost free access to Burma's resources in the past, the military regime was beginning to recognize this aggressive depletion of resources. The ordinary citizens of Burma also resented the Chinese as their projects did not benefit the locals and their communities as profits ended up in the corrupt generals' pockets. The Chinese companies also brought their own laborers, did not assimilate into local culture and community, overlooked rights of the locals, and disregarded social and environmental impact of the region. With Beijing's aggressive stance in SE Asia and Burma's increasing economic dependence on China, many believed *Than Shwe's* regime decided to open up to the West to counterbalance Beijing's influence.

Burma was increasing defense cooperation with its eastern neighbor, India, who offered to sell weapons and ammunition as it had in the past, supplying not only guns and rifles but war-gaming software and naval gunboats.[2] The new army chief *Min Aung Hlaing* has strengthened Burma's ties with India with his 2017 visit to India, during which a major deal was made to buy $37.9 million worth of military equipment, including lightweight torpedoes. India also provided night-vision devices, bailey bridges, rocket launchers, mortars, rifles, sonar tracking systems, radars, and communication equipment and directing gear to *Tatmadaw*.[3]

The New Tatmadaw Chief

On the eve of the 2015 elections, former general *Thein Sein*, the President, was approaching 75. His active political days were likely to be of short duration. Who would be the next dictator general? For years *Than Shwe* had been grooming a younger up-and-coming officer of the *Tatmadaw* who had become a five star senior general and chief of staff. General *Min Aung Hlaing* was the tough, confident military leader fully in control and well spoken. The world focus now shifted from President *Thein Sein* to the army chief. He was unknown outside Burma but was the most powerful man in the country. Son of a civil engineer and born in 1956 in Tavoy (renamed *Dawei*) *Min Aung Hlaing* attended Rangoon Arts and Science University as a law student and was admitted to the prestigious Defense Services Academy. He graduated from DSA in 1977 and became a second lieutenant in Burmese army. Through

[1] *Forbes Asia.* Eric Meyer: "With Oil And Gas Pipelines, China Takes A Shortcut Through Myanmar", February 9, 2015.

[2] *The Irrawaddy.* Aung Zaw: "India Courts Burma", July 20, 2017.

[3] *Sputnik News.* "India Bags Myanmar Torpedo Order Worth $38 Million", March 27, 2017.

various field positions and promotions he eventually replaced General *Shwe Mann* as joint chief of staff of the army, navy, and air force in 2010. He was promoted to commander-in-chief of *Tatmadaw* in 2011. The following year he was promoted to vice senior general and in 2013 he became senior general of Burma armed forces. He had voiced the army's responsibility and goal to rebuild Burma into a peaceful and modern developed nation.

However, since the 2015 election, the NLD administration and the military have so far failed to implement many democratic principles. *Aung San Suu Kyi* and *Min Aung Hlaing* have never been known to have a good relationship and few believed it would improve any time soon. The NLD's winning the elections in 2015 did not spell a true democratic victory without total support of *Tatmadaw*. Peace in ethnic regions would be unachievable if the Burmese military continued its barbaric acts of human rights violations and retained the power to block any democratic action, domestic or international, to end the civil war.

The senior general may not have the high public profile of the Lady but the world is beginning to recognize the supreme commander of the army, navy, air force and armed security forces as the most powerful man in the country. As the commander-in-chief he controls three key ministries, a quarter of parliament seats, and veto power over any constitutional amendments. The *Tatmadaw* chief advocates for continued military involvement in Burma's politics and has the sovereign power to control the legislature, executive and judiciary in emergencies or to take over the country in a military coup should democracy fall from grace. On the world stage, he was the statesman and often wined and dined with leaders from the US, Europe, and Japan and was welcomed by Austrian defense officials with an honor guard. As stated in the *Diplomat*, "Snug in its constitutional bunker, [*Tatmadaw*] can reap the fruits of improved foreign relations, a cooperative civilian government, solid public support for their crackdown on the *Rohingya*, and the increased revenue that comes with a rapidly growing economy. The taciturn senior general can afford a brief, complacent smile".[4]

The US and the International Outlook Post 2011

For decades the Western world and the United Nations have failed to act or been slow to act in response to abuses by Burmese dictators. World leaders have visited the country and UN envoys have met with the generals but nothing much seems to have changed. The only difference now is that those who have been wronged can protest or file grievances under the demo-

---

[4] *The Diplomat.* Ben Dunant: "It's Good to Be the *Tatmadaw*", May 11, 2017.

cratic government of 2015. Russia and China, acting as Burma's political allies, could block international intercession, and stronger and tougher action, not polite diplomatic words, needed to prevail to effect any change or improvement. The global community must use a language and implement action the Burmese military regime cannot ignore. Since the 1990s, the Western view on Burma has become narrow, as all information is cast as seen through the eyes of one Western-educated person who was recently released after 17 years of house arrest. The Western public views Burma as a country defined by the recent two decades of struggle between a cruel regime and a pro-democracy fighter. This black-and-white outlook obscures a deeper and more complex situation within the government and the complexities and dynamics of the myriads of internal social forces and cultural sensitivities. *Aung San Suu Kyi's* role has changed from that of a pro-democracy pro-human rights icon to that of a domestic politician, a member of the parliament, and since 2015, the head of a democratic civilian government.

In her new political role, can she support Western sanctions against the military of her own government? Obama's US policy under president *Thein Sein's* quasi-democratic government was based on a very limited dialogue with just a passing glance at the regime's gross human rights violations. By removing all sanctions, the US may have rewarded the regime for its democratic reforms prematurely. For decades *Tatmadaw* has been able to attract major investments from China, India and other Asian nations, many of them have been in partnerships with the military junta, owning real estate, mining, extraction and lumber deals while the West watched from a distance. Half a century later the retired generals made a few selective gestures and superficial reforms, and the Western world rewarded the token actions by removing sanctions and providing economic, financial, and military aid. Burma has not yet proven that its reforms will last and all reforms can be reversible in view of current power structure as written in the regime's drafted current constitution. US strategy for Burma today is to do more by opening diplomatic and commercial ties than by isolation. However, the Burmese regime has been generous with rhetoric but less substantial with agreed results. To maintain leverage and to ensure the US cannot reward the new regime too quickly, some sanctions should remain in place until the Burmese government takes more substantive action on human rights, releases all of its political prisoners, terminates press and media censorship, actively fights internal corruption, and transfers power to the people.

To maintain a balance of power with its chief rivals, US relations with Burma need to improve. The Burmese people hoped that the US could apply some pressure to reduce the regime's abuses in return for favorable treatment, but this presents a challenge. China is benefiting from Burma's energy. Russia is making lucrative arms deals. And despite repeated assurances that the Burmese government severed military relations with North Korea since 2011, the regime continues to engage in weapon and nuclear arms deals with North Korea. According to a report by independent United Nations monitors, North Korea supplied Burma with ballistic missile systems, conventional weapons, multiple rocket launchers and surface-to-air missiles.[1] Nothing much has changed.

[1] *The Sydney Morning Herald.* Lindsay Murdoch: "Fears *Myanmar* Buying Missiles from North Korea Raise Canberra's Alarm", February 6, 2018.

CHAPTER 9. FRONTIER OPPORTUNITIES AND THREATS

Burma has endured two world wars, two imperial occupations, civil wars, and several oppressive, corrupt and incompetent military regimes. Even with a deeply troubled economic past and violent history, many believe Burma has the resources to propel it to be Asia's next economic frontier, the next commercial engine in the region. With new investment and emerging growth, an unprecedented structural shift in the nation's economy is taking place in every sector. Since Burma opened its door and welcomed international investment, opportunities in infrastructure, healthcare, education, banking, manufacturing, construction, tourism and many other sectors are growing.

As Burma opened to the world in 2011, the International Monetary Fund estimated its GDP to be growing at 8.6%, making it the fastest-growing country in the world of the time. As US and Europe lifted many punitive measures, international investments increased over $10 billion in just three years, according to the Ministry of Commerce. Official figures declare Burma received approximately $9.4 billion of direct foreign investment in the 2015–2016 fiscal year, most of the investment being in the oil and gas sectors as several Chinese conglomerates, British Gas, Chevron, ConocoPhillips, Shell, and others entered the market. Other investment includes transportation, communications, and apparel manufacturing sectors.

According to the Investment Commission, direct foreign investment for fiscal year ending March 31, 2017 through 2020 is expected to exceed $6 billion, and projected to be $8 billion per year from 2021–2030 with tax breaks in health and education, tourism, IT, construction and many others.

US investment in Burma is minimal compared to that of China, India, Thailand, Malaysia, Singapore, Japan, Vietnam and Korea. In addition to assistance for economic growth and poverty reduction from the World Trade Organization, Burma also benefits from many foreign governmental organizations and NGOs who offer guidance and advice in political, social, and economic issues and help the country assimilate into the world community. With assistance from the Asian Development Bank, the NLD administration is revising the *Myanmar* Companies Act to ease some investment restrictions with the hope of attracting more foreign investment and to promote capital market. Even with global support, it will likely take a generation to achieve long term meaningful sustainable success. Burma needs human capital and expertise from pillar companies, universities, and talent from around the world who can assist and train Burmese people to become functional CEOs, vice presidents, engineers, marketers and other executives with expertise. They can mentor young talented Burmese people and build on their domestic strengths. Burma has profited from its exports of natural gas, oil, metal, apparel, jade, rice and other agriculture products. More than 30 countries have granted Burma special trading status and the EU has connected Burma to new markets in Europe with a GSP (Generalized System of Preferences) status.

Responsible Investment

All land and resources in Burma are owned by the state; villagers have no formal land title or rights to ownership for their ancestral agricultural land. Although new policies have been passed to allow private ownership, the country lacks the administrative and legal structures to enforce these provisions. Companies take advantage of this lack of enforcement and engage in profit-driven activities. Big corporations and businesses partner with the government and grab land from small farmers. Villagers have been losing their homes and livelihoods. Large cities like Rangoon have been experiencing an unprecedented construction boom with little consideration for long term environmental impacts and no investment responsibility. The gap between urban Rangoon and rural Burma has widened, in economic, political and social terms. With economic growth estimates hovering around 7–8% per year over the next decade, revenues from the sale of these resources could have been used to meet the basic needs of the people, such as health and education.

In fact, foreign investment in Burma has caused mass displacement and exacerbated poverty. As there is no formal legal system to safeguard people's rights, rapacious investments will go on causing further abuses, forcing more people from their homes and resulting in more poverty in affected communities.

Hypocrisy rules the day. Multinational companies from the West, Japan, Singapore and other nations pump millions of dollars into Burma while their leaders condemn the military for its human rights violations. With increasing global demand for commodity crops, MNCs continue to expand agricultural production and move to countries where environmental regulations are lacking or weak, land abundant, and labor cheap, as in Southeast Asia, South America and Africa, and it is not uncommon to see that profit is the only motive.

Foreign countries vie for access to Burma's natural resources and its strategic position. China's massive *Myitsone* dam in Kachin State would supply 90% of the electricity produced to China, and a few other hydroelectric power plants are being built at *Baluchaung* with Japanese assistance. The development of *Kyaukpyu* port in Arakan state is expected to displace around 20,000 people. The estimated $7.5 billion project threatens the environment and entails many negative socio-economic impacts, as reported by *Environmental Justice Atlas*.[1] That includes biodiversity loss, soil erosion, waste overflow, loss of landscape/aesthetic degradation, surface water pollution and decreasing water quality in addition to displacement, loss of livelihood, loss of traditional knowledge/practices/cultures, land dispossession, and other socioeconomic impacts.

As China expands its investment in Burma building dams, power plants, pipelines and seaports, India is harboring increasing concerns over China's growing presence in the region, not just around the India Ocean but across land connecting Burma, Bangladesh, and Nepal on the east and Sri Lanka in the south. India also shares a 1,021-mile border with Burma and has signed an agreement to build a $110 million *Kaladan* multi modal transport in Arakan state to connect the landlocked northeast Indian provinces to Burma's southern coast and the Bay of Bengal. The *Kaladan* will provide access to other Southeast Asian countries, opening new trading routes.

Other Indian strategic interests in Burma include a project to develop a Special Economic Zone, SEZ, and a seaport in *Sittwe*, the capital of Arakan (*Rakhine*) state similar to the deep seaport China is developing in *Kyaukphyu*. Thailand and Japan also plan to build a highway to connect with Burma's coastline of Andaman Sea. The construction plan includes an enormous $8 billion deep sea port at Tavoy (*Dawei*) to build a petrochemical facility, a

---

[1] *Environmental Justice Atlas.* "Socio-economical Impacts", January 14, 2019. ‹https://ejatlas.org/conflict/kyaukphyu-port›

fertilizer factory, coal based power station and a Special Economic Zone, with a capacity to hold 250 million tons of cargo. Little discussion has taken place concerning environmental impact to the pristine coastal region of *Dawei*.

Japan also invested in another SEZ development in the outskirts of Rangoon, and many other sectors from banks to breweries. Companies from Japan, Singapore, Thailand, Malaysia, Hong Kong, Philippines, Indonesia, South Korea, China, Taiwan, and a few Western countries are setting up factories to produce cement, garment, electronics and pharmaceuticals. Construction of industrial zones also results in environmental destruction and displacement of thousands of farmers. Companies profit from minority and marginalized communities without any consideration for the local people as no compensation is offered to them. Toxic chemicals from gold dredging have reportedly been dumped in the Irrawaddy River polluting the water, killing the fish and destroying the ecosystem of the region. Illegal mining of deposits and extraction of gemstones have created a huge black market of products on which the government loses large sums in unrealized taxes that could be used to fund the much needed healthcare and education for the people.

Globalization may create wealth and jobs but it also creates social changes. According to a Business & Human Rights Resource Center survey, few companies made available their human rights policies and due diligence efforts. Companies doing business in Burma ought to use their influence to promote respect and equal rights for local partners and workers. To understand the issues of the community, local people must be allowed to participate in two-way dialogues and community engagement giving their input and voicing their concerns with companies, governments, and NGOs. Companies should be made to pay taxes instead of bribes. They can not only hire but train the local workforce.

Confiscation and Environmental Destruction of Ancestral Land

The waters of Burma contain extensive marine biodiversity and aquatic ecosystems. The ethnic minority provinces, characterized by hills and mountain, dense forests and rivers, abound with vast raw material deposits in scattered remote villages. Control over these regions has been the major cause of conflict with the central government for decades. Villagers have been living and farming in these regions for generations without any ownership title to the land.

The largest revenue earner for the government has been its gas and oil sales to China and other Asian countries through MOGE, *Myanmar* Oil and Gas Enterprise, which bankrolls the abusive and corrupt military government. The regime also built hydroelectric power plants with China, India, Thailand and other neighboring countries since exporting electricity generates billions of dollars for the military. Past regimes have allowed mega foreign investments in large scale hydroelectric power dam projects without input from the villagers who live in those communities. Farmlands are destroyed without proper compensation, and the muddy polluted water from the dams damages crops and kills fish, destroying a valuable food source for the locals. Rivers are further polluted with discharge of waste chemicals and untreated sewage. The use of illegal, misuse and overuse of Chinese pesticides and herbicides in Shan state not only damage their ancestral land but affect the people's health living in the region. Many, especially children, suffer allergic reactions to these chemicals.

Government owned MEHL and MEC dominated the economy for almost two decades, controlling everything from imports, exports and natural resources to alcohol, cigarettes and consumer goods.

A JV between MEHL and China's Wanbao *Letpadaung* copper mine in the city of *Monywa*, near Mandalay, is another project which has caused massive human rights violations and irreparable environmental destruction of farmland, villages and religious sites. When local residents supported by monks protested the mine operators in 2014, a woman protester was fatally shot by security police. In November 2015, a waste leak from the mine ran into people's fields killing all crops but Wanbao remained silent about the spill, denying the villagers information about its cause, the content of the waste liquid, or whether it posed any health risks. The company has not cleaned up the area or compensated villagers for the devastation of their crops. The NLD-led government would not cancel the project due to concern it would hurt the economy and relations with China.

Gold mining in *Loi Kham* hills of eastern Shan state has polluted the main water supply with cyanide-filled and other toxic mining waste and made 300 acres of surrounding hillsides unstable. Farm land and livelihoods of people living in these eastern villages have been destroyed by the resulting soil erosion and water pollution. They have become destitute as their farm animals are also poisoned and their children sick and suffering from skin diseases from lack of clean water and needed medical treatment. Additionally the ecosystems in these areas are negatively impacted by soil erosion, landslides, sedimentation and climate change. In Karen State the use of mercury in large scale river dredging for gold is taking heavy environmental toll in the Salween River basin and threatening the health of living organisms in and along the river.

The mangrove forests of the Irrawaddy delta provide critical ecological services and habitats for a variety of wildlife species. Mangroves have dense and partially submerged root system which acts as extreme resistance to high winds and flood waters. According to the Environmental Rehabilitation Network of Burma, roughly 75% of the mangrove area in the Irrawaddy delta region has been lost over the past 30 years from intensive deforestation due to a lack of proper management and agricultural development. The impact of this has been devastating as the loss of a natural buffer protecting inland areas from erosion and flooding.

In 2008 Cyclone Nargis killed an estimated 200,000 people and destroyed the entire Irrawaddy Delta basin, further increasing the risk of droughts, floods, landslides, tropical cyclones and heat waves in the region. People living in these regions are as vulnerable as before to destruction and government must address these issues that threaten their livelihoods and loss of homes and lives. According to the Burmese government, floods and landslides of 2015 resulted in economic losses estimated to be 3.1% of Burma's GDP. Over 1.6 million people have been displaced many with total loss of income and livelihoods.[1]

A primary focus of the government on mainstream economic growth brings a high cost to the environment and livelihood of the people.

Jade and Other Resources

Under the existing constitution, the government owns all natural resources from the air, water, and ground. The people do not share the profits from resources extracted. Huge sums of money made from the sale of jade, ruby and sapphire were funneled through a complex system of government owned enterprises to line the generals' pockets.

Besides having the largest natural gas reserves in Asia, Burma is the largest producer of jade in the world, estimated to be worth at least $6–9 billion per year. This has been one of the driving forces of ethnic wars between *Tatmadaw* and armed minorities for more than half a century. Only a fraction of the thousands of jade and gemstone companies were recorded. The people resented the military families and the Chinese businessmen who enriched themselves by looting their land.

---

[1] *World Bank Press Release.* "Myanmar to Receive US$200 Million in Financing for Post-Disaster Recovery and Reconstruction", July 14, 2016.

According to Global Witness, mining of jade accounted for about half of Burma's annual GDP and over 46 times national spending on health, but hardly any of the revenue reached or benefited the Kachin people or the state budget. In 2014, the jade industry was estimated to be worth $31 billion; this may be the biggest natural resource heist in the modern history of Burma.

Today the lucrative trading remains largely undetected and severely under reported as it is outside the radar of the international trading and commercial networks and revenue flows. For decades the generals and high level officers of the military regime and affiliated drug lords have been looting Burma's resources using secret or hidden company ownership struc-tures. The business of extraction, production, polishing and sale of jade are based on private relationships among family members and trusted friends. These relationships spread out in many different locations and countries, making it difficult to trace or monitor illegal activities. The three top players alone, Generals *Than Shwe, Maung Maung Thein and Ohn Myint*, reportedly earned US$220 million from jade trade in 2014. More details about this shrouded trade, the key players and how the corrupt licensing system works, are available online at Global Witness website[1]. Villagers worked long hours in dangerous conditions for little pay and landslides caused by collapsing mountains near the mines account for untold loss of lives. Deadly accidents are a common and regular occurrence. Many miners have also died of mine pit collapses. In November 2015, a landslide near a jade mine in *Hpakant*, Kachin State killed over 100 people with hundreds more missing. Companies use dynamite and heavy equipment for large scale mining dumping huge quanti-ties of rubble available for scavenging. Unaware of the risks many migrant miners work or scavenge and live near unstable piles of waste dumped by the companies. Companies also introduced and smuggled opium to these mining towns, using their mining vehicles, causing an epidemic among the locals.

After General *Than Shwe's* retirement President *Thein Sein's* government signed the internationally recognized Extractive Industry Transparency Initiative, EITI, to be more transparent in the oil, gas and mining sectors and to promote good governance of natural extractives. Hopefully, the imple-mentation of EITI should make the jade trade more open with sharing data on policies, practices and, identify companies which control mines.

---

[1] *Global Witness.* Minzayar: "Jade: A Global Witness Investigation into *Myanmar's* 'Big State Secret'", October 2015.

Logging

Since independence the government has been exploiting forests, minerals, precious stones, gold and other natural wealth from the hills belonging to the Kachin and Shan ethnic nationalities. Military generals were giving their allies licensing rights to log teak, mahogany, exotic *padauk, pyinkado,* rosewood and other hardwoods for sale to foreign companies. Burma's tropical forests also support human life by providing water purification, flood control, and climate stabilization. As forests are cut down indiscriminately to make room for new construction and superhighways, this last great frontier will soon vanish.

Burma is an agricultural country with 70% population engaged in small-scale labor-intensive subsistence farming. Most of ethnic nationalities also depend on land for farming and forests for their livelihoods. Besides exploitation of their natural deposit wealth, illegal land grabs have exacerbated tensions with the Burmese army, as villagers and farmers were displaced without compensation.

In 2014 almost US$500 million worth of timber was smuggled into China. Traditional axes and handsaws have been replaced with modern chainsaws which cut down trees four times faster. Illegal logging practices have not only depleted the forests but posed a threat to national security by its own citizens within its own boundaries as ethnic minorities took up arms to fight the government who invaded and plundered their land. Lack of legal structure and strong governance emboldened corruption and criminalized local communities with unhampered profits for those engaged in the illicit trafficking of timber to international markets.

Villagers began to replace rice growing with illegal logging as a means of sustenance of higher income stream. Insatiable demand for logs from Burma has propelled illegal trade in the form of violence and conflict in the border region. Foreign companies operating in partnership with government should operate more responsibly and make investments that not only benefit itself but the local communities from whom resources are extracted. Responsible countries like Denmark halted teak imports from Burma due to lack of due diligence requirements. Since Burma became a member of EITI in 2014 and as NLD took reigns of the civilian government, major reforms are underway, even if at a snail's pace. All military owned companies and unreported revenues are being disclosed. It is hoped the new transparency measures should deter corruption and may provide an incentive to end armed conflict in these ethnic regions in the foreseeable future.

Exotic Wildlife

Due to its biodiversity, many exotic wildlife species exist in the jungles of Burma. Unfortunately, poaching is threatening some species to become endangered. Rare and exotic wild animals like red panda, red goral, takin, musk deer, Himalayan bear, serow and blue sheep are indiscriminately slaughtered. Their body parts are illegally smuggled through the southern border into China to meet their insatiable consumer demand for ivory, horns and other parts perceived to contain aphrodisiac elements and oils. Black markets thrive with stolen elephant ivory, leopard and tiger skins, rhino horns, bear paws, monkeys, rare tropical birds, prized Burmese star tortoises, lizards, geckos and snakes for sale as status symbols, Chinese traditional medicines, and aphrodisiacs. Illegal wildlife trade, smuggling of frozen foods, electronic goods, small appliances, clothing and household items from China contribute to growing black market in border towns. In the absence of alternative means of survival local residents hunt wildlife and sell them to earn easy money to support their livelihood. The new government must address these issues of wild life protection and creation of job opportunities to alleviate poverty and sustain livelihood in these regions.

Fishing

Burma's waters, once abundant in seafood, are being depleted due to use of illegal fishing gear and illegal methods of fishing, including electrocution or shock fishing. Fishing gangs use batteries and high voltage transformers to shock fish and maximize their catch using trawling nets. Such illegal methods have also killed dolphins in the Irrawaddy River.

Mercury and other toxic chemicals from gold mining in Kachin state also contribute to pollution, and run off from chemical fertilizers contribute to poisoning the river. In the open coastal sea the use of explosives kills ordinary fish as well as many exotic sea creatures that threaten extinction. Thai fishermen reportedly use illegal sonar to attract fish and other creatures from Burmese waters. As fish population declines many fishermen are using narrow sieve nets to increase yield, catching fingerlings and small young fishes before they have a chance to grow to maturity, threatening the availability of fish stocks. Lack of enforcement of fishery laws, shortage of cold storage facilities due to the high cost of electricity to run them, inadequate distribution and transportation add to exacerbate this industry.

Currently dolphins, porpoises, and sea turtles live unprotected in Burma's rivers, seas and oceans. With assistance from the Wildlife Conservation Society, WCS in the US and the University of Exeter in the UK, the new democratic government is planning to implement a program to protect the biodiversity as well as provide locals who rely on fishing a viable way to sustain their livelihoods.

Illegal Drugs

The drug trade which is inextricably intertwined with Burma's economy has tripled over the last half a dozen years, making Burma the second largest producer of opium and heroin, second only to Afghanistan. Burma is also a leading supplier of methamphetamine. By some estimates, poppy cultivation and meth synthesis has been reported to be worth over $30 billion.[1] The military regime, under the control of the army, used its state owned MOGE to launder drug money and control related activities.[2] Burma's under regulated financial system and lack of basic anti money laundering provisions facilitated the funneling of drug money into commercial enterprises and infrastructure investment. Laws were weak and vague and without any enforcement mechanisms to trace dirty money. The drug economy is informal, unregulated and cash based and allows criminal organizations to operate businesses and perform financial operations without legal requirement to maintain transaction or any written traceable records. The system perpetuates as farmers are forced to plant poppy as their best economic option of cash crop for opium production. With no governmental support such as social security, health or educational benefits, the poor ethnic minority villagers were forced to grow poppy as their only means of livelihood, survival and pursuit of economic stability. Even then, they had to pay huge sums as 'taxes' to corrupt soldiers, police and armed ethnic groups or their poppy fields would be destroyed. In the interests of its own survival, the junta has not only created a narcotic state where money laundering was accepted, but tolerated the unofficial policy of 'don't ask, don't tell' looking the other way. According to Wikileaks, a drug lord of Asia World, *Lo Hsing Han* referred to as the 'kingpin of the heroin traffic in Southeast Asia' has converted heroin proceeds into legitimate businesses. The Burmese junta granted heroin 'concession' to him and his son, Steven Law in exchange for negotiation with ethnic rebels for cease fire agreements. They were the ruling military junta's most important business partners and were awarded contracts to build roads, provincial seaports and other large infrastructure projects. Other companies with unexplained wealth also flourish, many with connections to the regime and narcotic trade and have built and operated

---

[1] *The Times.* Patrick Winn: "Drugs, Murder and the Real Leaders of Burma", June 2, 2018.
[2] *The Nation.* Dennis Bernstein and Leslie Kean: "People of the Opiate: Burma's Dictatorship of Drugs", December 16, 1996, 3.

housing developments, office towers, condominiums, hospitals, school and university buildings, television and radio production complexes.

Economists, real estate brokers, and current and former law enforcement agents have indicated the illicit drug money was the current major source of investment in rebuilding the country, and companies linked to the drug trade have been engaged in building new roads, rail bridges and sea ports. Rangoon, once with low run down decrepit buildings of colonial era was now buzzing with new construction at every corner reshaping the skyline of the commercial hub. But there are many dark aspects associated with illegal narcotic money. Money laundering leads to serious problems as it criminalizes Burma's economy and leads to inflation. It is bad for business, investment, development, and the Rule of Law.[1] The New York Times reports how the drug trade in Burma, according to analysts reinforces corruption, bolsters the power of the military and threatens to return Burma to a pariah state instead of a democratic country.[2] Those with large sums of dirty cash were developing shopping malls, commercial and residential plazas, condominium high rises and hotels driving real estate prices in major cities to triple and quadruple in the last six years.

The New Economy

Modern air-conditioned shopping malls, hotels and high end condominiums as well as lower cost apartment buildings were built all across Rangoon and surrounding areas, but the market could not be sustained after 2013. The global economic downturn hit hard. When the new NLD government came to power after a landslide victory in 2015, it began to implement new safety regulations and urban planning standards, and prices began to drop even further.

Since 2016 the administration introduced new real estate rules, including the Condominium Law granting foreigners property ownership in Burma, but many regulations are still unclear and confusing. Land ownership disputes are rampant due to potential legal complications and financial penalties. The demand especially by foreign investors may be limited as Rangoon is neither a vibrant cosmopolitan city nor an international economic engine like Singapore, Bangkok, or Kuala Lumpur. The city is plagued with stifling traffic congestion, lack of adequate infrastructure, poor internet connections, intermittent electricity and water supply, and a rudimentary financial system.

---

[1] *Burma Lawyers' Council.* Peter Gutter: "Legal Issues on Burma Journal No. 10", December, 2001, 8.

[2] *The New York Times.* Thomas Fuller: "Profits of Drug Trade Drive Economic Boom in Myanmar", June 5, 2015, 2.

Another impediment to the new economy is the ongoing Arakan crisis, making investors nervous. Burma is still a cash economy. Less than 15 percent of adults have a bank account. It is nearly impossible to trace where all that money comes from or goes in this economy.

According to the New York Times, a realtor in Rangoon reported that one home buyer paid a down payment in local currency *kyats*, the equivalent of US$200,000, in cash stuffed into rice sacks, which is not uncommon for home purchases.[1]

The gap between the haves and the have nots grows in this economy. The wide income and wealth inequality is the result of the ruling junta's decades of corruption, injustice, and market control and manipulation forming shell companies and sweetheart deals that benefited only the elite — the generals, their families and those connected with the top. They stole from the people and now it's time to give back, even reluctantly. The new democratic government must address these issues and implement solutions, not just voicing lip service commitment.

YSX

Launched in 2015, Burma's stock exchange or Yangon Stock Exchange, developed with help from Japan, began limited trading in March 2016 with one company listed. Five companies are now listed, but companies with foreign ownership are prevented from listing. Foreigners were not permitted to buy shares, and Burmese investors are small players. All this raises skepticism about the country's ability to foster a vibrant equity market.The Exchange Commission opened the bourse in May 2020 to foreign investors, hoping to bring an influx of foreign capital and inject more liquidity into YSX as a legitimate trading platform.

Tourism

Burma is one of the most exotic and unspoiled countries remaining on this planet. In many parts of Southeast Asia, modernization has destroyed most indigenous life and culture, but not in Burma, not yet. The diverse ethnic village hill tribes and sub tribes with distinct cultures, languages, and colorful costumes, isolated geographically, economically, socially and politically from mainstream Burma, are still largely living the way they have for centuries. The Golden Land is generously dotted with thousands of pagodas

---

[1] *The New York Times.* Thomas Fuller: "Profits of Drug Trade Drive Economic Boom in Myanmar", June 5, 2015, 3.

and historical monuments built by royal families of past dynasties; many are well preserved and ready to be explored.

The climate is just as diverse, with snow-capped mountains in Kachin State in the north, the Chin Hills on the northwest at the foothills of the Himalayas, the Shan plateau, Karenni *(Kayah)* and Karen *(Kayin)* states to the east, and the southern delta plains of the Irrawaddy River which meanders throughout the center of Burma emptying into the ocean. The hill tribes regions of Kachin, Chin, and Karenni states, which were closed to tourists for decades, have recently opened up. Also away from the tourist footprint are the jade-green paddy fields of the Irrawaddy Delta.

Since the country opened to the world in 2011, Burma has become a hot tourist destination. According to the Ministry of Hotels and Tourism, more than three million tourists visited the country in 2014.[1] It is Asia's version of Cuba, a land forbidden and forgotten, where tourists are now welcome with genuine curiosity and not just exploited for profit. Many airlines offer daily flights from Bangkok, Hong Kong and Singapore. With the unprecedented influx of visitors, Rangoon's 90-year-old *Bogyoke Aung San* Market is bustling with tourists shopping for Burmese souvenirs and products.

A visit to Burma must include Bagan, an ancient city with its splendor and remains of an extraordinary civilization that rivals Angkor Wat and Machu Picchu. Bagan was the capital of Burma during the monarchy that flourished from the 10th through 13th centuries, when a series of fifty Buddhist kings, the Bagan dynasty, ruled. It is situated on the banks of the Irrawaddy River, renamed *Ayeyarwady* River, and is home to the largest and densest concentration of Buddhist temples and shrines in the world. It has over 3,000 pagodas, Buddhist temples, monasteries, stupas and monuments. The Burmese kings erected over 10,000 religious monuments as a way to earn merit according to Buddhism. History records how the city prospered and grew in size and grandeur over two and a half centuries and became a cosmopolitan center for religious and secular studies for monks and scholars from all over Asia. Many of these free standing temples have survived over a thousand years of earthquakes and the invading Mongols of Kublai Khan. A hot air balloon ride enables a visitor to appreciate the true extent of *Bagan's* spectacular landscape of cultural treasures and the unforgettable, serene countryside.

During the decades of military rule, the authorities constructed a mishmash of new temples and stupas, in an attempt to increase tourism without regard to the area's historic architecture integrity. *Than Shwe's* government tampered with sacred archaeological sites and painted over ancient murals, built on top of old structures, or reconstructed them completely. They even

---

[1] *Myanmar Times.* Kyaw Phone Kyaw: "Tourism creates 50,000 jobs", January 23, 2015.

built a shrine dedicated to *Than Shwe*, who was never a patron of the arts or architecture.

The regime's application for UNESCO World Heritage Site recognition in 1996 was rejected as the new construction and restoration were completed without proper legal frameworks. An earthquake of 6.8 magnitude struck central Burma in 2016, but most of the historic sites have been restored. The government reapplied and Bagan received UNESCO world heritage site in July 2019.

Mandalay is a historic city and was the last royal capital of Burma, under the last king of Burma, King *Thibaw*. Mandalay is also the center of Burmese art and culture, including exquisite tapestry works, elaborate marionettes, stone sculpture, and the traditional gold leaf production. You can visit the area where traditional gold leaf makers pound the gold with hand-held hammer into paper-thin sheets. These are offered for sale as donations used to cover the stupa dome and other sacred or regal structures. The royal palace was extravagant with beautiful buildings elaborately carved with solid teak or fragrant tropical woods of Burma in traditional royal designs and completely gilded with 24-carat gold leaf over red lacquer. Many halls, royal chambers, palace pavilions and throne rooms are covered with intricate glass mosaics. Although most of the palace was destroyed during the war, when the Japanese invaded, the buildings have been rebuilt and restored painstakingly by local artisans, with manicured gardens and surrounded on four sides by a moat and defensive walls, recreating the glories of the royal family. Besides the white marble pagoda and the majestic teak monastery, Mandalay's landmarks include the world's longest teak bridge, three quarters of a mile long. Mandalay is also known for its jade market.

The 'Golden Rock' or *Kyaiktiyo* is another marvel. It is situated on a rocky mountain 3615 feet above sea level. The gilded stupa is built on top of a massive rock approximately 80 feet in diameter. The bell-shaped rock, miraculously balancing on the edge of a cliff, is believed to be sacred; it is completely covered in gold leaf. It is said that the rock is perched without falling due to Buddha's hair preserved in the shrine. The hike up is 10 miles through dense tropical forests and bamboo groves; once at the top, you are rewarded with an awe inspiring panoramic view and majestic scenery. You can also hire coolies or porters to carry you and your bags in hammocks attached to bamboo poles.

Inle Lake is a picturesque water village situated almost 3,000 feet above sea level in northern Burma, in Shan state. Here, fishermen and locals row their boats in a unique way, without using their hands. They stand on one leg and wrap the other around the oar, freeing their hands to do other things, such using their nets to catch fish. Rowing in a standing position also gives the boatman a better view over the floating vegetation. The lake is covered by reeds and floating plants.

The *Inle* people are water people, living on the water most of their lives. They plant their crops and vegetables on rafts of turf and soil that float on the lake like islands. They construct these floating islands and vegetable farms from vegetation, weeds and mud from the lake bottom and anchor them by bamboo poles. Houses on stilts are built on these islands and vegetables and fruits are grown hydroponically in these floating gardens that take water directly from the lake without having to be watered. These gardens and farms are protected from flooding as they rise and fall daily with changes in the water level. They are also very fertile due to the constant availability of nutrient-rich water. Daily transportation, is served by boat or 'water taxi', including shopping at these colorful floating markets, children going to school, and so forth. Buyers and sellers meet at traveling markets to do business in canoes and boats on the lake. Boats serve as grocery stores carrying fish, prawns, vegetables, fruits, flowers, toiletries, household items, apparel, shoes, and woven Shan bags for which *Inle* Lake is known.

Burma is blessed with over 1200 miles of coastline stretching from the Bay of Bengal on the west all the way south to the Andaman Sea. Much of the coastal area is still untouched, as it has been off limits to tourists for several decades. The unspoiled white sandy beaches lined with palm trees extend from the northwest *Arakan* (now *Rakhine*) Region to the southern Mon region of *Tenasserim* (now *Tanintharyi*). The stunning Mergui archipelago has become the world's best kept secrets with hundreds of dazzling islands and thousands of pristine virgin white sand beaches, cliffs, caves, sea tunnels and coral reefs swarmed with rare exotic underwater sea life. The Mergui Archipelago, called *Myeik* in Burmese, consists of over 800 predominantly uninhabited islands spreading over 10,000 square miles in the Andaman Sea. Due to their remoteness and difficulty of access, the islands have been well preserved. While many are uninhabited, some are occupied by local sea gypsies or the Mokens (*Salon* in Burmese) believed to have migrated there from China 4,000 years ago. They are skilled at deep sea diving in search of pearls and abalone. Mergui or *Myeik* is now open to visitors by several boat cruises and adventure tours. Historically, the city was a cosmopolitan hub for traders and travelers from both Eastern and Western countries, some have settled in the region adding a unique population mix and cultural flavor. Due to its location crossing the isthmus between the Indian Ocean and the Gulf of Siam, Mergui was strategically important on a global trade route of its time. Based on its many architectural styles, the Arabs, the Portuguese, the French and the British were all here trading and profiting from abundant teak, rubber, mining, rich fishing grounds and pearl harvesting. Since the Burmese government opened Mergui to tourists recently, modern recreation activities such as snorkeling, sailing, canoeing, deep sea diving and forest trekking are now available.

Tourism would boost economic growth in the country, creating new jobs and increasing revenues hopefully would benefit the common people and improve their standard of living in the long run. For now government has tentacles in every sector of the economy including tourism and many large tourism related business and hotels are still owned by the generals, their families and their connected friends. Nepotism and crony corruption need to be addressed and dealt with by the new NLD democratic government. Accelerated clearing of forests and land for construction of hotels, resorts, restaurants, golf courses and roads has displaced people and damaged the environment. These issues of developing tourism with environmental protection and preservation of culture and traditions must be on the government's plate to be addressed. Tourists insensitive to local communities and tribal way of life undermine their social, cultural and moral values, including sexual exploitation of women and young girls as prostitutes. Often modernization comes with unwanted culture shifts and unintended consequences. Indiscriminate and thoughtless tipping by many foreigners encourages children and poor grown ups to beg. The dark side of tourism industry includes sexual exploitation of local women and children and human trafficking as some 'rich' foreigners travel to poor countries like Burma and exploit the vulnerabilities of poor local families. As the country opens up and welcomes tourists, the government must recognize and respond to sex exploitation, not only in the streets and local communities but on the internet. The negative effects of tourism must be considered by both the host country and the visitors to maintain a balance between the benefits of tourism development and dignity of the people of the country.

CHAPTER 10. FACE OF THE STATELESS

Ngapali, Arakan (Rakhine) State

One of South East Asia's loveliest beach resorts is Ngapali. Located in Arakan or *Rakhine* State, on the Bay of Bengal coast, Ngapali is an idyllic two mile stretch of pristine white sand beach lined with palm trees and the small boats of local fishermen. It has the touch of local Burmese life and charming fishing village vibe with fishermen bringing in local daily catch of seafood for sale. It is the favorite beach of the military generals and the well-to-do Burmese. The sky is blue almost every day and the water is crystal clear and cobalt blue or turquoise. The beach is lined with coconut palm trees but no volleyball players, surfers, or noisy boats in sight, not yet anyway. No empty coke cans, cigarette butts, or paper trash. Ngapali is indeed an idyllic paradise. Under military dictatorship rule it was accessible only to the elite, high ranking military officers of Tatmadaw, their families, and the Rangoon upper crust society who were well connected and with abundant financial means. For children Ngapali Beach was unparalleled vacation spot with endless miles of undisturbed golden sand and no other person in sight. We spent hours with Mommy looking for hermit crabs and picking colorful rocks and exotic sea shells of all types, colors, shapes and sizes. Papa would hire a small fishing boat to venture out into the deep sea for fishing and exploring caves accessible only by boats. Meals with various curries were freshly prepared from the daily catch of seafood, including lobster, crab, squid, and fish. Try coconut prawn curry, made with prawns the size of my hand and traditionally cooked on charcoal with freshly squeezed coconut milk. Slurp it down with abundant fresh coconut water straight from the green coconut. Other exotic tropical fruits include sweet juicy mangoes, custard apples, yellow watermelon, papayas, and mangosteens all abundant and readily available. Our accommodations were simple Burmese style native thatched roof huts on the beachfront. Since 2011 construction of modern hotels and upscale resorts brought eyesores of thick brick fence walls and concrete retaining walls along the shoreline, many without proper permit. It may not be the Ngapali I visited with my family as the thatched roof huts on the beaches have been replaced by sprawling hotels, restaurants with Western cuisines, and tour offices offering sea adventures like jet skiing, fishing, kayaking, scuba diving, and snorkeling.

Less than 350 miles north of tranquil Ngapali is the violence-torn region of Arakan state with clashes between Arakanese Buddhists and Muslim minority in a multi decade long struggle. The military regime has marginalized the Muslim people turning a blind eye to the fighting and destruction. Their villages and towns have been burnt to the ground, forcing hundreds of thousands Muslim minorities to flee to neighboring countries. Over a million have ended up in squalid refugee camps. Who are these stateless Muslim people and why are they the most persecuted people on earth? How did so much hatred towards them originate?

Bengali or Rohingya?

Few people in Burma had heard of the *Rohingya* until the late 70s or early 1980s, and few people living in Burma had ever been to Arakan state or interacted with a Muslim from that region. The name *Rohingya* (as the Arakan Muslims are internationally known) came into play after the British colonial times. After independence Prime Minister *U Nu* promoted the name to gain votes in Arakan (*Rakhine* in Burmese) and since the name *Rohingya* has been adopted by many Muslims living in the state.

Under *U Nu's* government they were recognized as a specific ethnic group much like the Kachin, Chin or Shan ethnic nationalities and like them, they were granted citizenship. Most people in Burma dislike this group and spread unfounded hatred toward them on social media. They are seen as an alien population or illegal immigrants and as a threat to Buddhism and Buddhist culture. In post-independence Burma and especially under successive decades of military dictatorships, distrust and hostility toward them grew and a gradual hacking away of rights and dignity of this group of people began to take place.

In the mid-60s the military regime under General *Ne Win* began to isolate them and called them derogatory names like *kalar* and *Bengali*. Dark-skinned people are referred to as *kalar*, a deep seated racial slur derived from Sanskrit meaning 'black man'. The military government began to purge the Muslims in Arakan and marginalized them with persecutions as early as the mid 60s. They also committed human rights abuses against other ethnic nationalities living in bordering states of the country.

The military forced assimilation of these people to *Bamar* cultural norms, religion and language. They began implementing carefully crafted policies to coerce ethnic minorities into a homogenized *Bamar* group of people. Process of 'Burmanization' of ethnic nationalities to erase their identity began with repressive laws, economic exploitation, and religious persecution. Ethnic education and language instruction were removed from schools. Rigorous beating and kicking escalated into systematic spikes of torture, raping, killing, and destroying their homes, businesses, and villages in Arakan and other ethnic states.

In 1982, the army passed the Citizenship Law declaring Arakan Muslims to be foreigners from Bengal and revoked citizenship rights from the Muslims. They were denied access to health, education, and employment in public offices. The regime used many other less evident ways to mistreat and torture the Arakan Muslims. Over several decades, many violent incidents erupted in Arakan, each time killing a few to a few dozen, while the security forces failed to intervene to protect the fleeing Muslims. Human rights groups reported the army soldiers and police forces often fueled unrest either by standing by or taking part in violence. Regardless how long they have lived in the country, the Burmese government would not grant them citizenship as it considers them as *Bengali* or migrants from Bengal. (East Bengal was later made East Pakistan and became the independent nation of Bangladesh in 1971).

Over decades of army rule there have been killings, beating, raping and torturing of minority Muslims with carefully planned intent to destroy and eliminate the communities of Muslim minority from the state of Arakan. Many violent episodes erupted over the years under military regime forcing thousands and hundreds of thousands to flee from their homes and villages. The brutality did not end as the humanitarian crisis continues today. The UN has labeled the burning, mass killing, raping and torturing 'ethnic cleansing' with 'genocidal intent'. The US recently named the crisis a genocide.

The new NLD-led democratic civilian government inherited a daunting list of challenges including the long running Arakan crisis, but *Aung San Suu Kyi* remains silent about the mass killing and other horrors committed by *Tatmadaw*. She is strongly criticized by the international community for her failure to speak out and to end the violence. Those who admired her as a symbol for democracy and human rights are indignant as she remains tongue-tied in the face of this ethnic cleansing. She not only ignores the mass killing and human rights violations committed by the military but defends its actions, justifying *Tatmadaw* has legitimate right to carrying out a campaign against 'terrorists'. People begin to wonder if this civilian government can build a genuine democracy in Burma or provide what is required for democracy to evolve from decades of deeply authoritarian system. In addition to racial and religious overtones, the issues in Arakan involve details of Burma's history and geopolitics that are not always addressed by foreign press and media. An understanding of the historical and political develop‑ ment, cultural, religious, racial and psychological aspects is crucial to gain a better insight into the crisis of this bitterly divided nation.

Historians and experts on the Arakan Muslims claim their ances‑ tors arrived in the then kingdom of Arakan during the 8th or 9th century as seafarers and traders from the Middle East;[1] and that they had been settled in the Arakan kingdom for centuries, long before the Burmese army conquered the kingdom in 1785 and made Arakan part of the imperial Burma. Most of the people of Arakan were Buddhists, but a minority living near bordering countries became Muslims and Hindus, primarily due to intermarriage with Pakistanis and Indians.

'*Rohang*' is the Muslim name for Arakan and '*Rohangya*' means 'inhabitant of *Rohang*'. The name identifies them as a Muslim group and ties them to the land that was once the kingdom of Arakan.[2] They can identify with the heritage of the precolonial Muslim community in Arakan. The name *Rohingya* also sets them apart from other Indian and Pakistani Muslims in other parts of Burma. It is a basic right for them to self‑identify as *Rohingya* or any name they choose. In modern days, the name *Rohingya* is used by the international community including the UN and the West to describe Muslim minority people living in Arakan or *Rakhine* state. But the government of Burma and the country's predominantly Buddhist people dispute the name, and instead, call them *Bengali*, suggesting they are from Bengal and are illegally occupying Buddhist land. They are therefore regarded as stateless illegal immigrants.

This part of coastal Burma is not easily accessible due to the Arakan Yoma Range, a mountain range that separates western coastal Burma from the rest of the country. The physical barrier also fosters the development of a distinct culture and dialect in the state. Due to increasing conflict and violent fights with the Buddhists in Arakan, the Muslims began to migrate to neighboring countries.

At first, the disagreements ended up with beatings and kicking and destruction of property. Tension grew and by the 80s even a slightest provo‑ cation would erupt into full blown violence. Eventually, mobs would attack the Muslims, burning, raping, and killing while the army looked the other way.

---

[1] *The Economist*. "The Rohingyas. The Most Persecuted People on Earth?", Kuala Lumpur, Shamlapur and Sittwe, June 13th 2015.
[2] *Council on Foreign Relations*. Eleanor Albert: "The *Rohingya* Migrant Crisis", January 12, 2017.

A British Legacy

Looking back, violent conflict and frontier wars in bordering states of Burma date back to the pre-colonial era when the British ruled over the Indian subcontinent. The British settled people of Indian origin in that region, and many others, from other areas, migrated into the subcontinent for economic opportunity. In 1825, the British captured and annexed Arakan state and governed it as part of British India. Burma was part of British India until 1937 when it became a separate British colony.

The British Empire was divided into India and Pakistan in the subcontinent. The British then divided the Indian province of Bengal into two different entities, namely, East Bengal and West Bengal, based on religion. The majority of people in the East are Muslims while West Bengal is predominantly Hindu. When the British left India, Muslim-dominated East Bengal was given to Pakistan as a province and Hindu-dominated West Bengal became part of India. Later, East Bengal gained independence and became Bangladesh as it is known today.

Unlike other bordering regions of Burma like the Shan or Kachin state, Arakan lacks mineral wealth and is primarily reliant on fishing and agriculture although gas is found in offshore fields. During the colonial days from 1824 to 1948, the British brought hundreds of thousands of Bengali Muslims from East Bengal into Burma. The Muslim migration flooded Arakan state to work as laborers and farmers. The British wanted a cheap source of labor as they were constructing a waterway to connect the Mediterranean Sea to the Red Sea through the Isthmus of Suez. They needed rice to feed the workers during the construction of the Suez Canal. They also built a railroad between *Buthidaung* and *Maungdaw* to transport the rice and encouraged mass migration of Muslims into Arakan state. Colonial economy flourished but local Arakanese Buddhists resented it as their ancestral land and jobs were taken over by 'illegal immigrants' or so-called '*Bengali*'. This cheap source of labor for the colonialists fired up resentment toward the Muslims living in the state, continuing today. With the Bangladesh Liberation War in what was East Pakistan, a second wave of migration into Arakan took place in 1971–1972.

Fear of Secession

To add insult to injury, when World War II broke out and the Japanese invaded Burma and drove out the British, the division between the Muslims and the Buddhists intensified. The people of Arakan became politically, religiously and socioeconomically divided. The Muslims, armed by the British, helped in the fight against the Japanese while the local Arakanese Buddhists sided with the Japanese.

After the war the Muslims in Arakan asked Muslim-dominated Pakistan to help annex the territory of Arakan state. They wanted independence from the *Bamar* government. When Pakistan refused, they took up arms and created an internal rebellion. Confrontations with the Burma army grew in scale and frequency. The divide is not only about race and religion; it's also about an ideology and fighting for something tangible like a *Rohingya* state, a piece of land separate from the rest of the Buddhist nation and under its own regional control, self governing, like the ethnic Shan or Kachin state of the 135 officially recognized ethnic groups. Thus, the controversy is not just over the names *Rohingya* (people of 'Ro' or Arakan) and *Bengali* (from Bengal, now Bangladesh). It includes a demand for ethnicity to add *Rohingya* to be the 136th ethnic group of Burma — a status which the military government of Burma is unwilling to give.

The military has a deeply-rooted fear of a separatist rebellion. *Tatmadaw* portrays itself as the country's savior who fought for Burma's independence and as the only institution that could keep the country from splitting apart.

Marginalization under Army Dictatorship

After independence in the 1950s, under the civilian government of Prime Minister *U Nu*, the Muslims of Arakan were recognized as an ethnic group of Burma and granted equal rights as citizens. The teaching of Islam, its history, culture, and languages of Urdu and Arabic were permitted at schools and even Arabic newspapers were allowed publication and radio broadcasts were aired. Muslims and Buddhists traded with one another and there was communal interaction and some degree of social harmony. The children went to the same schools and studied and played together.

All that ended a few years after the military coup of 1962, when the army began segregation, isolation and persecution of the minority Muslims. Since then, this group has become a severely disadvantaged group of people under military autocratic rule. Ever since the mid-1960s systematic spikes of killing, beating, burning, torturing and raping of the minority Muslim have been taking place in Arakan.

Burma has a long history of communal unrest which was allowed to simmer, and periodically and systematically, exploited under military rule. When conflict or riots broke out between the Muslims and the Buddhists in the region, soldiers tended to side with the Arakan Buddhists while the security forces looked the other way. The systematic destruction continued for decades even under President *Thein Sein's* nominal civilian rule, while the abomination and violence increased in scale and intensity deepening inequalities.

In 2012, 2015, 2016 and 2017, violent bouts sparked by routine disagreement would explode into bloody massacres in the state. Resolvable internal conflicts ignited violence, and the army would intervene in the name of defending the faith and indiscriminately destroyed the whole community. A flash point would create a violence that quickly escalated into widespread communal clashes with deadly consequences. The conflicts escalated with hundreds of thousands Muslim fleeing across the border by foot or in rusty old boats out into the ocean and were abandoned at sea for weeks.

By 2017 a crisis of unprecedented scale erupted; roughly 750,000 fled their homes and tens of thousands were reported lost and presumed dead in Arakan state. Hundreds of villages were burnt and crops destroyed. The UN has described the military crackdown as ethnic cleansing with genocidal intent. Based on multiple visits by the UN and countless interviews and reports by journalists, historians, researchers, scholars, and human rights groups, the Burma army continues the indiscriminate killing today, seemingly set on the annihilation of the country's one million plus Muslim minority.

With the 1982 Citizenship Law the military junta compiled a list of 135 official ethnic nationalities and excluded this group, revoking their citizenship rights. They were classified as resident aliens and therefore were denied health and education benefits and were restricted from holding public office. They were declared migrant refugees from Bangladesh, brought in illegally by the British colonialists to work as colonial slaves and undocumented laborers.

After the 8.8.88 student uprisings more restrictions were imposed on the Muslims including movement and travel in and out of Arakan, and even marriage was prohibited without permission from the government. The Bangladesh government does not accept them either, as they are considered Muslim nationals of Burma. They have become the people of nowhere, that is, stateless.

Anti-Everyone

The ruling generals of *Tatmadaw* stirred up post war Burmese nationalism to create a mental split between Buddhists and Muslims, not just in Arakan but among the general population. 'They' are the 'perpetrators', they take our land, and want to 'Islamize' the nation. 'We' are the 'defenders', and we protect our land and Buddhism and we must destroy any existential threat from Islam. This psychological manipulation has expanded widely to the whole population throughout the country to gain people's support resulting in not just anti Muslim sentiment but also anti Western, anti UN, anti NGOs, anti humanitarian workers, and anti anyone who provides aid to the minority Muslim in Arakan.

Foreign aid to the refugees actually deepened the bitter Muslim–Buddhist division in the region. Many well intended projects funded by aid organizations to help the refugees have created negative perceptions within the Arakanese Buddhist community. They feel deliberately left out as beneficiaries of aid supplied by NGOs and this unequal resource allocation creates alienation and animosity between the two groups. Among the displaced in recent violence of 2017 over 30,000 Arakan Buddhists and other ethnic minorities also fled their homes and many of them were killed. No one outside of Burma has expressed support for them.

Many Buddhists grow up believing the *Bamar* race is blessed with national superiority over other ethnic nationalities. Instead of advocating equality, the army regime reinforces these biases in order to 'divide and conquer' and destroy potential unity. They propagate and expand people's prejudices through media, anonymous publications, the powerful Buddhist clergy, the *sangha*.

Over time radical nationalism brewed within the Buddhist clergy. A radical anti-Muslim 969 movement founded by militant monks began to sweep the country coincided with the rise of Buddhist radical group, *Ma Ba Tha*. By 2017, anti Muslim hysteria was at its peak and most people in Burma have become supportive of the government as protector of *Bamar* ethnicity and Buddhism. With the rise of radical Buddhist nationalism the *Bamar* Buddhists believe they are defending the *Bamar* army and the civilian government. International outcry from Western governments, media, NGOs and human rights organizations and criticism of the military and the civilian government are viewed as insensitive, biased and misguided. By now the citizens have been conditioned to believe these people are 'terrorists' who have illegally migrated from Bangladesh and India to usurp Buddhist land, that with four wives per Muslim man they will propagate to take over the country and destroy Buddhism!

Recent Escalation of Violence

In 2012, the rape and murder of a young Buddhist woman by an alleged Muslim assailant sparked widespread deadly rioting and clashes between

Arakanese Buddhists and the Muslim minority, killing an estimated 200–300 people and displacing 140,000 who ended up in IDP (internally displaced people) internment camps across the border. Witnesses reported riot police, local police, security forces and army soldiers on duty stood by or joined the Arakanese men armed with machetes, swords, and homemade guns and attacked their villages and assisted in the killing.

In 2015, waves of deadly violence engulfed villages forcing tens of thousands of Muslims to flee by sea, taking life-threatening voyages in overloaded, rickety boats to Bangladesh, Thailand, Malaysia, Indonesia, Vietnam and other Southeast Asian countries. Several hundred drowned or perished from starvation and dehydration and over 100,000 displaced and ended up in squalid disease-ridden IDP camps. Corpses were found in boats as people-smugglers abandoned their human cargo and left boats adrift in the sea without water and food. Security guards extorted payments at departure and illegally profited till the end from this mass exodus.

Their most recent plight made international news headlines but government downplayed the situation. Some human rights advocates believe communal violence was in reality a pre-planned state-led massacre. The news got the attention of global media but where is the West? Leaders of international communities were silent or slow to move while the Muslims were dying in the sea. International outrage was expressed in a few words of condemnation but little was done to help those fleeing persecution. Neighboring countries were reluctant to take in the refugees for fear of a migrant influx. Even India which has been a safe haven for thousands of Muslims from Arakan does not want more, as Indian public hostility towards the refugees grows. Increasing tensions between Hindu dominant India and bordering Muslim Pakistan also threatens the refugees. First they fled from Burma, then from Bangladesh, and now India wants them to leave. Where would they go?

ARSA

ARSA, or the Arakan *Rohingya* Solidarity Army, emerged in 2016. In October 2016, several hundred armed assailants attacked three Burmese border posts in northern Arakan State killing nine police officers and injuring many others. ARSA launched a three-month long attack, forcing nearly 70,000 Muslims to flee to Bangladesh, killing an estimated 1,000 and burning down thousands of homes. According to the International Crisis Group, ICG, the attackers were from the group known as *Harakah al-Yaqin* formed in 2012 after the deadly riots between Buddhists and Muslims which killed over 200 people and displaced 140,000, almost all of them Muslims.[1]

The group is well funded with *fatwas* from Saudi Arabia, United Arab Emirates, Pakistan and elsewhere. They are well trained and some have international experience in modern guerrilla warfare and use of explosives. They claim their goal is to secure the rights of the *Rohingya* as citizens of Burma rather than terrorists killing indiscriminately to establish a caliphate or an emirate. In August 2017, ARSA attacked 30 police posts and an army base in Arakan state in a daring and well-orchestrated assault. *Tatmadaw* responded with a full scale counter offensive, in disproportionate military force, without distinguishing attackers from civilians. Villages were burnt to the ground and both sides fired upon indiscriminately. The crisis forced three quarters of a million Muslims to flee across the border to Bangladesh. According to foreign NGOs estimation at least 6,700 to 7,000 were killed in the first month of violence alone. Most were gunned down while others were burned to death in their homes. Additionally, over 43,000 *Rohingya* parents have been reported lost and presumed dead in the six months since the Burmese military unleashed the crackdown of August.

The UN has declared the reckless devastation and destruction of life and property as ethnic cleansing with genocidal intent. Other researchers use the term genocide, defined as mass murder or deliberate killing of a large group of people. Genocide took place in Germany, Cambodia, and Rwanda, and most recently in Yemen, and is happening in Burma. The mass slaughter and human rights violations also got the attention of the Organization of Islamic Cooperation, OIC, founded in 1969, which represents the collective voice of 57 states of the Muslim world and the collective population of member states of over 1.6 billion. OIC's past effort to intervene through the UN's Human Rights Commission has not been successful but it has appointed an OIC envoy to deal with the Arakan Muslim plight just as OIC has interceded for the persecuted Muslims in Palestine and Kashmir.

The Lady is Silent

Aung San Suu Kyi was once a beacon of hope for democracy and human rights but now, as a politician, she has not only ignored the atrocities committed by the military but defended their actions and continued violations in Arakan. By not taking a stand on human rights, she safely avoided upsetting the military and the majority Buddhist community. By not making

---

[1] *Time.* Tim Johnson and Anagha Neelakantan: "The World's Newest Muslim Insurgency Is Being Waged in Burma", December 13, 2016.

any statements and gestures in support of the Muslim minority, she safely avoided political suicide.

Her refusal to acknowledge the scale of August 2017 crisis represented total disregard and disdain for domestic human rights issues. The 1991 Nobel Peace Prize winner has now been stripped of a series of international honors including prestigious human rights awards and honorary citizenship from Amnesty International, US, UK, Sweden and Canada. Her portrait was removed from St. Hugh's College at Oxford University. The Nobel laureate who represented non violence was now looking the other way while ethnic cleansing was taking place in her own backyard. By her continued silence and not speaking out about the violence that caused tragic suffering and immense loss of life, she was guilty of perpetuating human rights abuses against the Muslim minority. But she could not stop the refugees and the oppressed from talking.

The Government of Burma denied UN and human rights groups access to conflict zones but it could not prevent people who have escaped to neighboring countries from speaking out. Special rapporteurs like Professor Yanghee Lee are independent and not hired by United Nations. They report what they see and hear firsthand. The government's dismissals of unbiased third-party reports and its refusal of access to the affected regions were the identical to the tactics of *Tatmadaw* for the past several decades. *Tatmadaw* continued to justify its abuses in the name of protecting its sovereignty and rejected international investigative reports and outrage as unfair, harsh or even slander. In years past, the government also agreed to repatriate the 250,000 refugees who fled from Arakan to Bangladesh but only a handful, fewer than 50 refugees, were repatriated.[1] To quote David Scott Mathieson, a human rights researcher, "*Suu Kyi's* recent treatment of Yanghee Lee is a sadly consistent pattern of denial and diversion honed by Burmese diplomats and generals for decades."

Why is *Aung San Suu Kyi* silent? Is it out of fear of losing the support of the majority Buddhists? As a politician she is playing it safe. Any public criticism of *Tatmadaw* would have repercussion she cannot afford. However, she has the moral authority and has the right to speak out. Since taking over the civilian side of the government, she had vowed to push for national peace and reconciliation. Instead, she has remained quiet and even rejected the international fact-finding mission. *Aung San Suu Kyi's* office is quick to deny such reports as fabrications. Instead, state run newspapers and social media

---

[1] *Tea Circle Oxford.* David Scott Mathieson: "Burma's Lost Rapport on Rights Protection", April 2, 2018.

blame Muslim insurgents. What happened to truth, justice, and compassion she wrote in her book, *Freedom from Fear*?

However, UN representatives have interviewed hundreds of local residents and witnesses who testified to helicopter shootings and killing by dropping grenades on the people. They also witnessed methodical burning of homes and entire villages, and systematic abduction, torture, killing and gang rape of women and children. These acts of savagery committed by soldiers and police forces have been labeled crimes against humanity and ethnic cleansing by the UN and the international community. *Tatmadaw* declared they would investigate their own actions, and they recently released a report denying all allegations. They repeatedly claim the crackdown was a legitimate counter insurgency operation.

The powerful influence of the military is undeniable; it controls three key ministries that report directly to the military head and operate independently of the civilian administration. Therefore, *Aung San Suu Kyi* does not have free range to the executive and legislative branches nor does she appear to have the decision power or maneuverability regarding major crises like the Arakan issues.

Has *Aung San Suu Kyi* reached her limits dealing with Senior General *Min Aung Hlaing* and is her NLD government unable or unwilling to proceed? So far the Lady appears to be maintaining a cautious but cordial relationship with the *Tatmadaw* chief and the generals. As an astute politician she has not only defended the Burmese military but rejected international interventions, calling the Arakan crisis an 'internal issue' which should be handled by the Burmese government without international interference. She also rejected the proposed UN fact finding mission to the conflict regions which has been strongly supported by 23 international organizations including Amnesty International, Human Rights Watch, and Fortify Rights. Her office routinely responds to investigate any abuses reported and to take appropriate action in accordance with the law, but these assurances remain empty.

Rise of Nationalism and Militant Monks

Discrimination and persecution against the Muslim minority was increasing and new laws were being proposed to restrict their freedom of movement, the right of women to marry non Buddhists, and access to employment, health, and education. The government expelled the humanitarian healthcare group Médecins Sans Frontières (Doctors Without Borders), leaving the marginalized people with no other source of medical care.

In recent years Buddhist nationalism and anti Muslim sentiment in Burma have surged as the army continued its propaganda, slowly but systematically, spike by spike. Meanwhile anti Muslim pamphlets and fliers were distrib-uted widely throughout the country by Buddhist extremists portraying the Muslims as an enemy and threat to the *Bamar* people, Buddhism, and the nation.

An anti-Muslim campaign headed by a Buddhist monk, dubbed 969, a named based on Buddhist principles, urged Arakanese Buddhists to boycott Muslim owned shops and businesses. The 969 movement incited the local people to attack Muslim shops and properties and punish those that did business with them. The provocation caused riots and mass destruction, and often while the police and security forces watched or looked the other way. *Tatmadaw* soldiers often participated with the mobs in the attacks against the Muslim minority, burning mosques and houses, driving them from their homes, and preventing people from helping the injured and dying.

Just a couple of decades ago there were no ultra-nationalists but now there is a growing Buddhist radicalism, Buddhist cleansing and other anti Muslim radical forces. Now, *Ma Ba Tha* is a powerful nationalistic Buddhist movement against Muslims founded in 2012 by members of 969 movement and radical monks. The group harbors strong discriminatory bias as it spreads anti Muslim sentiment with fiery rhetoric and inflammatory hate speeches and sermons fueling more violence and escalating more conflict in greater intensity. In the three years of NLD administration, nationalism, radical Buddhism and anti Muslim fervor increased. The radical monks, intoxicated with nationalist fervor, deliver un-Buddhist disgraceful hate speeches and publicly stir up animosity that disrespects Buddhism.

Past military regimes allowed a permissive environment in which hate speeches and incitement in these communities were tolerated and even encouraged. *U Wirathu*, the instigating monk and leader of *Ma Ba Tha* (also known as 'Burmese Bin Laden') incited violence with his paranoia, muddled with racist stereotypes. He ferociously called the UN special representative a 'whore' when she was commissioned to inspect and report human rights abuses in western Burma. He also publicly praised and thanked the gunman who fatally shot the NLD Muslim advisor *U Ko Ni* and defied the government in other ways as if he was above the law.

In the context of a powerful military, *Aung San Suu Kyi* is afraid to speak up in defense of the Muslims but by being silent she has also angered the radical Buddhists for not supporting the militant monks of *Ma Ba Tha*. Defying threat of arrest, *U Wirathu* also made personal verbal attacks and obscene remarks about the state counselor. *Ma Ba Tha* and other nationalist groups have been staging pro-military campaigns across the country criticizing the civilian government of prioritizing human rights over Buddhism. These campaigns are beginning to resemble political rallies to agitate the people rather than a religious crusade to protect Buddhism.

As an astute politician, the state counselor is cautious not to support 'illegal immigrants' against the mainstream Burmese community.

Under immense pressure from the international community the government finally allowed a group of independent journalists to visit some villages in *Maungdaw*, the conflict-ridden region in Arakan. True, villages have been burnt, women and children raped and villagers killed, but government denied these allegations and claimed many are fabricated by Muslim sympathizers in collaboration with insurgents who are linked to Islamist terrorists overseas. Some unofficial reports do contain factual inaccuracies and there are also exaggerated reports and fabricated photos and video footage to exert pressure for intervention at the global level. On the other hand, many observations are true and reported accurately, investigated, verified and witnessed by survivors; for example, a video of policemen caught beating Muslim villagers was investigated and proved to be true. The military has closed off the conflicted region citing security concerns to justify its continued viciousness and access denial to media, human rights organizations and international investigating groups.

Unless government allows human rights groups to visit the region and inspect the areas, it is difficult to know which news, photos and video images are true or fake. The government cannot credibly or reasonably offer a blanket denial or allegations without full verification. These human right abuses and allegations must be investigated openly and proactively. There are no easy fixes or quick solutions for these complex issues but a defensive approach of Burmese army promulgates and disseminates perception of cover up. These hideous acts must be addressed, investigated, and the perpetrators disciplined as a first step for sustainable peace to be achieved. People need to live without fear and with equal rights and freedom.

Whatever they are — *Rohingya* or *Bengali* — they have been living in Arakan, Burma, for generations, and therefore should be given, at the very minimum, some clear guidelines to non-citizen rights and rights of residency status. As members of the human race they have basic rights to be treated with dignity and respect. It is unfathomable they have been physically abused, mistreated, marginalized, and stigmatized in a peace loving Buddhist country by people who are taught the core humanist qualities of Lord Buddha's teachings to embrace Buddhist principles of non-violence, tolerance, mercy, kindness, and compassion.

The Rise of Terrorism

The Muslim population in Arakan is estimated at 1–1.3 million but roughly 750,000 have fled due the recent crisis of 2017 and military crackdown. Another 4–500,000 lived in Bangladesh prior to the crisis and about 600,000 live abroad in other countries. They speak a dialect of Chittagong, a coastal seaport and financial hub in southeastern Bangladesh. The Muslim minority in Arakan state live in towns and villages with predominately Arakanese Buddhists, some Hindus and a few other minor ethnic nationalities of Burma but in *Maungdaw* and *Buthidaung* the population is predominately Muslim.

Most villagers are farmers, fishermen and some run small family businesses and open shops. Although most inhabitants are unarmed villagers there are militant groups from both sides, Buddhists and Muslims, who are armed with knives, machetes, homemade explosives, slingshots, and sticks, ready for attack. Today's militant Muslims include outside elements like ARSA instigators who are more sophisticated and better trained. They receive financial support from other Muslim groups outside of Burma and weapons and jungle war training from foreign Muslim groups. They attack all opposition including the Burmese military, Arakan Buddhists, and other nationalities. ARSA has declared they are fighting the Burmese military and others to establish a 'Rohingya-only territory', a potential fertile breeding ground for terrorists that threatens the security of the nation. ARSA has expressed its political aspiration beyond human rights to build 'an Islamic State for the *Rohingya*' and gain autonomy and self rule free from the Burmese government. There are other foreign terrorists who could attack in coordination with radical groups inside Burma such as IS sympathizers and other groups from majority Muslim countries like Indonesia, Malaysia and the Middle East. The threat of resurgence of radicalism is real and not limited to Burma as violence against the encroachment of Islam spreads in other Southeast Asian countries like Indonesia and Malaysia that were formerly predominantly Buddhists. Burma expert journalist Bertil Lintner discusses the on-going violence and alleged atrocities in the region as well as the growing sympathy for the militants in the Muslim world outside of Burma.[1]

Muslim dominated countries like Indonesia and Malaysia have publicly pressured Burma over the Arakan crisis. Malaysian police also reported the Islamic State is planning *jihadi* attacks against the Burmese government as part of establishment of an ideological global jihad. An Islamist militant inspired movement is also seen to be emerging in this region which could

---

[1] *The Irrawaddy.* Bertil Lintner: "Militancy in Arakan State", December 15, 2016.

lead to an *al Qaeda* type terrorist network. According to the Irrawaddy news, Brussels based International Crisis Group, ICG, even suggests the attacks in Arakan are linked to Muslim insurgent group in Saudi Arabia.[1] Some claim the foreign militant involvement also has links to Pakistan. The Saudi-backed attackers with international fighting experience have been recruited and well trained in guerrilla warfare and use of explosives.[2]

The rise of extremism in Arakan is real, and fear of international terrorism is genuine as the crisis has provoked antagonism in the Muslim world with growing sympathy for the militants. The situation risks making Burma a breeding ground for jihadist-type terror. The risk of attacks on pagodas, temples, monasteries and large public gatherings is becoming real, as hostility from the Muslim world grows.

Anti Buddhist sentiment, anti Burma political rhetoric and strong confrontational language are prevalent from leaders of many Muslim countries. In neighboring Pakistan, thousands of demonstrators rallied against the Burmese government protesting the Arakan crisis and posing potential threat of attack on the Burma embassy.[3] The West reinstated sanctions as the crisis continues. The military generals and border security police officers are under scrutiny for murder and other rights abuses committed and the international community is increasing pressure to prosecute them before the International Criminal Court. Burma urgently needs to cultivate beneficial relations through dialog and diplomacy with the Muslim world if long term peace is to be achieved. Regardless of what they are called — *Rohingya*, *Bengali*, or Muslim minority of Arakan, and regardless of who is responsible for atrocities — the Burma army, ARSA, militants, Muslims, Buddhists, vigilantes — they are being killed, burnt, tortured, and raped and they need and deserve the world's help to end the violence in the name of humanity. Regardless who is to blame in the current Arakan crisis Burma needs global cooperation and strategic partnerships to achieve peace, and economic and political stability. International aid and support through positive relations with other countries is not only essential to successful transformation to democracy, but imperative to Burma's geopolitical stability and economic development through foreign investment.

---

[1] *The Irrawaddy*. Tim Johnston and Anagha Neelakantan: "Arakan Attacks Linked to Group in Saudi Arabia", December 15, 2016.

[2] *Time*. Tim Johnston and Anagha Neelakantan: "The World's Newest Muslim Insurgency is Being Waged in Burma", December 13, 2016.

[3] *The Irrawaddy*. "*Myanmar* Embassy in Pakistan Undergoes Emergency Security Upgrade", May 21, 2018.

Peaceful Coexistence

Peaceful coexistence and inter racial and religious mutual assistance existed in Burma in the past, as reported by Tea Circle Oxford[1]. People of different faiths not only coexisted, but have come together in times of crisis such as during the natural disaster of Cyclone Nargis or in a major fire, or to celebrate festivals with mutual goodwill and shared interests of bonding. There are villages that are predominantly Muslim and those that are predominantly Buddhists. In Arakan state, there are Muslim villages, Arakanese Buddhist villages, and mixed community villages where all people of Arakan — Muslim, Buddhists, Hindus and other minor ethnic nationalities live together.

In many parts of Burma, people of different ethnicity, cultures and faiths co exist. The authors of Tea Circle Oxford cited the importance of these memories and experiences as powerful tools of de-escalating tense situations, conflict prevention, and peace building. In a country which has endured decades of repression and suffering, it would take years to heal old wounds inflicted on the complex basis of ethnic, religious, racial and political differences.

As indicated by philosopher Charles Montesquieu, people are much less likely to wage war if they rely on each other economically. When a buyer and seller come together to exchange goods or services, they form a trade union based on mutual economic necessities. In the past, in rural villages of Burma, various ethnic communities came together to trade and shop in the marketplace; there was communal rejoicing when they gathered to celebrate holidays and harvest festivities; there was deep sense of collective ownership of goods and property as they worked together planting, cultivating and harvesting crops; and there was long-standing tradition of providing communal labor freely as the men cleared trees to build roads while the women cooked and fed the community. The Burmese, Chinese, and Indians live and work side by side in communities of Buddhists, Christians, Muslims, Jews, Hindus, Sikhs, Baha'is, Confucians, Zoroastrians, and Animists in many parts of the country.

In cities and urban environment like Rangoon, many Muslims coexist with non Muslims. Many are bilingual, speaking their mother tongue — Hindi, Urdu, Chinese, but they also speak Burmese as a common language of trade and commerce conducting daily businesses. Many, if not most, are

---

[1] *Tea Circle Oxford.* Matthew J. Walton, Matt Schissler, and Phyu Phyu Thi: "'Peace Memories' in *Myanmar*", April 21, 2017.

given legal status and citizenship, even if they practice a different faith and follow other religions, traditions and customs.

There were other religions in this is predominantly Buddhist nation, and Rangoon was once one of the most liberal cosmopolitan cities in the region, a thriving multi-cultural city with churches, temples, mosques and synagogues. According to the 2016 published national census, the population comprised 6.2% Christians, 4.3% Muslims, and 0.5% Hindus.[1] Today there are splendid Buddhist shrines, fine mosques, churches with magnificent steeples, elaborate Hindu temples, Joss houses, synagogues and other gathering places of worship in the same cities. In parts of Burma, Buddhists who are predominantly *Bamar* ethnicity coexist with the Muslims without serious conflict, even though there are regional differences, each with different needs, aspirations, goals and challenges. Many other minority religions also coexist with the Buddhists and conduct businesses daily with one another openly and freely. They intermarry and many are citizens, including Muslims. Peace can be achieved and multiple religions of all faiths can coexist in harmony as represented in other parts of Burma and under different administrative rule. Not everyone in Arakan is a militant Muslim. Why are these *Bengali* Muslims discriminated against? Why are the *Rohingyas* not entitled citizenship when other Muslims in other parts of Burma are granted citizenship with equal rights?

---

[1] *The Irrawaddy.* Tin Htet Paing: "Nationalists Oppose NGO's Curriculum for Including Religious Education", March 7, 2017.

Chapter 11. The Exodus

Ethnic Cleansing and Genocide

In 2017, the crisis in Arakan reached unprecedented proportions, forcing roughly three quarters of a million Muslim minority to flee from their villages across the river to Bangladesh. It is estimated over a million have so far been displaced from Arakan, fled across the border, and are forced to live in disease-ridden makeshift camps in Bangladesh. UN has labeled the military crackdown a 'textbook example of ethnic cleansing' and some even described the abuses as war crimes against humanity and genocide.

These attacks destabilized the fragile transition to democratic civilian administration in Burma. There was no one strong voice or leadership other than *Aung San Suu Kyi* who seemed unwilling to speak up loud enough for the Muslim minority. As an MP and leader of the civilian government, she was now part of the establishment. Arakan state had caught global attention in 2017 after the mass exodus of Muslims fleeing the Burmese military crackdown in response to ARSA militant attacks. The same year Kofi Annan, then UN Secretary General, and its Advisory Commission visited the conflict zone in Arakan. The Commission proposed several long term solutions to resolve conflict issues and urged the Burmese government, among other recommendations to grant citizenship to children of *Bengali/Rohingya* born in the state. Further, the Commission suggested amendment of the existing citizenship law to be in line with international standards and norms.

The military supported USDP strongly rejected Kofi Annan Advisory Commission's suggestions stating prioritizing human rights over national security would threaten Burma's sovereignty but *Aung San Suu Kyi* and her civilian government agreed to implement the Commission's recommendations. The US, UK, Australia, Indonesia, Turkey, and Germany also supported the full implementation of the Advisory Commission's recommendations. The ten member international advisory board was formed to support *Aung San Suu Kyi* with counsel for genuine policy changes addressing peace and stability in the Arakan crisis. The state counselor has endorsed the 88 recommendations of Kofi Annan although the army chief criticized several recommendations of the report. Government's plans were underway to form a new committee to accelerate the national verification process for the minority Muslim and to provide equal access to education and healthcare regardless of religion, race, citizenship or gender. Months went by and as summer of 2018 rolled in, few of the recommendations have been implemented.

Meanwhile back in northern Arakan within hours of the release of the Commission's report, ARSA attacked 30 police stations and an army base of the Burmese military. In retaliation the Burma army launched an all-out counter attack creating large scale war zone violence and triggering the biggest mass fleeing of hundreds of thousands of predominantly minority Muslims across the border to Bangladesh. The army's stated goal and justification for the excessive counter attack was to protect the country and safeguard its territorial integrity and national security. Several thousand *Tatmadaw* soldiers and security forces retaliated against ARSA's series of coordinated militant attacks with full military might and unrestrained military force killing villagers, both Muslims and Buddhists, and savagely crushing anyone in their way. Many unarmed villagers were caught up in the deadly crossfire. Collateral casualties were heavy as both sides did not, could not, or would not distinguish between insurgents and villagers, or terrorists and civilians.

Tatmadaw and ARSA accused each other of setting the fires and burning down the houses. Journalists who risked their lives met with and interviewed many sources including Arakanese Buddhists, Muslims and Hindus who confirmed that arson was carried out by both sides. In some instances, to complicate the matter further, there were locals acting as vigilantes and taking justice into their own hands.

All media sources have to be kept confidential as witnesses risked their lives and many have been beheaded in the past when suspected of speaking with the authorities, the Muslim militia, or the media. Many informants were also executed by ARSA. Fleeing Muslim minority and human rights watchers said the Burmese military and security forces deliberately set fire to buildings, houses, and shops to drive out the Muslims.[1] Satellite images from Human Rights Watch confirmed the account. Some claimed Arakanese Buddhist vigilantes were also involved in a campaign of arson to drive out the Muslims.

The military claimed the culprits were ARSA terrorists and that many Muslim militants also participated and were guilty of arson. Within ten days of the clashes, at least 500 people have been killed in the conflict zone. The number of Muslim refugees fleeing across the border to predominantly Muslim Bangladesh grew quickly from 200,000 to 370,000 within days, over 400,000 within a few weeks and over 500,000 rapidly climbing to over 660,000 before the attacks deescalated but continued. In the chaos an estimated 30,000 Arakanese Buddhists and Hindus have also been internally displaced and evacuated. The intensity and scale of this violence was alarming the UN and the international community as the crisis reached unprecedented proportions and magnitude with headlines flashing across the world. The violence not only consumed Arakan state but has engulfed the entire geopolitical region.

The UN is considering taking R2P (Responsibility to Protect) action to stop 'genocide' and mass atrocity crimes of total destruction of a national, ethnic, racial or religious group. Hundreds of thousands have fled their homes and tens of thousands have been reported lost and presumed dead in this killing field of Arakan. The international community was outraged and vowed to take action to stop the barbaric acts. However, China with its massive economic and geopolitical interests in Burma and in competition for geopolitical influence with the US in the region, will defend Burma at the UNSC. Both Moscow and Beijing backed the all-out military operations with disproportionate force in Arakan in the name of counter terrorism attacks.

ARSA declared a ceasefire for a month, but the government did not recognize it dismissing them as terrorist groups. ARSA has threatened to attack again after the month long ceasefire expired and this was driving the continued mass exit of refugees as more people abandoned and left their villages for fear of another series of ARSA attacks and *Tatmadaw* all out violent retaliation. Some villagers were forced to join the militants and fought against *Tatmadaw* forces while many were manipulated and threatened to leave their villages by ARSA. Those with relatives already living in Bangladesh went to join them. Meanwhile the military operations continued. The West began to impose restrictions and bans on the Burmese military.

---

[1] *Reuters.* "Rohingya Muslims Flee as More than 2,600 Houses Burned in *Myanmar's Rakhine*", September 2, 2017.

By the end of October the US rescinded invitations for high level Burmese military officers to travel to the US and was considering other action such as imposing asset freezes, visa bans and prohibiting US citizens from doing business with the military leaders. The civilian government of *Aung San Suu Kyi* declared ARSA as a terrorist group, meaning that the violence and mass killing in Arakan state was no longer a domestic issue and that it has reached the international stage. The Arakan conflict was more than just an internal crisis as the minority Muslims were fleeing as refugees and asylum seekers in neighboring countries of Bangladesh, India, Pakistan, Malaysia, and Indonesia. The plight of these Muslims could possibly engender more insurgencies against Burma's security forces and even extend southeast to the terrorist domain of jihadist groups in other Muslim dominant countries. Recently an *al Qaeda* leader has called for attacks on Burmese authorities and hundreds of Muslim activists protested at Burmese embassy in Jakarta.[1] *Al Qaeda* militants were urging Muslims in Bangladesh, Pakistan, India and elsewhere around the world to support the Muslim *Rohingya* with humanitarian aid or with guns and weapons.

As Burma's de facto leader, *Aung San Suu Kyi* must bear the brunt of international condemnation for her sustained silence. The army's violent attacks on ethnic minorities in bordering states has eroded the people's trust and respect for her. As champion of peace and non-violent fight for democracy she has failed to speak out overlooking the atrocities committed against the Muslim minority. She condones the gross human rights violations of Burmese military against a minority population. As international pressure increased so were mounting calls from protesters for the withdrawal of her Nobel Peace Prize. Several Nobel laureates suggested international support and financial aid to the Burmese government should be conditional on a major positive policy shift towards the Muslim minority in Arakan. The Indonesian President has sent his foreign minister to urge the Burmese government to end human rights violations against the *Rohingya*.[2] The burning of villages and indiscriminate killing was condemned by All *Myanmar* Islamic Religious Organization, the national Islamic organization in Rangoon who pledged collaboration with the government and interfaith groups to end these inhumane acts. Where is the international peace icon that represents non-violence and human rights? The one who professes love and kindness of Buddhism? Is all that traded for cooperation with the military? Has power

---

[1] *Reuters.* "*Myanmar* Urges *Rohingya* Muslims to Help Hunt Insurgents amid Deadly Violence", September 3, 2017.
[2] *Reuters.* "Indonesian Envoy to Urge *Myanmar* to Halt Violence against *Rohingya* Muslims", September 3, 2017.

and position taken a higher priority over the horrific abuses of some three quarters of a million people?

Although the US in the past has strongly spoken in support of *Aung San Suu Kyi* and Burma's transition to democratic rule, with continued conflict in Arakan state Washington was considering to end the proposed expansion of military-to-military engagement. Deputy Assistant Secretary of State for Southeast Asia Patrick Murphy visited Burma after a month of the crisis. British government also proposed suspension of its officer training program with Burmese military, and Australia and France have called for the end of military operations. In December 2017 US imposed sanctions on thirteen serious human rights abusers including General *Maung Maung Soe*. Although the military denied all allegations against it, the general was replaced in the midst of the crisis without giving any reason. The US announced sanctions on Commander-in-Chief *Min Aung Hlaing*, his deputy General *Soe Win* and two senior commanders Brigadier Generals *Than Oo* and *Aung Aung* and their families, barring them from entry to the United States. Governments of the 'free world' that condemn human rights transgression should not trade freely with the government of Burma.

The Burmese government blocked Dr. Yanghee Lee, the UN special rapporteur, from visiting Burma again because they didn't like what she said in her findings. This is a sign of disrespect, an insult to Professor Lee, who is a reputable respected independent auditor with expertise in international human rights work. Meanwhile, the Burmese military signed an agreement with India to train *Tatmadaw* officers and for them to study in Indian military academies. China and Russia were also open to train Burmese officers as they have in the past while fresh human rights violations and continued abuses were being reported.

Thousands of Muslim fleeing Burma to Bangladesh ended up in make-shift camps of plastic sheeting and tree branches. They faced another hurdle as stateless refugees in no man's land, as both countries regard them as the other country's nationals. *Tatmadaw* soldiers have been seen installing land-mines to prevent the refugees from returning. Even those who made it across into Bangladesh faced being sent back to the killing fields, despite UN pleas to grant safe shelter and humanitarian support to the refugees. They were caught between a country that wanted them out and one that did not want them in.

Due to grossly unsanitary living conditions, those who ended up in these camps continued to suffer, not only hardship and lack of food and water, but illnesses and tropical diseases without any available medicine. International aid programs such as World Food Program (which provided essential aid and life saving food assistance) have been suspended due to the renewed fighting.

Journalist Bertil Lintner estimated ARSA to be about 500 fighters strong[1] and reported ARSA has connections with foreign extremist groups and a Pakistani named *Abdus Qadoos Burmi* has called for jihad in Burma on social media. Other reports stated ARSA was using children and women as human shields. ARSA wanted *Tatmadaw* to respond to its attacks with its full military might to create criticism against the Burma army from the UN and the international community. *Tatmadaw* reported ARSA has established a '*Rohingya*-only area' in the region destabilizing the situation and threatening national security. Media and political analysts believe blanket counter terrorist attacks as military response alone would not solve the crisis. The Belgium-based ICG also stated a disproportionate military response without any overarching political strategy would play directly into ARSA's hands as in October last year.[2] The crisis in Arakan state has reached a scale of monumental proportion in terms of intensity, casualty and scope.

And it isn't just the Muslims; the Burma army is now attacking the Arakanese Buddhists as well. A wave of violence began in 2019 between another armed ethnic group Arakan Army and *Tatmadaw* and has continued with increasing intensity and casualty. In 2019, AA, comprised of 7,000 member strong ethnic *Bamar* Arakanese Buddhists attacked police outposts in Arakan causing thousands more villagers to flee from their homes and plunging the state into deeper war zone mired in violent conflict. AA formed in 2009, is a Buddhist insurgent group who recruits and trains Arakanese Buddhists and is fighting for an independent Arakan waging wars against Burma army and security forces, adding another complicated dimension to the already complex conflict zone in the state.

Domestic Affair

Tatmadaw, the NLD civilian government and the people of Burma increasingly feel the current criticism from the global community against the Burmese government's handling of the Arakan crisis is unfair, unfounded and one sided. They say the West does not understand the historical, political, racial, and religious complexities of the situation and declare they don't need Western help to solve internal crisis. They say the Arakan crisis is a domestic affair and don't want any Western or external foreign interference.

---

[1] *The Irrawaddy.* Bertil Lintner: "ARSA Linked to Foreign Extremist Groups", September 22, 2017.

[2] *The Irrawaddy.* "*Rakhine* Attacks: How Should the Military and Government Respond?", September 2, 2017.

True, that is their right just as others have rights as well. Rights are respected and honored as long as they are reasonably free of biases and emotionally charged prejudices. The authoritarian leaders of *Tatmadaw* seem to believe they can do whatever they want to do within their own borders in the name of protecting the nation's sovereignty. Diplomacy and soft words from the free world fall on deaf ears with *Tatmadaw* and embolden them to continue the violence and commit crimes against the Muslims in Arakan. Blanket denial of the heinous acts committed in the region as fake news would produce no solution to peace. Lack of transparent and objective third party investigation only result in condemning and finger pointing at one another. *Tatmadaw* leaders, the military backed USDP and the militant Buddhist group *Ma Ba Tha* strongly object to foreign interference and Burmese government declared they would do their own investigations. Would you ask a criminal to investigate his own crime? This would be the equivalent to the fox guarding the hen house. To be credible the investigation process must be unbiased and independent using international standards for collecting evidence. We cannot sit back and do nothing when people are being slaughtered and violently violated. In the chaos of killing and burning that took place in Arakan no one knows for sure what happened in the weeks and months following the crisis but overwhelming evidence shows soldiers and security forces were involved in the burning, murdering and raping of villagers. True, there were other criminal elements from ARSA, armed militants, and other rebellion activists so it would be incorrect to say the military is 100% responsible. But everyone knows *Tatmadaw*'s actions drove hundreds of thousands unarmed villagers out of the country and thousands have died in the days following the crisis. We must each feel a deep concern and powerful compassion for the suffering humanity and do our part to end the utter savagery and meaninglessness of this ordeal.

The world today is much more globalized than in 1962 or 1988. No country can ignore the implications of international relations especially with global powers and survive in self isolation. The Arakan crisis of 2017 deteriorated Burma's relationship not just with the West but the international communities as a whole as terrorism and counter insurgency attacks became a reality. Past efforts by UN to end the atrocities failed mainly due to Chinese and Russian support for Burma's military and their vote within the UN Security Council to oppose any punishment of the military regime.

This time the government of Burma again looked to China for continued support within the UNSC. However, for Burma, financial and humanitarian aid from international donors, the UN, and NGOs are a significant consideration and it needs to balance its relations between China and the West.

Although China and Russia had been key supporters of past Burma military regimes in foreign investments, weapon deals, and protection from UN punitive action, Burma's dependence on these two eastern blocs significantly reduced in 2011 when *Thein Sein's* quasi civilian government took over. Since, the relationship with the West improved dramatically attracting a flood of new foreign investment from Europe and the US. But the unprecedented violence and savagery that began in August 2017 got the world's attention and have outraged the international communities. The UN has suspended its humanitarian assistance and related operations in Arakan since the crisis began due to accusations from the Burmese government that the UN was supporting 'Rohingya insurgents', thus leaving Red Cross as the only major provider of humanitarian aid to the state. Western support has declined, sanctions re engaged, and travel bans and criminal action against the senior generals imposed. The global reputation of the civilian government and the military have been severely damaged, trade negotiations suspended, and economic development through foreign investment has nearly ceased.

With perspective on democracy and human rights the goal of the international community is to increase humanitarian aid and access to the refugees, to investigate atrocities, and to repatriate them back to their homes in Arakan. The US, UK, Japan, and other European and Southeast Asian countries are coordinating their collective response to the crisis agreeing to target punitive action on the military chief and its generals. The West must find a balance in its disciplinary measures against Burma as too severe correction could force the Burmese military to turn to China for stronger diplomatic, economic and military support. Under most recent international pressure Burma is turning again to China with increasing economic and military cooperation. Both China and Russia have veto powers in the UN Security Council. The leverage of the US and Europe is limited due to their relatively small economic and military engagement with Burma. They intervene on human rights grounds and provide humanitarian aid in the name of democracy, freedom and equality. Burma should exercise caution before sliding into a total return to dependence on its next door neighbor for diplomatic protection. A better option is to balance its strategic relationship with world leading powers for continued aid, economic and diplomatic support; improve relationship with the Muslim world to prevent attacks from militant jihadist groups and terrorist organizations; and to repatriate refugees giving them a genuine stake in the country's future.

Sanctions

Since the 2017 crisis erupted in Arakan, the international community has been awakened to the plight of the minority Muslims on a grand scale. *Tatmadaw*'s excessive military counter terrorism attacks against ARSA militants only goaded them to strike back harder with both sides destroying and killing unarmed villagers for months following the initial attack and counterattack. US, UK and EU are considering reimposing sanctions targeting the military and *Tatmadaw* leaders that most likely would affect the relationships between the Burmese military and the West and the international community.

Decades of past sanctions had not been effective with the Burmese military as the generals were no stranger to Western punitive measures. Since the early 1990s, the EU had imposed sanctions including an arms embargo and visa bans on senior level military officers and their families. The US even blacklisted former dictator Senior General *Than Shwe*, his generals and crony business allies, but these sanctions were lifted when the quasi civilian government of President *Thein Sein* took over in 2011. In reality sanctions never hurt the generals and their billionaire crony allies. They may only negatively impact the image of a military institution in the eyes of the global community. This time leaders of the world pressured to hold powerful military generals accountable for barbaric acts against Arakan Muslims. The UN mission called for military chief *Min Aung Hlaing* and five other generals to be prosecuted under international law for crimes against humanity for gang rapes and mass killings with genocidal intent. SE Asian nations also wanted those responsible for the atrocities held accountable and punished and Muslim majority nations are demanding criminal charges and punitive measures against the generals of the military. EU extended its arms embargo against Burma and sanctions against individual army officials. Switzerland also added sanctions banning the military generals already imposed by the EU. All were accused of acts of brutality against the Muslim minority in Arakan by the EU as well as human rights groups including Amnesty International. The US have already imposed sanctions on a key army general and have scaled back already limited military ties with *Tatmadaw*. Later seven more generals and eleven officers were added to the US sanction list.

In September 2019, the US House of Representatives passed the Burma Act holding *Tatmadaw* military leaders accountable for human rights abuses and crimes committed against the ethnic minorities and to provide humanitarian assistance in Arakan, Kachin, and Shan states.[1] The Burmese government continued to deny entry to UN investigators and rejected their findings, insisting that government security forces conducted a legitimate counter attack operation to wipe out terrorists.

The US team investigated the atrocities, with over 1,025 interviews with refugees who escaped across Naf River and are living in refugee camps. The US also used statistical data analysis tools to accurately decipher conclusions about the perpetrators, their methods and patterns of crime so that the world could seek justice and accountability. After a thorough investigation and refugee interviews, the US government released a 20-page report showing a pattern of planning and premeditation of large scale and a widespread campaign to terrorize and drive out the Muslim minority.

About 80 percent of refugees surveyed said they witnessed a killing, most often by military or police, including soldiers killing infants and small children, the shooting of unarmed men, and victims buried alive or thrown into pits of mass graves. Some were captured and mutilated including the cutting and spreading of entrails, severed limbs or hands and feet, pulling out nails or burning beards and genitals to force a confession, or being burned alive. Girls were abducted, tied up with ropes and raped for days and then left half dead. Facebook shut down more than 60 pages and 20 accounts including that of the army chief, Senior General *Min Aung Hlaing,* who contributed to human rights abuses. The military under *Min Aung Hlaing* is no longer isolated as previous dictatorial regimes, hence, much more assertive and vocal on mass media. These organizations and individuals are responsible for spreading military viewpoints and misinformation on social media without support of reliable independent research.

Facebook has been the main communication tool for the army chief with the people of Burma and is the primary official channel for news releases in the country. It is a powerful communication channel used by the military and its supporters to disseminate hate speech, inflame ethnic and religious tensions, incite violence and spread false rumors to the public.

New sanctions from the West pushed the regime closer to China and the generals continued to prosper, selling raw material to neighboring countries to lessen the impact of Western pressure. They diversified trading partners and established even stronger economic and political ties with China, India and other Asian countries that did not impose sanctions. Economic sanctions only impact ordinary people as factories slow down production and

---

[1] *Burma Unified through Rigorous Military Accountability Act of 2019 or the BURMA Act of 2019.* H.R.3190 — 116th Congress (2019-2020) Passed House (09/24/2019). ‹https://www.congress.gov/bill/116th-congress/house-bill/3190›

lay off workers. People have become disappointed by the economic down-turn resulting from Western sanctions and this has gradually diminished the popularity of the NLD administration. Meanwhile support for *Tatmadaw* would likely increase, making the fragile democratic transition more difficult. With the World Bank withholding US$200 million and declining foreign aid and investment, Burma's economic development would probably be negatively impacted as well. Neither China nor India joined in the Western condemnation for obvious strategic, political and economic reasons. For China, Burma is vital for its access to the Indian Ocean. For India, Burma is the gateway to Southeast Asia.

The Two-Headed Beast

The state counselor and the army chief were never known to have a good relationship and the civilian government never did see eye to eye with the army. In her speeches and campaigns prior to the 2015 election, *Aung San Sui Kyi* had asserted that achieving peace was a top priority of her government and vowed to continue democratic reforms and end the country's decades of civil wars. As much as she would like to see peace during her current govern-ment term the probability was appearing dim. The relationship between *Aung San Sui Kyi* and army chief *Min Aung Hlaing* has deteriorated further and the trust and confidence between the state counselor and ethnic leaders has also eroded.

She knew she had to get along with the generals, and so she has resigned herself to building a culture of consensus with them, avoiding a confronta-tion. She must cooperate and support the system and accept the status quo. People are becoming disillusioned with her administration as the conflict in Burma's north and west has intensified since her government took over. All ethnic minorities lost hope and confidence in her and her international popularity was also evaporating. But *Aung San Sui Kyi* knows she has her father's great name, the most valuable and priceless asset. With that name and as the daughter of *Bogyoke Aung San,* she will continue to inspire devotion among many ordinary citizens.

Even so, she has been criticized for her arrogance and perception of herself as above others. But unlike her father General *Aung San* she has no executive power and has no control over the armed forces. *Tatmadaw* still controls the three key ministries of defense, home, and border affairs, and a quarter of parliament seats, thanks to the 2008 constitution the generals have struc-tured. *Tatmadaw* not only firmly supported a strong military solution to the Arakan crisis, the same former military men who now occupied high level parliament positions also opposed any in-depth inquiry into rights abuses demanded by the international community. Everyone in the government supported *Tatmadaw's* actions and use of excessive security forces against the minority and no one questioned the army's conduct. Any investigation of any military action would be done by the military instead of a third party raising serious conflict of interest issues and credibility of the investigation process.

Aung San Suu Kyi has filled ministerial and other senior level positions based on trust and loyalty rather than knowledge and skills needed to rebuild the country. Her appointees are people who have served her well as loyal supporters of the NLD party but as cabinet ministers, her appointees have been ineffective. They were unprepared to tackle the country's economic, legislative, political and social challenges and have not been able to bridge the gap between *Tatmadaw* and civil society, or to negotiate effectively on ethnic issues and national reconciliation. Additionally many former military officers occupy powerful positions in the current ministries who are capable of blocking or at least hindering the civilian government's action for change. *Aung San Sui Kyi's* ministers have been accused of being media shy or intimidated as the newly elected NLD government issued a ban preventing lawmakers and MPs from speaking to the media, while parts of the parliament are off limits to journalists and reporters. As the state counselor 'above the president' and as the minister of everything, she runs her party with total autocratic control.

On the military side, the army is here to stay, both in the government and in politics. *Tatmadaw* chief Senior General *Min Aung Hlaing*, relatively unknown outside of Burma, is now calling the shots. No one knows for sure how many former army officers are holding civilian posts and in control of the ministries of the NLD government. Observers report an estimated 75% parliamentarians in the civilian administration are former military officers of the previous regime. Tension and conflicting policies between *Aung San Suu Kyi* and the General *Min Aung Hlaing* are major challenges to collaboration and their relationship continues to deteriorate with disagreement regarding foreign participation in what the military considers domestic affairs. The two-tier civilian/military decision-making organization structure is an uneasy partnership like dealing with a two headed beast, each one wanting to go a different, sometimes opposite, direction. The divergent goals and approaches of the two leaders complicate issues facing the nation. The military supported by USDP will safeguard the 2008 constitution it has written while *Aung San Suu Kyi's* civilian government wants to amend it to more democratic terms.

The two sides are therefore in direct conflict. Until the two government heads of Burma share the same vision for the future of the country, it would be difficult to find common ground resolution to issues that have plagued the country for generations.

In February 2017, ten Arakan Muslim men and boys were hacked to death by Buddhist villagers and security force members. The bodies were found buried in a mass grave. Witnesses who confirmed the accounts included not only the Muslim refugees but also the Burmese army soldiers, police officers and local Buddhists who admitted to participating in the bloody murder.[1] Two Reuters journalists *Ko Wa Lone* and *Ko Kyaw Soe Oo* risked their lives to investigate and expose the massacre. Instead of applauding them for their courage, they were framed, charged and sentenced to seven years imprisonment. *Aung San Suu Kyi* did not object, which may be interpreted as a tacit approval to hush the truth.

Exercising freedom of speech including exposing the truth or criticism of those in power is not a crime. It is the essence of democratic principle. Dissent is not a crime and those who speak out against powerful people of authority are not criminals. They should be lauded, not incarcerated. Under global pressure from the international community, the Burmese government launched an investigation into the killings and declared dismissal of seven unnamed soldiers from the military 'with ten-year sentence of prison with hard labor for their involvement in the murder'. Two prison officials and two fellow inmates told Reuters the seven imprisoned soldiers were well-known among prisoners and were kept in separate cells provided with prison banned indulgences like beer and cigarettes.[2] The seven were released six months later while *Wa Lone* and *Kyaw Soe Oo* spent 17 months in prison for reporting the killings. After more than 500 days behind bars they were released from prison in a presidential pardon around the Burmese New Year, *Thingyan*. Is it a gesture of renewed commitment to press freedom? Critics believe the release was deeply entwined with political preoccupations and a political motivation for the 2020 election. Not everyone who voted *Aung San Suu Kyi* into power in 2016 is blindly devoted to her. Peace seems elusive as ever. The crisis in Arakan continues while the economy weakens and foreign investment plunges. A small but growing movement of young activists is emerging who are disenchanted with *Aung San Suu Kyi* for her handling of ethnic minorities in Kachin and Shan states and the Arakan crisis. They also claim her government is becoming more authoritarian, beating and jailing

---

[1] *Reuters.* "US Team in Refugee Camps Investigating Atrocities Against *Rohingya*", April 26, 2018.

[2] *Reuters.* Shoon Naing and Simon Lewis: "*Myanmar* Soldiers Jailed for *Rohingya* Killings Freed after Less Than A Year", May 26, 2019.

protesters and journalists.[1] During the most recent Burmese New Year the young student activists sprung up into action by conducting traditional *Thingyan* performances to highlight current political situations in satirical performances and jokes. They were charged with defamation under the Telecommunication Law and arrested and imprisoned with a potential two year jail term plus penalty.

---

[1] *Reuters.* Shoon Naing and Poppy McPherson: "Lost idol: New Wave of *Myanmar* Youth Activists Look Beyond *Suu Kyi*", December 1, 2018.

Chapter 12. The Civil War

Complexities of Civil War

Burma has a highly complex mix of ethnic and religious minorities; more than 30 percent of the population represent non *Bamar* ethnic groups and sub groups who live in remote rural parts of the country. The north and northeast border regions of Kachin and Shan states have been unstable since Burma's independence. First, the British separated ethnic minorities and the *Bamar* or Burman majority, as they viewed the latter as rebellious and disloyal. They also recruited and trained ethnic minorities to serve in the colonial army, creating division between the majority *Bamar* and the minorities. Colonialism not only destroyed the unity of the nation but created an anti-ethnic nationalism among the majority *Bamar* people.

True, the colonial government enacted laws to stifle dissent but post colonialism, an independent government of Burma should not use these repressive laws against its own citizens. Regardless of religious and cultural differences all ethnic nationalities – *Bamar*, Shan, Kachin, Karen, Chin and other minorities are equal citizens. To build a democracy these archaic laws and legislation of the colonial era need to be amended as they no longer fit the goals of democracy of today. After independence, General *Aung San* signed the *Panglong* agreement with ethnic leaders to build a federal union after ten years on the principle of equal political rights for all nationalities. The Ethnic Armed Organizations, EAOs, and the people want separatism, self-determination, equal rights, human rights and citizen rights, not just gender equality as discussed at peace negotiations. The *Panglong* agreement was never honored by General *Ne Win* or his successive military regimes. For decades all military regimes discriminated against ethnic and religious minorities and the hope of secession for ethnic minorities along with the stated equal rights was doomed ever since. The armed struggle between *Tatmadaw* and the EAOs is one of the longest running civil wars of the century lasting seventy years at this writing but international awareness of these domestics wars was limited or none until recently. For over half a century these remote ethnic regions were inaccessible due to government restrictions and the regime's self-isolation from the world making it difficult for journalists, human right organizations, the UN, NGOs or any interested party to gain deeper understanding of Burma's civil war. In addition to decades of restricted access to the conflict zones, reliable data and statistics of conflict were unavailable. Ceasefire between *Tatmadaw* and the ethnic groups has been unsustainable and peace process with ethnic minority nationalities less than effective. The civil war between *Tatmadaw* and 20 or so armed ethnic groups continues today and numerous ceasefire proposals and peace conferences have taken place without success.

Bogyoke Aung San had pledged equality for all nationalities, but his promise remains unfulfilled. *Tatmadaw* became an enemy of all ethnic nationalities, an occupying army in their ancestral land. The new civilian government of *Aung San Suu Kyi* seems unable or unwilling to stop the abuses and the fighting. Intensified clashes between *Tatmadaw* and ethnic armed groups erode confidence in the Lady. They also raise international concern posing a serious challenge to *Aung San Suu Kyi* who swept to power in 2015 on promises of national reconciliation and peace.

It remains unclear how the armed struggle between the military and the EAOs can be resolved to the satisfaction of both sides. Religion, ethnic racism and Buddhist nationalism are tightly intertwined in this civil war and supernatural thinking is deeply rooted in ethnic culture and in the form of worship. Tangled into this web of complexity is the deep seated *Bamar* superiority complex over other ethnics. This delusion even justifies the *Bamar* Nobel laureate to remain silent or look the other way in the face of rising violence as the world watches the defiance of respect for human rights. In addition to deep rooted multi-ethnic, multicultural, and multi-religious differences among heterogeneous people in a pluralistic society, it also involves control of natural resources.

Both *Tatmadaw* and the local armed EAOs profit from the mining and extraction of oil, gas, gemstones, jade, gold, precious metals, minerals and tropical hardwood timber found in these remote hilly regions. Opium and methamphetamine production is another source of cash. Ethnic minority farmers in Shan and Kachin states resorted to opium poppy cultivation as the only sustainable cash crop for food security and survival. Poppy fields are controlled by opium kings, many in partnership with the regime. The drug money not only funds rebel armies and camps but *Tatmadaw* also directly profits from it and therefore has little incentive to stop the cultivation in these remote poppy growing regions. No one has a real incentive to end the conflict, so the fighting continues to this day as one the longest civil wars in the world.

Among the various armed ethnic groups there are different and often conflicting goals, political motivations, and leadership styles that further fragment the alliances. Peace talks between *Naypyidaw*, NLD government and ethnic resistance armies have been less than effective while economic and humanitarian conditions have not improved. The military and the civilian government share different views and interpretations of the meaning and definition of self-determination, federalism, and non-secession terms. So do the various armed ethnic armies. Decades of negotiation have not worked and now, under *Aung San Suu Kyi's* leadership, the peace process is floundering.

Meanwhile, UN remains ineffective with its own internal scandals with envoys criticized for accepting lavish gifts from the government and some accused of conflict of interest involving in lucrative business deals. Funding from the West is squandered away on meaningless peace projects without real peace building or any benefit to the villagers facing the refugee crisis in the conflict zones. The hope of any armed conflict resolution and national reconciliation toward building a democratic federal union seems as remote as ever today in the country at war with its own people. Peace remains even more elusive in Burma's borderland under the new democratic civilian government.

There are over 20 armed ethnic organizations in Burma and not all armed ethnic groups have agreed to participate in government proposed peace talks or signed the Nationwide Ceasefire Agreement, NCA initiated by President *Thein Sein's* government in 2015. Originally 16 groups signed the first draft in 2015 but some have dropped out. So far only eight of more than twenty ethnic groups have agreed to sign the finalized NCA so far.[1] Two of the most powerful groups, FPNCC, Federal Political Negotiation and Consultative Committee, the seven-member northern alliance led by the United *Wa* State

---

[1] The eight groups who have signed the NCA are: *All Burma Students Democratic Front, ABSDF; Arakan Liberation Party, ALP; Chin National Front, CNF; Karen National Union, KNU; Democratic Karen Benevolent Army (Karen National Liberation Army), KNU/KNLA; Pa-O National Liberation Organization, PONL; Democratic Karen Buddhist Army, DKBA; and Restoration Council of Shan State/Shan State Army-South, RCSS/SSA.* By early 2018 two more signatories were added to the NCA.

Army in the northeast, and UNFC, United Nationalities Federal Council, the five-member alliance based in the southeast have yet to sign the NCA. Also abstained from signing the NCA are the United *Wa* State Army, believed to be the largest armed ethnic group, and the Kachin Independence Organization, KIO. They refrained due to government's refusal to acknowledge three other ethnic armed groups, the *Myanmar* National Democratic Alliance Army, the Arakan Army, and the *Ta'ang* National Liberation Army. By summer 2018 at *Panglong* 21, only ten EAOs have signed the NCA. Ending the seventy-year-old civil conflict and achieving peace with the EAOs seem far-fetched without meaningful collective negotiation. EAOs are also not unified with conflicting agendas and goals with vast differences between and within groups. Although a coalition of major armed ethnic groups exists within the armed rebellion factions, there are many smaller less organized groups with widespread aspirations and sometimes, conflicting agendas and political motivations, incompatibilities and fragmented strategies. Each group has a different survival strategy, living in vastly different geographical regions with different political and economic goals. Even within same groups disagreements among factional leaders due to different policy approaches and leadership styles can result in internal battles, divisions and assassinations. Internal power struggles are common and lead to splits within organizations and fragmentation of groups. Some switched sides and left to join opposition groups. Often internal divisions and in-fighting among groups or clashes between two armed ethnic groups over territorial disputes occur, compounding the difficulty to reach any consensus or agreement for government dialog and peace talks. The disunity among the many EAOs makes peace negotiation process much more challenging. Not every ethnic armed organization is genuinely seeking peace with the *Bamar* central government as their survival goals are not the same. *Tatmadaw* also sees them as armed rebels wanting to break away from the country, to separate from the Union and a threat to its sovereignty. The military insists on one army, namely, the Burma army or *Tatmadaw*, for the whole country. The army also requires non-secession assurance from all EAOs even though the 1947 *Panglong* agreement provided secession option ten years after independence. None of the ethnic nationalities can accept both terms without adjustments, equality guarantee and negotiations. The EAOs never accepted the army written 2008 constitution as it was drawn up without any input or ethnic participation. Minority ethnic nationalities want more than just working toward a ceasefire. They are demanding local autonomy and federalism from the central government, but neither side has clearly defined what a federal union means. What is the distribution of power and the relationship between different levels of government? How do democracy, freedom, equality and self-determination fit within federalism context? Instead, both Burma army and EAOs blame each other for lack of trust and genuine interest for peace. By mid 2017 the military, the civilian government, parliament, political parties, and participating ethnic armed groups reached partial agreement on terms of the NCA but exclude non-secession from the Union, federalism, equality, and self-determination.

Due to the unprecedented Arakan crisis of 2017, the international focus has shifted from the civil war between *Tatmadaw* and the EAOs. Armed conflict with *Tatmadaw* actually intensified since NLD government took office and heightened rural insurgency is renewed. The number of human rights violations almost doubled, from 84 in 2015 to 154 documented in 2016, due to escalation of conflict between *Tatmadaw* and ethnic armed groups in Kachin and Shan states. Hundreds of villagers are still being killed or injured by landmines buried in these regions, with about 150,000 internally displaced people, IDPs in more than 160 camps scattered in areas under the control of either the Burmese army or EAO groups. Additionally, more than 110,000 IDPs live in camps in Karen and Karenni (*Kayah* in Burmese) states in the southeast and another 100,000 refugees live on Thai–Burma border. The numbers do not include human rights abuses of the Muslim minority in Arakan state, otherwise they would be enormous. *Tatmadaw* projects itself 'as savior of the country,' giving it every right to shoot and kill anyone deemed 'the enemy' or perpetrator, in the name of protection of national security and the sovereignty of Burma. Meanwhile, all stakeholders, domestic and foreign, political parties, civil organizations, the government, the army, EAOs and the international community cannot seem to corroborate, participate and contribute toward finding resolution to end this prolonged violence.

China's Role in Burma's Peace

Immediately following World War II, civil war broke out in China between the Chinese Communist Party, CCP and the Nationalist Party, or Kuomintang (KMT). The Communists defeated the KMT, leading to the fall of mainland China to communism in 1949. This led the US to suspend diplomatic ties with China and to support the KMT, both as its former war ally and as the sole option for preventing Communist control of China. The KMT fled across the border into Burma and established stronghold bases in the hills of the northeastern Shan state occupied by the ethnic *Wa* people.[1] Burma was also invaded by *Mao's* communist forces.

---

[1] *The Irrawaddy*. Bertil Lintner: "Who Are The *Wa*?", May 26, 2017.

After Burma's independence from the British, the Nationalist Chinese KMT continued to thrive in the densely forested impenetrable *Wa* hills and began to fight the Burmese Communist Party insurgents who were supported and equipped by communist China. China has actively supported the Burmese Communist Party, BCP, since independence and during *Ne Win's* era in the 60s and 70s. The Chinese communists poured arms and weapons to help the BCP insurgents in their armed struggle against *Tatmadaw*. China not only provided BCP with rockets and machine guns, armored trucks and tanks, radio and anti-aircraft equipment and air defense systems, but sent fighters from the People's Liberation Army to reinforce the Burmese communist rebel forces. With superior war weaponry provided by China, BCP eventually defeated the KMT and captured the *Wa* region.

After the KMT was defeated and pushed out of Burma, BCP began to recruit the ethnic *Wa* and trained them to be fierce fighters in the rebel army against *Tatmadaw* with weapons supplied by China. For over two decades BCP expanded their well-equipped army and occupied territory inside Burma. They controlled the *Wa* hills region and unquestionably posed a formidable threat. Eventually, friction between the aging *Bamar* communist leadership of BCP and the *Wa* hill tribe troops resulting in a mutiny in 1989 and the formation of United *Wa* State Army. UWSA signed a peace treaty with the Burmese government and agreed not to fight *Tatmadaw* in exchange for control of its territory in the northeast hill region of Shan state. The UWSA-occupied territory continued to expand and thrived, establishing its own army, local civil administration, hospitals and schools and operating, as journalist Bertil Lintner describes, a 'mini-state' within the Shan state.[1] The military's 2008 constitution officially grants the territory controlled by the United *Wa* State Army as the *Wa* Self-Administered Division. It is a de facto independent territory believed to have the largest and best equipped armed ethnic groups with 30,000 soldiers, operating outside the sphere of the central government.

China has been a key player and supporter of Burma's peace process since around 2014 and has invited both the civilian government leaders and the army chief to Beijing to make economic deals and discuss military cooperation. As escalating clashes between non-signatory EAOs and *Tatmadaw* erupted at the China–Burma northeast border, thousands of minority Shan refugees fled to Yunnan Province in southern China. China wants these clashes to stop as heavy shelling and bombing destroyed roads and bridges disrupting border trade worth millions of dollars. Beijing also does not want an influx of Burma's ethnic refugees. Realizing its national interests were best

---

[1] *The Irrawaddy.* Bertil Lintner: "Who Are The *Wa*?", May 26, 2017.

served from long-term stability in Burma, especially along the border, Beijing shifted focus to ambitious infrastructure investments, mining and extractive projects, as described in Chapter 8, page 156, the BRI 'grand strategy'.

According to a 2018 government report, half of Burma's total foreign debt of over US$9.1 billion was a loan from China, its largest lender.[1] Beijing's most recent shift has been to show willingness to abandon the completion of the controversial $3.6 billion *Myitsone* dam project in exchange for other even better economic and strategic opportunities in Burma. China also wants to implement a SEZ in Muse on the Shan state–China border, but heavy fighting is preventing that for now. Beijing also wants to see an end to ethnic conflicts along the Burma–China borders to prevent potential interference from the West.

Beijing also wants to increase its influence as a peace broker between EAOs and *Tatmadaw* and to broaden its contacts by strengthening connections with both the civilian government and the military leaders of the community, including political activists, and the media — particularly the press and journalists. While Beijing nurtures its relationship with, and increases its support for the new democratic civilian government of Burma, the Western world is focusing on human rights issues in the ethnic conflict regions of the country. Although the new leadership in *Naypyidaw* is sensitive to China interfering in its internal affairs, both sides want border stability for mutual economic interests. US also want to develop bilateral military engagement with Burma army and Washington DC-based United States Institute of Peace, USIP, have met with State Counselor *Aung San Suu Kyi* and Burma army chief Senior General *Min Aung Hlaing*.[2] However, China is strategically located as Burma's next door neighbor, the Western world is across the ocean. Moreover, the West lacks the shared history and depth of China's relationships with Burma. Beijing has funded armed ethnic insurgents like the Northern Alliance and United *Wa* State Army along the Burma-China borders for decades and has been supporting the *Wa* and *Kokang* EAOs in Shan state who have close racial and cultural affinity to the Chinese, speaking Mandarin and having strong ethnic and clan ties to families living in Southern China. More recently, PRC also witnessed the signing of National Ceasefire Agreement in 2015 and continues to encourage all armed ethnic groups to sign it today. Using its relationship with the ethnic groups as leverage China also participates in many peace talk meetings and conferences and has conducted multiple political dialog directly with both

[1] *The Irrawaddy*. Nan Lwin: "*Myanmar*'s Foreign Debt - The Big Picture", July 10, 2018.
[2] *The Irrawaddy*. Sandy Barron: "China's Complex Role in Burma's Peace Process", March 17, 2017.

the leaders of the civilian government and *Tatmadaw*. Beijing also knows of Burmese power center with Burma military's grip of three key ministries controlling the defense, home and border affairs and is fully aware that *Tatmadaw* takes orders from the commander-in-chief, not the president or the state counselor of the elected NLD civilian government. International institutions, NGOs and donors have provided help but their failed interventions are obvious when it comes to peace negotiations in the conflict borderland. Intercession from the UN and other Western countries has been unsuccessful in finding a resolution to bring peace to the region. Soft diplomatic language sprinkled with diplomatic etiquette niceties, subtle nuances and global standards of competence frequently lose relevance and end up as ineffective global democratic rhetoric. This is not the language that military tyrants and autocratic dictators understand and UN and the West's peace talks, engagement and sanctions have been complete failures. As Burma's best ally and biggest trading partner China appears to be the most powerful player in Burma's peace process and can be more effective than UN, international NGOs, or any Western peace making institution to date.

Forget and Forgive

Aung San Suu Kyi encourages the citizens of Burma not to dwell on the military regime's past abuses. Unlike her previous statement to "not forget the past...we must learn from history", she now wants no accountability for past crimes. "Whatever we do we must not take grudges against each other. We will have to heal the wounds the country suffered by showing love and compassion."[1] *Aung San Suu Kyi* asked the suffering people to forget the past or they would be 'hindrances' to the democratic transition. On one hand, the lack of desire for retribution is admirable, perhaps even noble, but it also demonstrates a careless disregard for those who have suffered past wrongs, not only the abuses of *Tatmadaw* but those committed by EAOs. People lived through imprisonment, injustices, torture and exile and want some form of acknowledgment for these past abuses inflicted upon them and an assurance that the atrocities would not be repeated. Their families also need closure and peace at heart that their loved ones did not die in vain or unrecognized for their sacrifices. *Aung San Suu Kyi* wants to reconcile ethnic armed groups and *Tatmadaw* but she also must reconcile oppressors with victims in a free democratic society. Justice for victims and their families must be addressed to build trust and achieve a genuine reconciliation between *Tatmadaw* and

---

[1] BBC. *Aung San Suu Kyi*'s speech commemorating 8888 Pro-Democracy uprising 25th anniversary. August 8, 2013.

the ethnic people. Only then can they heal their wounds, bury the past, exonerate the perpetrators and move forward as an undivided community to rebuild their beloved country together to its new glory. To achieve long lasting peace, national reconciliation and democracy, Dr Yanghee Lee, UN special rapporteur on human rights, aptly described how justice must be served which includes an acknowledgment of responsibility, restoration of damaged relationships, recognition of suffering and forgiveness by sufferers, and rehabilitation and reintegration of both victims and perpetrators.[1]

Lacking accountability as human rights violations go unpunished and impunity continues to flourish, the army finds different ways to obstruct, harass or intimidate those who try to pursue justice. For years HURFOM, Human Rights Foundation of Monland (referring to Mon State in Burma) has documented widespread and systematic violation of human rights by the Burma army and EAOs, such as arbitrary arrests, detention, and torture; extrajudicial killings and forced disappearances; rape and other forms of sexual violence; and land, property, and housing rights violations.[2] The military repeatedly denies these abuses and no one has yet been prosecuted. For those stolen generations who lost everything and have suffered prolonged maltreatment, they cannot forgive the unforgivable, or heal the unhealable without justice or acknowledgment of past abuses. Burma is a nation emerging from decades of dictatorship and repressive rule and compassion is vital in a land that seeks to heal its wounds. The people need to deal with their past and pain, and move forward with new hope and trust to rebuild their lives into the future.

Sacrifices for Democracy

The barbaric crack down on unarmed protesters of past authoritative army regimes deepens and exacerbates long held grievances of the citizens. Thousands of student activists and other pro-democracy protesters were brutally gunned down by the Burmese army during demonstrations of 8.8.88 and ensuing weeks. These people gave their lives for the good of the country and to end an unjust and autocratic military rule. Thousands were arrested, incarcerated and tortured in jail, all because they exercised their democratic and human rights. Many who were tortured brutally perished in prison while others suffered and were scarred for life. Many were traumatized and went in hiding or ran across the border into Thailand. They suffered and

---

[1] *Time.* Yanghee Lee and George Drake: "There Can Be No Peace for *Myanmar* Without Justice", September 26, 2018.

[2] *Tea Circle Oxford.* Janeen Sawatzky: "Justice and National Reconciliation: Why Looking at the Past is the Key to the Future", January 18, 2018.

died for the cause of democracy in 1988. So many students had died who were studying to be doctors, scientists and teachers who wanted to help the country.

Because of their sacrifices, Burma today has a new civilian pro democratic administration. This path to democracy in Burma was built on the sacrifice of thousands of lives. The legendary leaders of 8.8.88 democracy movement, *Min Ko Naing* and his fellow activists, *Ko Jimmy, Ko Ko Gyi, Min Zeya, Ko Htay Kyweh, Hla Myo Naung, Tun Myint Aung, Aung Naing Oo, Nyo Ohn Myint, Moe Thee Zun and Nyo Tun*, naming a handful from an unending list of dedicated peaceful warriors, helped set the stage for *Aung San Suu Kyi* to be the new democracy leader. Their sacrifices must be recognized and remembered by all those who believe in democracy. Those responsible for the brutal and senseless killing must face the truth, not for revenge, but to take ownership of their acts and responsibility to ensure these heinous acts would never happen again. To achieve a genuine reconciliation, the questions of who bears the responsibility for the thousands of deaths of unarmed protesters must be addressed. Who in the military junta were responsible for the brutal crackdown? Who gave the order to gun down the unarmed civilians? Who ordered *Tatmadaw* to murder the very people it was supposed to defend? As Buddhism teaches forgiveness, most families lack a desire for retribution nor do they seek revenge, but they need to hear the truth and put the past to rest in order to heal and forgive, find peace and move on with their lives. The people want an official, meaningful recognition from the government and apology for the loss of loved ones and the abuses they have suffered. They want assurance that their sacrifices are recognized, that future abuses by *Tatmadaw* would not be tolerated, and that the new government is committed to justice, equality and human rights for all.

Development of NLD Administration

In 2015, when the NLD won with a landslide, the people of Burma were ecstatic, filled with renewed hope for a freely elected democratic government. Following the sweeping triumph the new democratic government released many political prisoners, eased both printed press and internet censorship and numerous newspapers and magazines are now available. But that euphoric sense of increased political freedom soon gave way to the realities of a country beset by crushing poverty, internal ethnic wars, the Arakan crisis and many national issues.

Three years into NLD administration, little progress has been made on legal and judicial reforms. Not only are the laws unclear but they are applied selectively and discriminately on individual basis and situation. People are still being arrested under defamation laws and repressive tactics of past military regimes and journalists imprisoned under the Unlawful Association Act when speaking out about human rights abuses or critical of the military or NLD civilian government, jeopardizing press freedom. In 2017 about 20 journalists were prosecuted many of them under Article 66 (d) of the Telecommunications Act which criminalizes online defamation. International investigative teams are denied or restricted access to the region and witnesses are coerced with fear from speaking to them as they or their family members could be arrested or harassed. Those who participated in 1988 pro-democracy protests, including prominent political activists like *Min Ko Naing*, *Ko Ko Gyi*, *Min Zeyar* and many other fellow activists have been involved in democratic rights discussions, the 2008 constitution amendment reducing the role of Burma's army in politics, resolving ethnic armed conflict, environmental protection, rebuilding the nation and other national issues confronting the new democratic civilian administration. They expressed disappointment and frustration at the government's low achieving performance since taking office in 2015, including a stagnant economy, the continuing civil war, and the human rights crisis in Arakan. Changes and improvement *Aung San Suu Kyi* promised in her election campaign have yet to have any impact on day to day lives of ordinary folks. People want visible, tangible, faster and greater democratic changes with more opportunities for youth and women and improvements in living standards.

In January 2017 *U Ko Ni*, a prominent Muslim and highly respected NLD legal advisor and a leading advocate for democracy and human rights, was brazenly assassinated at gun point in broad daylight. He was a courageous and outspoken critic of the army and was deeply involved in constitutional reform. *Aung San Suu Kyi* remained noticeably silent over *U Ko Ni's* death, with no contact made with the grieving family after the assassination. She was also criticized for her noticeable absence at his funeral but under strong negative public scrutiny, she later declared him a martyr. The murder was never solved but an alleged key perpetrator who was a former army officer has disappeared and was never apprehended. Was it a politically motivated murder? Who could afford to pay the assassin almost US$100,000?

Dire economic hardship of the people and failure to bring peace in ethnic states continue to plague the nation and the civilian administration but *Aung San Suu Kyi* expressed her desire and goal to achieve peace in Burma in her lifetime. Good words are no substitute for good deeds and action and she may have put peace goals ahead of economic reforms but violence has escalated in conflict zones under her leadership. Her relationship with the commander-in-chief Senior General *Min Aung Hlaing* has reached an all time low over the Arakan crisis. Although her willingness to sacrifice her own family in the passion of service to her country is unmatched by any rival politician, many have lost hope in her as a local hero as she no longer represents the hope of freedom and peace for the ethnic minorities. Her government does not seem to have real commitment or priority to genuine peace. Has NLD's leadership lost the steam and political will to stop the persecution and human rights abuses in Arakan and the ethnic states of borderland?

Mining operations pollute surrounding areas and landscape with toxic chemical runoff flowing into local streams, rivers and other drinking water resources and detrimentally impacting the health of local residents. Thousands of families living in villages near the *Letpadaung* copper mine in central Burma risk losing their homes and farms due to damage caused by exploitative resource extraction. The authorities declared the project must continue, stating that abandoning the project would hurt the economy and relations with China. The project was resumed, causing wrath among the populace who saw *Aung San Suu Kyi* as representing the establishment and no longer protecting their rights. In previous elections of 1990, 2012 and 2015, voters including ethnic nationalities had unanimously backed the NLD, but their support today has dwindled to 50% as they feel betrayed by the civilian government. The NLD only won 9 seats out of 18 in the by-election of 2017 versus 79% votes in the 2015 general election.

During her reign of the civilian government there is no shortage of reports on human rights violations but little on real conflict resolution and creation of racial harmony and peaceful coexistence. No effort has been made to amend the outdated 1982 Citizenship Law for the Muslim minority which is pivotal to making real needed change in line with international human rights standards. With respect to other ethnic minorities the civilian government's recent naming of the bridge in Mon state as the '*Aung San* Bridge' instead of the suggested name in Mon language demonstrates insensitivity to minority culture and rights and could further exasperate racism and societal division. The government has not taken responsibility to promote sensitivity and multiculturalism, racial harmony and social justice in ethnic regions.

The economy is in dire need of reform. Foreign investment is dwindling and Western tourism is drying up. Many, including some *Bamar* political thinkers, are losing confidence in the government due to inefficient, unproductive and incompetent ministers. Much of the economy is still controlled by the military regime, their families and their super wealthy crony friends. They own agricultural companies, supermarkets, cement and toothpaste factories, transportation and telecommunication companies. For over three years of NLD administration the nation's economy shows no signs of improvement and escalating inflation drives consumer prices up to record highs while direct foreign investment and trade volume plunge. *Aung San Suu Kyi's* appointment of cabinet officers based on personal loyalty instead of skill, management experience and competence has failed. As untrained ministers not familiar with government policies, they were unable to manage the economy and move it to an open market system effectively. She boasts of her cabinet members being corruption free, but tolerates their incompetence and lack of clear vision and economic policies of what and how they are trying to achieve their goals. Political will alone is not enough to rebuild the country and a clean uncorrupt but ineffective government cannot move it forward. As a micro manager who finds it difficult to delegate, most decisions require her approval creating overwhelming bottlenecks that clog up the already stifling bureaucratic process. Her economic policy is unclear and lacks direction to address impending issues of international trade and domestic economic issues: foreign investment, banking and financial management systems, trade deficits, taxation, inflation and more. She has never formulated a policy program beyond vague promises of democracy and peace, rule of law and economic reform.[1]

Many people have lost confidence in doing business in Burma due to NLD's lack of business know how and poor economic management. Her ministers and high ranking cabinet officers still operate with old fashioned bureaucratic attitudes of by gone era which slow economic growth and stall peace process with EAOs. Ineffective and inefficient management and weak governance affect every economic sector and investment environment scaring off potential investors. Lack of cooperation among government departments and ministries also hinders development progress and many lucrative business sectors of the economy and major resources are still controlled by *Tatmadaw*.

The civilian government also faces obstacles and resistance from officials who are loyal to the previous military regime. Political tensions exist between NLD on one side and *Tatmadaw*, the Union Solidarity and Development Party and their allies on the other. After half a dozen years into transition from authoritarian military rule to a democratic civilian administration, economic growth in Burma is slow compared to other transition societies in Asia which achieved double digit growth in relatively short times. Foreign investors are shying away from Burma as it has become one of the least favorite Southeast Asian countries in which to do business. The

---

[1] *Foreign Affairs.* Zoltan Barany: "Where *Myanmar* Went Wrong From Democratic Awakening to Ethnic Cleansing", May/June 2018, Vol.97 Issue 3, 141-154.

shortcoming in the economy is blatantly visible with slow trickling stream of foreign investment while prices of basic commodities are rising dramatically without corresponding similar wage increases. Business and investor confidence is at a low in the face of these escalating prices of basic commodities. The crisis in Arakan and the civil war in Kachin and Shan states are also destroying Burma's reputation with the outside world and scaring away foreign investors especially from the West. Recent surge of violence in Arakan has alarmed the international community and foreign investments have retrenched further. According to a report by Roland Berger of Germany, the confidence of business people and investors has declined dramatically since NLD takeover. Even former corrupt military officers and their crony allies who pocketed huge sums under previous army regimes are holding off on major investments under the new NLD government. Other investors, both domestic and foreign are adopting a wait and see approach. As the West imposed sanctions investors from Western countries retrench holding off their investment while Asian investors are moving ahead as China, India, Thailand, Singapore, and Japan have never imposed sanctions on Burma and they are not about to start now. The crisis is also stifling tourism, especially from the West.

When NLD won the 2015 election, there was renewed hope for a genuine democracy and reuniting the nation's fragmented society of ethnic groups. Internationally, the new government has achieved some major success in foreign relations due to *Aung San Suu Kyi's* outside contacts and influence in the global community. However, several years into the administration, peace is not only elusive but nationalism, radical Buddhism and anti-Muslimism have increased, and she is now a fading international star as her reputation with the outside world has been tarnished.

Not everyone is happy since the NLD came into power including the opposition party USDP, radical Buddhist clergy group *Ma Ba Tha*, and other radical nationalist groups. Within parliament the military representatives and USDP party members behave more like an opposition to the pro democratic party law makers, making any consensus difficult or impossible to reach. Former generals, now MPs, their crony business associates and many powerful politicians are facing losses in unfair special privileges they used to enjoy under previous dictatorships as transparency and responsible investment are encouraged by the new government in business and investment dealings. They dream of the good old days when *Tatmadaw* was the supreme ruler and the elite class of generals and officers lived lavishly above the law. Although NLD government would like to amend the constitution and put the three key ministries under the elected civilian government instead of the military chief of *Tatmadaw*, that is highly unlikely to happen under current *Min Aung Hlaing*'s military term. Additionally, the relationship between *Aung San Suu Kyi* and Senior General *Min Aung Hlaing* has been a tug of war and she knows she must maintain a delicate balance between democratic reforms and not upsetting the army chief who could launch a coup and take over the country again as *Tatmadaw* has done in the past.

Burma, the new democratic nation and Jewel of Asia, is tainted by the violence in Arakan. Tourists, visitors and investors have begun to shun the country. Fresh systematic serious human rights violation by *Tatmadaw* continues to be widespread in the region. Press freedom has become more restrictive and those critical of the NLD civilian government or military, including journalists, are still being arrested, imprisoned and tortured or simply disappeared. Rape and confiscation of property and land from the villagers also are still prevalent in ethnic regions in the north and northeast. Although international pressure is on *Aung San Suu Kyi* regarding the Arakan unrest and lack of progress on peace with ethnic groups, the world knows she is not in charge of *Tatmadaw*, who reports directly to army chief *Min Aung Hlaing*. Her government has no control of the army, and *Tatmadaw* will protect the constitution at all cost to remain in politics. Nevertheless, as the political and moral authority, *Aung San Suu Kyi* is still the best and perhaps the only democratic leader Burma has to offer, at least for now. Outside of Burma *Aung San Suu Kyi* is a fading democracy icon as her reputation and global image has been seriously damaged involving the Arakan crisis, but at home she still has the support of the majority *Bamar* people. She is practical and knows she must find common ground with the *Tatmadaw* chief and the generals and has transformed into a pragmatic politician from a symbol of democracy and human rights as she continues to support *Tatmadaw* actions against the ethnic and Muslim minorities and remains uncritical of the army chief.

Disarming Armed Rebels

For decades *Tatmadaw* has been fighting some two dozen ethnic armed organizations in remote bordering states. How can a government disarm a population of armed ethnic people who spend their life fighting and defending their ancestral lands? As Bobby Anderson pointed out in his article, having a weapon taken away from a soldier can be a traumatic experience for him.[1] He discusses the issues involved in the reintegration process of disarming and repatriating the armed ethnic insurgents into their local communities

---

[1] *The Irrawaddy.* Bobby Anderson: "*Myanmar's Post-Panglong* Problems (Part 2)", August 30, 2017.

and economies. Since most ethnic nationalities live in remote borderlands, they rely on low-productivity subsistence agriculture. Armed fighters whose livelihood is fighting and killing cannot be expected to become subsistence farmers or bicycle-riding vegetable sellers overnight. Although some EAOs have ownership interests in real estate, shopping malls, hotels and other lucrative investments, the majority of their cash economy is illicit. A large amount of cash is generated from organized criminal activities such as opium poppy cultivation, exploitation of gemstones and hardwood timber, extortion, gambling, forced taxation and smuggling. They generate these revenue streams to survive and fund their rebellion.

Can the Burmese central government change and transition their cash streams from illicit to legal? Peace may be achieved in other tangible ways not just laying down guns and weapons. Long term durable peace is attainable when the local people in the inflicted war zones in bordering regions have vested interest to improve their lives and standard of living. As part of conflict resolution program, the central government of Burma can support the EAO territories with better access to health and education, and employment opportunities with real income-producing work. All stakeholders must collaborate toward finding resolution to end this multi decade long violence. It is critical that activists, politicians, economists, journalists, scholars, leading thinkers and public intellectual, professionals, teachers, monks and students work together. They must continue to push for greater democratic change so that in the years to come the people of Burma can live in harmony, fearlessly, productively and peacefully.

Repatriation of Refugees

Decades of military oppression forced millions of Burmese people (including students, activists, ordinary folks) to leave their homeland to escape the acts of brutality of the Burma military. Ethnic minorities were forced to leave their homes as their villages were destroyed by *Tatmadaw*. Many end up as refugees living in various encampments in Thailand along the Burmese border. They have nowhere to go as their homes and villages have been burnt to the ground and many villages are littered with landmines. Families have been killed, girls forced to become sex slaves and boys kidnapped as child soldiers. The government of Burma must take responsibility to move them out of their deplorable existence and to repatriate them. Every human being has universal right to freedom and pursuit of happiness, a good education, adequate health care, and equal opportunities. Hundreds of thousands of exiles who end up in refugee camps in Thailand and other neighboring countries have been displaced permanently with physical, emotional and financial hardships. Many ethnic nationalities had dedicated their lives during the War to fight for Burma's independence and freedom from foreign occupation. Now the military government destroyed their lives and slaughtered their loved ones. They have lost their families, material possessions and livelihood. They should be allowed to repatriate, reunite with families and come home without fear of repercussion. Justice for victims and their families must be addressed to achieve a genuine reconciliation between *Tatmadaw* and the people they were supposed to protect. Denying the past is not worth sacrificing the future.

Like many who suffered during 8.8.88 and other uprisings against the brutal military regime, the ethnic nationalities suffered killings, raping, and land confiscation, at the hands of *Tatmadaw*. To date no one in the uniform has come forth with an apology and no perpetrator has ever been reprimanded for past abuses committed. Article 43 of the military backed 2008 constitution states, "no penal law shall be enacted to provide retrospective effect" giving the military impunity under any present or future government. The 2008 army written constitution was not designed to serve the interests of the people, but to protect *Tatmadaw*. No one can ignore the fact that not one of the uniformed men has ever been tried or brought to justice for the past abominable acts. Army generals, field commanders and officers need to atone for their past sins even in the absence of formal criminal tribunals and retribution in international criminal court of law. They need to build trust first with the people by acknowledging the pain and suffering of those whom they and their men in uniform have inflicted. Continued blanket denials destroy trust and make forgiveness unattainable and peace unachievable. People want government recognition, a public acknowledgment and an official apology for past wrongs committed. As author Janeen Sawatzky pointed out, justice does not always require criminal prosecutions and tribunals. As a symbolic form of reparation in the healing process public apologies can begin to heal wounds. It is the government's responsibility to help them rebuild their lives by other material forms of reparations, including monetary compensation, community development, access to land, and guarantees of non-repetition of past atrocities.[1] Loss of lives can never be replaced but, the government can ease the physical pain by providing material needs such as food, housing, medical care, education, pension and other material support as a starting point goodwill gesture to the remaining members of the families of those who were tortured, raped, beaten, imprisoned, exiled or killed.

---

[1] *Tea Circle Oxford.* Janeen Sawatzky: "Justice and National Reconciliation: Why Looking at the Past is the Key to the Future", January 18, 2018.

Tatmadaw must take the responsibility to provide medical and financial assistance to victims who suffered at their hands just as they support their wounded and disabled soldiers who participated in these brutalities. As many who survived prison torture also lost their sight, hearing, limbs, or became permanently disabled. Many ethnic villagers who survived barbaric attacks and abuses also became permanently disabled, some with mental illnesses contracted during their long hardship imprisonment and others became afflicted with incurable diseases infected during their struggle to survive in harsh jungle life. For those who have become unable to work or support a family government must provide financial reparations to recover lost wages of years of unemployment and denial of work for political prisoners. Professional licenses lost by lawyers, engineers and doctors during arrests must be reinstated and the courtesy extended to reintegrate them back into society to live a productive life.

Such people should be commemorated and celebrated, focusing on the bravery and sacrifices of the victims as democracy heroes and freedom fighters. They deserve government help to reenter society, and engage with full participation in economic, social and political life of their motherland. They must be repatriated from exile, their citizenship restored, their criminal records eradicated so they can be employable again. In ethnic regions, land grabs by the military were common occurrences. Due to fighting in many states, villagers fled their land but upon returning found their ancestral land had been permanently taken over for government development. Like those who survived the brutal crackdown of *Tatmadaw* during past uprisings, the minorities also need to be repatriated, starting with material support and compensation including return of properties and land confiscated and sources of livelihood as farmers, fishermen, and shop owners.

More intensified fighting in 2017 and 2018 between *Tatmadaw* and ethnic insurgents in Kachin and Shan states continues to force people in these regions to flee. Thousands have fled and thousands more have been displaced, including 90,000 residing in IDP camps living in the region.[1] Decades of ongoing clashes and civil war in bordering states have largely been unknown or ignored by the international community. Today, the world is preoccupied with the minority Muslim crisis in Arakan and has shifted its attention away from the other violent ethnic conflict regions in other states. Due to recent renewed raging fighting in Kachin state and widespread reports of human rights abuses by the Burma army, 150,000 ethnic Kachins had to flee their homes but nothing was heard outside of the country. Meanwhile, *Tatmadaw*, as the aggressor and invader continues to intrude their ancestral land and

---

[1] *UNDP/AFP Services.* "Thousands flee fresh clashes in northern *Myanmar*", April 28, 2018.

commit persistent human rights abuses where they live. With increase in the fighting the number of IDPs rapidly rises to thousands in the region. Fighting between *Tatmadaw* and Arakan Army, AA, an EAO headquartered in Kachin state, also intensified in recent months with landmine explosions and attacks on government security posts in Arakan state.

In addition to the civil war refugees scattered across north and north east borders Muslim minority refugees also need to be repatriated from Bangladesh. Since 2012 at least 120,000 displaced Muslim refugees have been living in concentration like camps in western Burma. Across the river in Bangladesh an estimated 870,000 Muslim refugees already live there in overcrowded unsanitary refugee camps with make shift tents and another roughly 750,000 who recently fled across the border in 2017 making it the world's largest and fastest growing refugee camp.

Past regimes have restricted their travel, mobility, health and education, births and marriage and prohibits citizenship regardless how long they have been living in Arakan with all civil rights taken away from them. There were routine extortion by soldiers and security forces for minor 'offenses'. Decades of movement restrictions prevented them from finding jobs, selling their farmed crops and fishing products at local markets and obtaining supplies and basic necessities for daily livelihood, causing crippling poverty, malnutrition, and illnesses. Now their villages have been completely razed and reduced to ashes leaving nothing left to return to and no access to fields, markets and services to start a new livelihood.

They live with catastrophic rains and face monsoon worries causing potential mudslides, cholera epidemic, hunger, robberies and abductions. Since August 2017, about 300 killings of refugees have been reported with possibly many more unreported murders, kidnap for prostitution, and other crimes. The gigantic isolated refugee camp is target for terrorist groups like ARSA to recruit radicalized refugees to fight against the enemy of Islam in the name of Jihad. In response to international outcry and diplomatic protestations, Burma and Bangladesh agree to make plans to repatriate the refugees from Bangladesh camps but so far not a soul has returned. The refugees still harbor memories of previous expulsions and subsequent repatriations by *Tatmadaw* in 1978, 1991–1992 and 2012–2013. Many are reluctant to return to the so called model villages constructed recently by the government. The Muslim refugees fear for their safety as they have no guarantee of protection from the government or from anyone, for that matter.

Tatmadaw is still in control of the state, their land, and crops and they have no freedom of movement or access to basic services. They have been through unprecedented horrors as family members are murdered, wives and daughters are gang raped, and their babies are drowned, cut into pieces or tossed into fires. Their villages and homes have been razed and destroyed, their crops and properties stolen, they have nothing left to come back to. They fled with nothing and now they have nothing to return to – no house, no land, no farm, no crop, no job, no means of survival or support and no guarantee of safety, citizenship or freedom. Returning refugees have no hope of any government support or restitution for farmland and crop losses, houses burnt and other damages to lives and property. Government built model villages are no better than internment camps like IDP camps where over 120,000 *Rohingya* refugees still live today since 2012. Many of these camps are flooded with sewage and curable diseases run rampant and untreated. Living in government planned Muslim ghetto like villages is no better than current overcrowded, unsanitary squalid living conditions across the border. They have no assurance that if they were to return to Arakan they would be allowed to settle back to their original villages.

The laws and policies which discriminate against the Muslims have not changed and there is no guarantee that the Burma army will not attack them or destroy their homes and livelihood again. *Tatmadaw* could cut off access to food and force them to starve as they did before or prevent them from their daily livelihood consisting of farming, fishing and foraging, as *Tatmadaw* soldiers had in the past. Arakan is a poor state with limited infrastructure and opportunities for education and advancement. Its geographical location also makes the state disaster-prone and the people vulnerable to the force of nature. Furthermore, ongoing fighting, conflict and violence take their toll adding extraordinary burden on these vulnerable communities and villages. Refugees are demanding their rights, freedom, security and citizenship guarantee before making the decision to return under those provisions. They rejected *Aung San Suu Kyi's* offer of the National Verification card which is only an alternative identity and residency document allowing them to reside as new immigrants with no citizenship rights or freedom of travel outside of Arakan state borders without restrictions. The NV card has nothing to do with citizenship and they want the government to directly address the citizenship issue and offer real citizenship cards.

According to an expert on refugee studies, many refugees ask for resettlement in a third country, but no country is willing to accept them. In Arakan *Tatmadaw* has reclaimed the region of the destroyed villages and built security bases and rows of half-finished houses attempting to obliterate the past with denial of ethnic cleansing. A New York Times team led by Hannah Beech and Adam Dean recently visited the area and were shown fictitious scripted propaganda by the Burmese government. Using maps, diagrams and slideshows the security officials dressed in crisp uniform and neatly combed hair described how the Burmese government was preparing for the *Rohingya* refugees to return[1]. A charade of security forces regurgitated the official story, but as soon as the team left, the officials "turned off the lights; the generator juddered to a stop; men slipped out of their uniforms; and the computers supposedly meant to record all the returning *Rohingya*, were never even turned on".[2] Of the 750,000 minority Muslim who fled Arakan in 2017, only a few, a handful at best, have returned. Bangladesh said Burma lacked will to repatriate the refugees. Dhaka wanted them to return as its resources has been severely strained by nearly a million refugees living in camps. Past attempts of repatriation have failed as not one refugee turned up to the waiting buses arranged by Bangladesh. The refugees said they did not want to go home until their safety was guaranteed by the Burmese government and they were recognized as citizens. To be meaningful to returning refugees, repatriation plan must include a safe place to live with schools and clinics, a means of subsistence, freedom of movement and equality in all aspects of life. Repatriation must contain a provision for vested interest to improve the refugees' lives and standard of living. The Burmese government needs to demonstrate a real commitment to basic humanitarian rights including access to health, education, job training, employment and economic opportunities. Long term investment in human and social capital is the assured way to end suffering, conflict and violence and may be the only way to sustain economic stability and genuine peace.

---

[1] *New York Times.* Hannah Beech and Adam Dean: "How *Myanmar* Covered Up Ethnic Cleansing", October 15, 2019. ‹https://www.nytimes.com/interactive/2019/10/15/world/asia/*Myanmar*-ethnic-cleansing›

[2] *New York Times.* Hannah Beech and Adam Dean: "How *Myanmar* Covered Up Ethnic Cleansing", October 15, 2019. ‹https://www.nytimes.com/interactive/2019/10/15/world/asia/*Myanmar*-ethnic-cleansing›

CHAPTER 13. THE BURMESE WAY TO DEMOCRACY

Understanding Burmese Style Democracy

The generations of Burmese people born since the military regime took over the country in 1962 have never seen democracy, justice or freedom. They have only seen authoritarian control, repression and corruption. They don't know what it's like to live without fear, censorship and harassment. But they know what it means that healthcare, education and employment are inaccessible.

For the average person in Burma today, democracy is an empty buzzword associated with more sophisticated and advanced countries. The people of Burma just want to be able to work freely so they can provide for their family, educate their children, and have healthcare.

A nation governed by democracy means a system of government by the people and for the people, equality, freedom of speech, freedom of thought, press and mass media, religious liberty and freedom to vote and pursue happiness. It includes participation of the people and therefore power is to be decentralized. It means the right to differ and disagree to encourage exchange of viewpoints and to negotiate through peaceful dialogue. In true democracy the people of Burma have the right to change their government and implement any constitutional reform, but that is not the case here. Democracy in Burma operates at a different level. The fledgling Burmese style democracy is not well defined or understood as the majority of the people are still dealing with survival and basic human rights to life – the right to live without fear and oppression. Previous autocratic regimes treated any criticism or opposition as threat and confrontation and would crush all dissent with guns. To repressive regimes peace means silencing all opposition, security means absolute control and power. To enrich themselves the regime's generals exploit the resources of the land profiting huge sums in their hidden bank accounts abroad while the people and the country remain poor and destitute.

In their book, Bruce Bueno de Mesquita and Alastair Smith describe the resource curse of resource rich nations. They have worse economic growth, more civil wars, and become more autocratic than resource poor countries. They discuss how taxation provides government with a revenue but it is one that requires people to work and pay taxes. An easier alternative is for the government to extract revenue directly from the land cutting the ordinary people out of the equation altogether.[1] That is precisely what the military dictatorship regimes of Burma have done for over five decades. Today, although the country is under an elected democratic civilian government it must share power with the military. Repressive tactics of past autocratic army rule still operate today to intimidate, manipulate, arrest, discriminate and persecute its people. The deep-rooted systems of exploitation and corruption will take years to overcome. Today the military presence in Burma's parliament acts as a powerful obstacle to open uncensored public discourse. The constitution revision is necessary to reduce the military's executive dominance in politics in order for the democratization process to take place in parliament.[2] In short, Burma is still a quasi-military state today.

Many citizens and residents of Burma are not familiar with the principles of democracy, social equality, or citizenship rights and responsibilities nor do they understand the nuances of politics. To them democracy is an empty word. Two thirds of the people live in rural areas, they are largely uneducated and work in low subsistence agriculture. They lack political literacy and care little what the ideology or name the government chooses—USDA, SLORC, or SPDC. Unlike Africa and other dry regions of the world Burma is blessed with fertile land, monsoon rains and abundant natural wealth and people are able to sustain themselves given land to farm and grow crops and support their families. Regardless what the government calls itself – socialist, dictatorship, republic, or democracy, all they want is peace and freedom to pursue their simple livelihood on their land and raise their children. Farmers and villagers in rural regions live in hard conditions and occupy their day with survival issues. They pay little attention to politics. They toil in knee-high

---

[1] *The Dictator's Handbook Why Bad Behavior is Almost Always Good Politics.* Bruce Bueno de Mesquita and Alastair Smith; New York: Public Affairs, 2011, 88-89.

[2] *Asia Foundation-sponsored report.* Renaud Ergreteau: "Parliamentary Development in Myanmar: An Overview of the Union Legislature, 2011-2016", May 2017.

rice fields often infested with leeches, oblivious to issues discussed in *Naypyidaw*. They are simple folks that struggle to survive day to day and do not understand their legal rights. The few that do, they have been conditioned by decades of autocratic rule and repressive military dictatorship not to question or exercise their rights nor challenge the authorities. Few understand the democratic principle of power limitation and constraints of the rulers or the concept of tolerance of minorities.

The gap between big urban cities like Rangoon and Mandalay and rural Burma is widening at all levels, economic, political and social. Farmers and peasants in villages are losing their homes and livelihoods as government-supported foreign investments (nominally joint ventures) seize their land for development and building of dams and other projects. They have lived in a world where they had no voice or political participation. With successive regimes of authoritarian rule, they live with diminishing hope of seeing freedom in their lifetime. In this multi ethnic, multi cultural, and multi religious pluralistic society, many political groups and civil organizations have different understandings, interpretations and definitions of democracy, human rights, or respect for the environment. Western models of democracy with total separation of civil and military institutions may not fit here, at least not for now.

Since taking office, the NLD's democratic civilian government has left much to be done on the issue of human rights and democracy. *Aung San Suu Kyi*, despite world criticisms against her, remains the best hope for democracy in the nation. Unprecedented changes have taken place, with some semblance of democracy appearing in the country since 2011, even if the signs are superficial.

Under NLD's civilian administration, people enjoy more social and political freedom. Hundreds of political prisoners, student activists, and journalists have been released, media censorship relaxed and people can even criticize the government, albeit mildly and with caution, without being harassed or arrested. Many oppressive and controversial laws have been amended, education and health budgets increased, and public healthcare has improved especially fight against diseases like tuberculosis and malaria and growing HIV.

But the government's regression in these improvements becomes apparent with new arrests and attacks on the media, inaccessible education and healthcare in rural poor, and the continuation of the status quo conditions of quasi military rule politically, economically, socially and environmentally.

The Constitution Obstacle

Since independence from the British, Burma, has had three constitutions. The first constitution, drafted in 1947, was abolished in 1962 when the military took over with a coup d'état. General *Ne Win* drafted a new constitution in 1974 to establish the Burmese Way to Socialism. That ended in 1988 after the 8.8.88 uprising when the ruling military junta, State Law and Order Restoration Council, SLORC, seized power again. Burma did not have a constitution again until 2008 when General *Than Shwe* drafted one guaranteeing *Tatmadaw* protection from prosecution for any actions committed while in military service. The military wanted to secure immunity in any international court of law for decades of human rights abuses committed during the military reign. To date not one general has ever been held accountable for the transgression of the past in any court of law. In the event of instability, uprisings and chaos, this constitution allowed the army to stage a coup at any time and take over the government.

That constitution is today the biggest obstacle to full-fledged democracy in Burma. Ironically, the military objected to the NLD's attempts to reform the constitution. What does it mean when Senior General *Min Aung Hlaing* stated the military will leave politics after peace has been restored to the country? Or that *Tatmadaw* will retreat when the country is stabilized? Translation: as long as there is ethnic conflict the military remains in power and will not withdraw from politics. Civil war between the military and about twenty EAO's has been ongoing since 1948, and the military has no incentive to bring it to an end.

It was also enshrined in the constitution that *Tatmadaw* could take over anytime to 'safeguard sovereignty of the nation'. In the current political power-sharing system, the civilian government is weakened as it must share both executive and legislative powers with the military. The military has not collaborated with NLD government as it has no interest to amend the 2008 constitution that guarantees the military's role in politics. The constitution not only enshrines *Tatmadaw's* involvement in the country's politics it gives the military veto power over any proposed constitutional amendment of the civilian government.

The current constitution also gives *Tatmadaw* constitutionally privileged position of power, reserving 25 percent of parliament seats to be occupied by non-elected military appointees and three key cabinet positions to be filled by military officers. The army written constitution makes the military the most powerful institution in Burma reporting directly to the commander-in-chief, and not the civilian government president. In a military dominated parliament civilian administration can become a toothless institution with no real power to amend, adopt or endorse constitutional changes.

The NLD democratic government and the people of Burma want to amend the existing constitution including provisions for the military to retreat from politics and ethnic issues of equality and self determination. Many agree the army should return to its barracks and withdraw from the political arena. At some point in the future NLD would likely propose constitutional amendments putting the three key ministries under the elected government, not the *Tatmadaw* chief. For over a year all substantive constitutional amendment proposed by NLD to reduce the military's role in government have been rejected. The military maintains its grip on National Defense and Security Council and the power to take control during a state of emergency. The constitution not only guarantees veto power on amendment, it shields junta generals and officers from future prosecution of human rights violations. Meanwhile, under the constitution, *Aung San Suu Kyi* remains banned from the presidency.

It is highly unlikely the military will agree to change the constitution, at least not before the 2020 election. For now no one could challenge *Tatmadaw* as the constitution guarantees its power and control and the military is immune and untouchable by any court of law, domestic or international. *Tatmadaw* takes the position that its primary responsibility is to safeguard the nation and as long as there are EAOs they will remain in politics with the current constitution intact.

Sustaining Peace

For decades of armed struggle, organized demonstrations and people's uprisings, intercession from the global community, international sanctions and peace treaties have been tried and failed. Continued international participation and support remains crucial to Burma's successful and smooth transition to democracy. The Arakan crisis and ethnic minority issues in Kachin and Shan states are both a humanitarian crisis and a threat to the country's fragile transition to democracy and it is vital to resolve them for genuine democracy and to achieve sustainable peace.

The civilian government must stop denying and defending the inhumane acts committed by the military and begin meaningful dialog in support of those who have suffered. The road to peace, however, is complicated further with power sharing between the civilian government and the military. As Burma liberalizes its economic and social policies the past grievances of the brutal military regime can now be voiced but everything is at a standstill without any effective mechanism in place yet to process and rectify complaints of the ethnic nationalities. Not only is the government-led peace process in deadlock, within the parliament the two sides are in a power struggle gridlock. At *Naypyidaw* the civilian government and the ethnic parties on one side and the opposition with the military and its party, the USDP on the other, have been stuck in a head-on impasse during parliament sessions. The democratic side would like to amend the constitution removing or reducing the role of the military in politics while *Tatmadaw* resist the amendment wanting to preserve the status quo and their unfair unconstitutional privileges, including the possibility to retake the country via an army coup. The mindset of the old establishment still prevails as the generals have never ruled out the option of staging a coup if threatened by uncontrollable rebellion to separate a state from the Union. Additionally, the relationship between *Aung San Suu Kyi* and Senior General *Min Aung Hlaing* has deteriorated further over international involvement in the Arakan crisis, the divergent approaches of the two leaders undermining and complicating finding solutions to the peace process. In an effort to maintain good relations with the army chief the de facto leader has avoided sensitive or confrontational issues. She never questioned the military's use of excessive force and brutal crackdown against Muslim extremists in Arakan causing mass exodus of refugees to Bangladesh. Instead she supported the military by refusing to grant visas to UN workers investigating allegations of human rights abuses in that state. So far she managed to maneuver many delicate situations but their relationship remained testy.

Aung San Suu Kyi has many unrivaled political strengths at her disposal and silencing and acquiescing to *Tatmadaw* is not the only option. In the past as an international icon and Nobel laureate she had the stature and enormous support from the international community but failed to capitalize on her unmatchable strengths in light of the military's weak global position. Although her international reputation has diminished, domestically she still has the support and is the best hope of the people as a democracy leader. These sources of strength combined with many others that come with her name, Western education, high level global profile and personal charisma, give her unbeatable combination to take charge and lead the country. *Tatmadaw* may have guns but the generals lack the support of not just the West or the Muslim communities but all citizens of the world who believe in freedom, justice and democracy. Using force against unarmed citizens is not a sign of strength but it is a sign of insecurity and fear. In spite of these competitive advantages *Aung San Suu Kyi* chose to be silent. With growing international pressure including condemnation from the Islamic countries the military generals are increasingly concerned of being referred to the UN Security Council and International Criminal Court. Peace and economy are intertwined and the government cannot choose economic development at the expense of peace. Peace and democracy are also interdependent and mutually reinforcing processes. Without peace democracy is not sustainable. Economic success can postpone the democratic moment but it ultimately cannot replace it.[1]

Although Burma was one of the fastest growing economies in Southeast Asia its image was severely impaired in the wake of the Arakan crisis. The human rights abuses have caused a decline in direct foreign investment and participation from the West is diminishing as it is withdrawing its support to Burma economically, politically and militarily. Unlike the West, however, the economic giants of the East are adopting the reverse approach to increase their strategic geopolitical interests far beyond mere investments in infrastructure, seaports and industrial zones. Beijing's ambitious Belt and Road Initiative (BRI) includes the 1,700-km (10,563 miles) China–*Myanmar* Economic Corridor (CMEC) connecting Mandalay to Kunming, east to Rangoon and west to the *Kyaukphyu* Special Economic Zone (SEZ).

Another ambitious economic corridor is India's Act East Policy which includes the *Kaladan* Multi-modal Transit Transport project through Burma and connecting India with Thailand, Laos, Cambodia, Vietnam and China for trade development. Japan's grand plan includes railway, road and energy networks. The East–West Economic Corridor to promote trade and foreign investment with five Southeast Asian countries — Burma, Thailand, Laos, Cambodia and Vietnam connects Vietnam's Dong Ha City with Rangoon's *Thilawa* Special Economic Zone, SEZ via Cambodia and Thailand, and the Southern Economic Corridor connects central Vietnam, Cambodia and Thailand to the *Dawei* SEZ in southeastern Burma. It is more than a resource war. It is a competitive game of strategic dominance in Southeast Asia. Economic interests do reign supreme, and political, religious and ideological differences proved no barrier to doing business.[2] CNN cited China's increasing influence and power and the waning reputation of the US as a reliable ally. With shrinking direct foreign investment from the West and their re-imposed economic sanctions, Burma is looking east to China, India and Japan for economic, political and military support.

---

[1] *The Dictator's Handbook Why Bad Behavior is Almost Always Good Politics.* Bruce Bueno de Mesquita and Alastair Smith; New York: Public Affairs, 2011, 279.

[2] *CNN.* Tamara Qiblawi: "Muslim nations are defending China as it cracks down on Muslims, shattering any myths of Islamic solidarity", July 17, 2019.

Broken Health and Education Systems

Like everything in Burma, healthcare has been neglected for over half a century. According to 2000 ranking of healthcare systems of 191 countries, the World Health Organization listed Burma's healthcare system as the worst overall. The military government spends less than 3% of the national budget on health care, and well over 40% on military, consistently ranking the lowest healthcare budget in the world. Even the biggest and best equipped medical facility, Rangoon General Hospital, is a dilapidated colonial era building with intermittent electricity. The lobby smells of urine and is overflowing with the sick, the elderly and the injured. For the two thirds of the population who live in rural Burma, basic healthcare is non-existent or unaffordable with a ratio of 1 physician per 2,500 people. In rural areas the shortage of trained medical staff is so severe a nurse often has an overwhelming responsibility to handle ten villages. People tend to wait until the very end to seek medical help since they must travel long distances to reach a hospital or clinic in the nearest towns. Most healthcare workers are unwilling to live in rural areas with low standard of living and also for monetary reasons as private hospitals and clinics in cities pay higher salaries. Many physicians emigrate abroad to earn high wages compounding the shortage of healthcare providers in the nation. In rural areas, even when patients reach a clinic in a town, they are faced with widespread corruption having to give money under the table to workers in order to receive any treatment. If surgery is required, the doctor will write a prescription with all the required disposable materials used during the procedure and the patient or his family must purchase these at a local medical supply store and return for the procedure. Some clinics are so under equipped that patients have to provide basic surgical tools needed for surgery as they provide only services. Facilities are poorly equipped as much of government's meager spending often never reached its intended target due to corruption and dysfunction that characterize Burma's military regime. Patients have to pay for everything including doctor's fees, clinic charges, medication, and medical supplies such as syringes, bandages and even blankets and linens. As a tropical country Burma is plagued with malaria, typhoid, tuberculosis, diarrhea, respiratory infections, and HIV/AIDS, and vaccines, tests and treatment programs are limited or not available to the mass. Diseases like HIV spread as needles are reused without sterilization. Leprosy also plagues Burma. In a country steep in superstition, cultural practices, and astrology, the majority of the people who live in rural areas, including ethnic nationalities, tend to seek medical help from medicine men and religious healers of traditional remedies rather than medically trained healthcare providers. They seek advice and treatment from astrologers and fortune tellers for spiritual solutions to health issues instead of seeking medical help. Outreach programs to give the rural population better understanding of contemporary medicines and remedies are needed desperately. For the majority including orphans and street children traditional medicines provided by the monasteries is the only available health services. On the other hand, the privileged group of generals and the elite class can afford to travel abroad for state of the art medical services or surgery and other more serious medical treatment in Singapore, Bangkok, Japan and other major Southeast Asian cities. It is only a small percentage of the people who are wealthy and live in cities, who can afford private schools for their children and private medical clinics for health issues.

Under decades of isolation and oppressive military rule education in Burma experienced a catastrophic journey into decline. Burma's education system ranks among the lowest in the world. According to UN, Burma's human development index ranks 146 compared to 26 for neighboring Singapore. As Burma transitions to democracy educating and training successive generations of Burma's youth are crucial to rebuilding the country, its development and growth. It is also a key to democratization as only educated citizens can rise up to the challenges of rebuilding Burma and creating a productive future workforce. It may take more than a generation to reform the education system fully when the primary school students of today graduate from high school and universities fully trained, employable and productive.

Monastic Education

There are three distinct education systems, namely, monastic, public, and private education. As a Buddhist country the monastery is the center of culture and moral, ethical, and religious education. Traditionally, Burmese monarchy had been strong supporters of the *sangha*, building pagodas, temples and monasteries. The royal families were patrons of Buddhist faith and therefore sponsored monasteries where free education is provided to everyone to study Buddhism. Historically the literacy rate in Burma was one of the highest in Asia, as children received free religious teachings in Buddhist monasteries. Burmese universities attracted Asia's best and brightest. The tradition carries on today with monasteries providing free education including basic reading, writing and math based on syllabus from the Ministry of Education and Buddhist teachings, contributing to a surprisingly high literacy rate of 90% in Burma. Monastic education also includes school supplies and lunches provided free of charge and supported by donations from the Buddhist community. Monastic schools play indispensable role in the education system because they provide the only opportunity to learn for many children. For the lower economic tier majority, monasteries offer the only viable source of education for the economically disadvantaged children and the rural poor living in small towns, city outskirts and villages. Many poor families send their children to the monastery not just to be educated but also to be well fed. In return, the parents help the *hpongyis*, the monks with the chores, shopping, cooking, cleaning, and maintenance and repair.

Public Education

Government subsidized public education in state schools is also free but is so severely underfunded as the military regime chooses to fund *Tatmadaw* rather than schools. In current public schools funded by the government text books are in short supply and are severely outdated most of them written during the military junta era, emphasize the political climate of recent past decades. About 70% of the population live and work in the agricultural sector, a way of life that is manual labor intensive and children are expected to help with farm work, tend animals, doing chores at home, or taking care of younger siblings while parents are at work. Besides, many rural poor families still cannot afford the cost of uniforms, school supplies, lunches, bus fares, and incidentals. Military education has been glorified and developed to the detriment of the civilian education system. The curriculum focuses on military life promoting patriotism, nationalism and isolationism to defend the country against intruders. Burma was isolated from the world for so long few people knew a man had walked on the moon.

Corruption is another plague prevalent throughout the state education system where money and influence can acquire good grades and test scores. Some even use bribes to get their students exam scores raised. Another disconnect in current school curricula is the focus on learning by rote and memorization of text with the primary goal of achieving good scores in exams. In addition to learn-by-rote education, Burma's school system is afflicted with teacher shortage, poorly trained teachers, bribery, and old or obsolete resources. Students are taught using outdated learning methods designed to regurgitate class room theoretical concepts with no true understanding of their real life applications. Without critical thinking, knowledge and use of practical skills students lack connection to how the real world works, and lose motivation to learn. Government needs to address and respond to education challenges by designing programs to promote skills like critical thinking, creativity, empathy, and complex problem solving. These programs will enhance lifelong learning systems going beyond school education and training. Text books need to be revised and the scope of education broaden to include arts and sciences, technological development, world history, geography, literature, economics and politics, business and global events.

Private Education

In the latter part of 1800 Roman Catholic and Protestant Christian missionaries began to establish private English schools. These English private schools offer world class education in English language instruction with a curriculum generally patterned after the British education system and meeting international standard, like Methodist English High School and St. Paul Boys School. They charged high tuition but the students got a solid foundation with an education based on international standards. Many wealthy families sent their children to these Western style private schools with Christian roots in preparation for higher education abroad. Shortly after the 1962 coup when General *Ne Win*'s regime took over schools, English was eliminated from school curriculum as it was a 'colonial language'. The regime mandated Burma should use Burmese as the language of instruction at all schools. Unfortunately, many textbooks and other literature were not available in Burmese restricting available teaching material. School curriculum was censored and rewritten and textbooks were changed to emphasize army unity and solidarity with large doses of propaganda widening the gap between textbooks and reality. Current curricula teach detailed history up to independence but modern Burmese history since the army regime of 1962 was skewed with brainwash of socialistic views, omission, gaps and propaganda with twisted justification.

The generals were making teachers teach what they wanted the people to believe rather than preparing students with skills to build a better country and a better future for the people of Burma. The regime's ideology was forced on the people through the educational system, teaching blind obedience and loyalty to the junta and brainwashing Burma's youth through the regime's tampered school curricula. There was no independent thought or critical thinking, only rote memorization of what was allowed to be taught in schools. The education system was based on total memorization of given established knowledge with no encouragement for analysis or to develop a new approach to find solutions. When creativity is stifled the whole generation of young people becomes less effective to engage in problem-solving capacities. After half a century of low quality public education under military regime Burma decided to open up to allow private schools. Parents who could afford, send their children to private schools with higher education standard and quality curriculum, which better prepares them for further study abroad in Singapore, Japan, UK, US and other countries. Beginning in 2005, a surge of private schools sprang up at all school grade levels to cater and meet the demands of the growing market for English language in businesses, science and technology and to prepare a generation of uneducated young adults. Recognizing the importance of English as a language of commerce and international communication, private adult language schools began to appear around 2009 and some are offering local businesses with corporate skills and business English for their employees.

Higher Education

College level education is available at Rangoon and Mandalay Universities, founded in 1920 and 1925 respectively, and several other institutions and technical colleges. Prior to the military take over Rangoon University was one of the top universities in Southeast Asia with affiliations and exchange programs with prestigious higher learning institutions like MIT and John Hopkins University. Medical schools of Rangoon and Mandalay Universities were considered among the best in the region. Before the military junta era universities in Burma attracted Asia's best and brightest but all that changed under repressive regimes of Generals *Ne Win* and *Than Shwe* for five decades. Since the military regime took over starting in 1962 it destroyed the education system through neglect and frequent closures of universities. First, the junta abolished the colonial legacy of English schools for the elite and made Burmese the only medium for instruction at all schools at all levels. In higher learning, however, this had serious repercussions as textbooks, literary texts and other publications were not available in Burmese. The junta ordered textbooks to be translated into Burmese but many technical, medical, business and political terms do not have Burmese translation equivalent. When scientific and technology texts were too cumbersome to translate into the Burmese language, they were either omitted or discarded. Translation often strips the true meaning of the words and phrases of a language. Hence, the meaning of some texts was also lost or modified in translation. Seventeen years later, when *Sanda Win*, General *Ne Win*'s daughter failed her entrance exam to a British medical school due to poor English, the general reinstated the teaching of English in the school system. By then, many English speaking teachers have already left the country creating a shortage of quality English proficiency teachers. The quality of education has deteriorated to the point some university students could not even use an English dictionary. To the military junta college students are always a source of threat and Rangoon University has always been the center of political opposition since the days of General *Aung San*, Burma's independence hero. Under military rule the junta wrecked the higher education system with frequent closures of weeks, months, and even years to eliminate any rebellious student opposition and uprisings against the regime. Campuses were decentralized and scattered and small fragmented campuses were built on the outskirts of cities and satellite towns to prevent students from group gatherings in urban major cities like Rangoon and Mandalay which could lead to potential student led demonstrations and protests. Those who participated in anti government organizations were locked up in prison and given decade long sentences to intimidate them from future political activities. Between 1988 and 1998 universities were closed for seven years. The repeated cycles of opening and closing of universities and colleges made serious study virtually impossible. The buildings are dilapidated due to abandonment and the grounds have been overgrown with weed. Distance study became the norm replacing on site campus classroom instructions. Students were getting only a few days per month in class teaching and lectures with no access to laboratories, research facilities or library. When universities reopened students were often shortchanged getting only a few months classes for yearlong courses, six year technology programs were reduced to four years, and four year Bachelor's degree shortened to just three years. When students protested the downgrading of the education level, classes were canceled indefinitely. When in session the regime focused on suppression of student activism rather than on quality of higher education. Teachers were not only required to teach government approved curriculum and regime's propaganda but they were asked to patrol campuses for potential student political activities and organized group gatherings. Military intelligence was also widespread on campuses acting as janitors, gardeners, and maintenance crew intimidating the students and faculty.

The government has treated universities not as sources of higher education crucial to the country's future development, but as potential threats to its rule. There was little incentive to pursue higher education as there were few jobs for university graduates. Many students gave up on obtaining a college degree or left for neighboring countries to work resulting in loss of more than a generation of educated young Burmese nationals. Decades of closure and isolation from the world community left the people out of touch, ill informed, and socially, technologically, culturally, and mentally deprived and impoverished. With severe education neglect Burma has fallen behind other Southeast Asian countries by several generations. Internationally, education is regarded as an indispensable human right but in Burma, it is marginalized and inaccessible to most citizens. The ruling generals believe education is dangerous to their grip of power and control because educated people question the government and demand their rights. Military regime did not want people to be highly educated or to be taught how to think critically and independently for fear of potential threat they could organize an opposition to overthrow the authoritarian rule. Many senior ranking army officers rose to higher positions but have little or no formal education and do not want subordinates to be more educated than they themselves. Young people also became discouraged to attend colleges and universities, as education had little to offer collegians since there aren't enough career jobs in the country to cover the output of university graduates. Consequently, many Burmese left their homeland to escape arrests, grinding poverty, lack of employment, and to seek better educational opportunities abroad.

Ethnic Languages

Another challenge for the Ministry of Education is the previous military regime's ineffective way of dealing with ethnic minority education. In an attempt to suppress political and cultural identities of ethnic nationalities past regime has banned minority languages from state schools. For decades Burmese was the only language taught to promote *Bamar* identity and culture with Burmese as the unifying language. In bordering states of the country ethnic languages are penalized as the curriculum is taught only in Burmese, another reason many of the 135 ethnic nationalities do not attend school. In view of such diversity of ethnic minority nationalities, education to enhance understanding of different cultures would reduce prejudices and promote empathy, respect, open-mindedness, curiosity and anti-discrimination.[1] History has shown in other parts of the world with conflict regions, education linked to peace building process was effective in conflict resolution and reduction. An educational system overhaul is not only overdue but the need for repair is doubly acute in the ethnic regions. Burma with so many minority nationalities and multiple conflict regions could learn from historical events and conflict resolution based education curriculum. Recognizing their social, political and economic differences, an education program incorporating ethnic history, culture, faith, language, and customs will help the young people of today and future generations understand one another,

---

[1] *Frontier.* Ewan Cameron: "Rethinking ethnicity in the classroom", March 28, 2017.

respect diversity and live in harmony and peaceful coexistence. A curriculum that embraces tolerance, anti-racism, and multiculturalism may not only reduce tensions and violence but helps promote peace and understanding among various nationalities and religious faiths. It would be productive for the government to reach out to underrepresented minority ethnic communities with education assistance such as setting minority quotas and offering scholarships, grants, stipends and work-study programs at all levels of education. Education reform must be ethnic inclusive. It must address social, cultural, and political needs of all people of the country. Teaching minority languages in schools would instill respect and tolerance among the ethnic nationalities which would contribute to establishing peace and goodwill in the conflict regions of Burma. The teaching of ethnic languages in their regions is a bridge to better understanding, building peace, and resolving conflicts. Education inclusiveness is not just part of the educational process but it is part of the overall peace process and rebuilding of the nation.

Military Culture of Blind Obedience

For generations Burmese schools taught government propaganda by repetition and memorization. The army not only brainwashed soldiers but also ordinary people through propaganda in the media and school curricula. The military culture promoted blind obedience and unconditional loyalty to the regime. As a Buddhist country, Burmese society has been traditionally shaped by Buddhism discipline, and respect for seniority and obedience were taught and valued. The government used Burmese tradition of respect for elders and superiors to instill unquestioning respect and blind obedience. Army soldiers working as government officials have been conditioned not to think independently and to ask for permission from superiors for any and all decisions. Consequently, they no longer think or decide for themselves, solve problems, or find solutions independently. As insubordination was not tolerated and superiors could not be challenged, no one could perform effectively; everyone reported what the bosses wanted to see or hear, often concealing real issues and problems for fear of retribution.

When minor issues required layers of higher decision making, efficiency was sacrificed for bloated bureaucracy. This was reflected in every level of the government, public education and the culture. Questioning or mere suggestion of a different option became a threatening challenge to superiors rather than a positive contribution of a new idea or solution.

The army recruited poorest young men and women with low education level who have limited work opportunities. They lured them with government funded schools, housing, healthcare and other material privileges. Orphans were targeted as recruits and *Tatmadaw* became their only family support and reliance. The regime has set up the elite Defense Services Academy where promising recruits and young soldiers were trained to be army officers and brain washed with intimidation and anti foreign propaganda in exchange for lifelong loyalty to the army. Many parents made the painful decision to encourage their children to join *Tatmadaw* as the only way for them to succeed and for the family to be protected from harassment and intimidation. Some families ended up with a son in the military and another fighting for democracy, resulting in a bitter split. Living in constant fear took a huge personal toll. Brutality made people internalize fear and distrust and silenced their minds permanently. Over generations, fear has taken roots in the minds of the people of this nation and would take decades to erase it. To recondition a generation of people to learn to think would be a challenge of future generations to come. Starting with education, changes in school curricula, teaching methodology and reforms in learning systems are critically needed to be addressed.

Under decades of harsh military rule citizens were being watched and spied on every waking moment and followed everywhere by MI officers and plain clothes spies and informants. The people lived in an invisible prison suffocating as if living in a fish bowl under a microscope. Decades of living in fear and silence created a sense of hopelessness in a generation of people who no longer could talk or think freely even in their own homes. As Christina Fink aptly said, the people of Burma are 'living silence.'[1] The constant and widespread presence of military intelligence agents or secret police silenced the community. The regime employed a vast network of plain clothed informers who passed on information about colleagues, co-workers, friends, neighbors, and even families who criticized the junta. No one could be trusted as plainclothes informers were everywhere, in community, workplaces, hospitals, tea shops, restaurants, schools, and even homes. There were block police and block informers watching and spying everyone and everything. Families began to mistrust one another, as parents tended to conform to government order even if they harbored a deep rooted dislike for it. The younger generation, especially students, often retaliated and engaged in anti-government political activity, putting their parents, siblings and other relatives and family members at risk. Stories of betrayal and treachery, brother against brother, abound. Anyone protesting peacefully or speaking out against the government could be arrested and imprisoned. Once arrested

---

[1] *Living Silence Burma Under Military Rule*. Christina Fink; London and New York: Zed Books, 2001.

there was no legal recourse and they were black listed for life and barred from graduating from school, gaining employment, and harassed severely so even close friends would shun them for fear of retaliation. Any overnight guest, even a close relative must be reported and registered with the authorities.

Friendship with Old Allies

With rising global pressure against large scale violence in Arakan and the government's growing aversion to external intervention against human rights crises, Burma is shifting its strategic alliances with leading global powers. Lack of progress toward internal peace, faltering foreign investment, plummeting Western aid, reinstated sanctions by EU and US, condemnation from the UN and the Muslim world, and increasing threat of terrorism, are challenges that push Burma to rely more on its old allies.

As a last Asian frontier and its strategic location between two economic giants, both China and India are hungry for Burma's rich deposits of raw material. Its fertile alluvial soil can be developed again to feed the two most populous countries in the world. China does not want Western influence in Burma and has encouraged the Burmese government against signing the Memorandum of Understanding agreement with UN agencies which will allow deeper international involvement from the West. In exchange for unrestricted access to its natural assets and weapon deals, the government of Burma is turning to China and Russia for diplomatic protection against international criminal action at the UN Security Council, and for political, military and economic support, primarily from the PRC, and to a lesser extent, Russia.

Beijing has economic and geopolitical interests in building Burma's infrastructure to haul oil, gas, timber and energy to Southern China. Russia wants to sell arms (fighter jets, aircraft and combat helicopters) to Burma and may include submarines in the near future. Russia was recently rewarded with a contract to supply over $200 million of fighter jets. In the past, both Russia and China have supplied the majority of *Tatmadaw's* arsenal, and therefore Western sanctions and an arms embargo would not seriously affect the generals. But Burma does not want to become a puppet of any country and wants to maintain a good relationship with both East and West.

Recent intensified clashes in northern Arakan and Shan states are creating a growing sense of mistrust with China among *Tatmadaw's* generals and Beijing's role and influence as a mediator in the conflict regions. According to published reports, the PRC is believed to be supplying the armed rebels with grenade launchers, mines and other weapons seized during recent attacks with Burmese military.

Burma's strategic location at the center of Southeast Asia has attracted many players in the region. China, India and Japan are competing for influence in Burma in order to access strategically located ports, its abundant natural resources, agricultural commodities, cheap labor and untapped new markets. It is vital to maintain a balanced foreign relation not just with the superpowers of the East, but with the US, UK and Eu countries. Other countries are recognizing the increasing dominance of China in the region and US, France, Japan and Australia are forging stronger defense ties in the Asia–Pacific region by combined naval drill to counterbalance China's increasing influence in the region.[1]

Rebuilding the Country

Due to decades of isolation and mismanagement, Burma fell behind other Asian countries in vibrant economic growth, but many believe and hope it can rebuild itself with blazing double-digit growth if properly managed. This brings the focus to the 2020 election. *Tatmadaw* and its party USDP would like to retake the presidency of the civilian government and already more than two dozen political parties have been formed by former generals and party officials to run against NLD.

The military also has the unfair advantage embedded in the constitution whereby it holds a quarter of parliamentary seats, which could certainly help it to unseat NLD at the next election. Could General *Min Aung Hlaing* run against *Aung San Suu Kyi* to regain the supreme position as the next president? Lately he has been courting non-Buddhist religious leaders, visiting churches and traditional mosques (not affiliated with the *Rohingya*) and making donations. Some believe this PR campaign is designed to offset international allegations of religious persecution, others say he is merely wooing voters for the 2020 election.

The *Tatmadaw* chief also knows *Aung San Suu Kyi's* popularity has declined, especially among the minorities. The civilian government is beset with trade and economic issues and incompetent and ineffective cabinet officers and lawmakers. Under the current government, violent clashes between *Tatmadaw* and EAOs intensified, human rights atrocities in Arakan created a mass exodus, and the peace process is dead. The majority of the people live

---

[1] *Reuters.* Tim Kelly: "US, France, Japan and Australia Hold First Combined Naval Drill in Asia", May 17, 2019.

in dire poverty. In spite of this, the Lady is intent on fulfilling a deep seated personal aspiration and will run again at age 75.

In the absence of any other potential leader, she and her NLD party may still win. This time *Aung San Suu Kyi* will have four years more experience and another chance of transforming the country into a democracy and restoring some form of peace. Her administration can begin rebuilding by focusing on issues under its jurisdiction such as improving the economy, infrastructure, electricity shortages, land ownership disputes, healthcare and education. By defending Burma against charges of genocide at the International Court of Justice in the Hague, she stirred up unparalleled nationalism at home, unleashing a frenzy of public support. Her popularity shot up with the people, the military, and the *sangha* as they see her as a defender of a faith besieged by Islam and protector of Buddhist land.

A valuable untapped human resource and capital pool for nation building is the Burmese expatriate community. Burmese living overseas have been foreign trained and educated; they can provide fresh ideas, new technological know-how, and analytical and critical thinking. They are bilingual, bi cultural and have an understanding of both Eastern and Western business practices. They should be encouraged to return home. With sound, responsible investment, Burma can become an economic hub in the region, raising the standard of living of its people. Opportunities abound for building infrastructure, renewable energy, mining and extraction, construction and manufacturing, telecommunication, power generation, tourism, food processing, financial sector, education, medical and health related fields and many more.

The Burmese Way to Democracy

Burma is setting out on a new path out of autocratic military control to a democratic style government charting a new course for its people. It is a dynamic and evolving nation that's changing economically, socially and geopolitically. Much has improved in the private sector of small businesses, while much remains status quo and non-transparent, leaving the democratic government to grapple with the legacy of decades of dictatorial military rule and fundamental human rights issues.

Tatmadaw retains control of key government ministries and dominates the most lucrative economic sectors. The military is still clinging to power, ceding only a small degree of control in matters they are not interested in such as social, health and education. Political prisoners are still in jail and repressive laws continue to restrict people's rights. Peace is still out of reach and the Arakan crisis continues with more than half the population displaced and homeless.

Burma is not yet fully democratic but it is no longer a dictatorship. What sort of democracy Burma might pursue is up to the people of this nation. Since 2010, many political, social, and economic changes have taken place and the people have tasted some resemblance of democratic life. They no longer want or accept *Ne Win's* ideology of the Burmese Way to Socialism, the total nationalization and control of businesses, and economic isolation from the world. Nor do they want the State Law and Order Restoration Council era with rampant corruption and cronyism under General *Than Shwe*, plundering Burma's natural wealth for the generals' personal profit. They are demanding change. Burma needs to find a democracy that works for the Burmese people and one that fits their way of life.

Many are wondering if *Aung San Suu Kyi* has the power, will or skill to bring the promised peace to her motherland. Her name, Western education, and charisma all contribute to her strength in government but these are qualities of a different nature than institutional leadership qualities like vision, values and principles that drive the actions of a leader and inspire more respect than idolization. Indeed, can the civilian administration sustain continued success for democratic principles and programs of free political competition to shape public policy? Can they continue without a burnout or a downward political spiral post *Aung San Suu Kyi*? Changing a political system is an arduous process requiring unflagging persistence, sustained sacrifice, unwavering commitment and strong effective leadership. In the end it is up to the people of Burma to continue to fight for democratic principles and speak out for freedom, human rights and justice.

It would take many years, but success is achievable. We learn from past world events and global history that peace is attainable to nations that are socially, economically and politically free, with stable societies that do not propagate domestic or external terrorism or cultivate aggressive attacks against one another. It's more important to strive for realistic attainable objectives than overarching democratic ideals. It is vital to focus on finding ways to enhance societal health, education and economic benefits for the people and to improve the economy, social welfare and employment opportunities, particularly in the ethnic regions. These benefits would also bring within reach stability, security, peace and harmony among different racial and religious communities.

Regardless who the perpetrators are, killing and raping in Arakan must stop. They have endured enough violence and humiliation as "aliens in their own land, homeless at home".[1] Most important of all they belong to the common race called human and they have rights and deserve to be treated with dignity and decency. The atrocities are so horrific in their utter savagery and meaninglessness and each of us must bear a deep concern for the suffering humanity. We cannot tolerate a system that degrades human beings on the basis of race, origin, or whatever human characteristics, and perpetuates violence, exploitation and injustice. All *Bamar* and non *Bamar* ethnic people deserve to enjoy autonomy and equality without civil wars in their home states. Investment in human and social capital is the assured way to create a cohesive society with a shared sense of identity, a shared understanding, shared values, trust, and cooperation. It may be the only way to sustain economic stability and genuine peace in Burma.

As the new emerging democratic government seeks economic, political, diplomatic and moral guidance the West can provide support for democracy without imposing values that work in the US or Europe. Western ideas and concepts about democracy may not necessarily be applicable within the framework of Burma's agrarian culture, religion, history, and tradition. For now, it may be an imperfect democracy as the country is still in its fragile democratic infancy and the people need time to understand, grasp and assimilate its principles. Many, including the rural poor, struggle to survive day to day lacking any understanding of their legal rights or political participation. Living under decades of repressive army rule they have learned to accept that only an elite could make decisions impacting their lives. But everyone and every group wants freedom, justice and equality defined as democracy.

The powerful *Tatmadaw*, the militant clergy, hard line Buddhists, and opposition groups have all capitalized the anti Muslim sentiment for political purposes to suit their ends. This must end first. Democracy requires active political participation from its citizens, with rights and responsibilities for its citizens. The ethnic minority nationalities continue to fight for democracy and federalism as embodied in General *Aung San's Panglong* agreement. Many surviving students of 8.8.88 revolution ended up in the jungles and joined the EAO's sharing common goals with the minorities toward a free Burma with a peaceful and better future. Like myriads of community based organizations working on both sides of the Thai–Burma border the *Bamar* people and all ethnic nationalities must work together to rebuild this country as a free united nation. Burma cannot rely solely on the cult personality aura of one icon and democracy cannot be defined synonymous with *Aung San Suu Kyi* or any one person.

---

[1] *New Internationalist*. Parsa Sanjana Sajid: "Fleeing *Myanmar*", April 1, 2018.

Democracy as defined in the Burmese context must come from within, endorsed and supported by the country's most powerful institution, *Tatmadaw*, but without a return to authoritarian military rule. Looking ahead, the NLD civilian government is likely to win the upcoming election again. Can they reconcile with *Tatmadaw*? Can the undemocratic constitution be changed? Can the NLD deliver what it takes for democracy to evolve from a deeply authoritarian system?

The people hope for a government that they can trust. The people of Burma are resilient; they may live in fear but never give up hope. They hope for a land that is a safer, kinder and happier home for their family regardless what the government calls its political system. They hope for peace, freedom, justice and end to suffering.

As the new emerging democracy of Burma matures, the government can continue to seek aid from the international community for economic, political, diplomatic and moral support. Peace, human rights, equality and freedom for all will come in baby steps through implementation of democracy principles and democratic rule of law as the nation integrates into the free world. The people of Burma must find their own way to self-determination, free expression and happiness. In their own terms, the people of Burma must define the Burmese way to democracy.

BIBLIOGRAPHY

Unsourced or unreferenced materials are from family accounts, perspectives and knowledge, family archives (including *Aung Gyi*'s letters to *Ne Win*), face-to-face interviews with assurances of anonymity, and personal experience and observation.

Bandow, Doug. "A Brighter Dawn In Burma: *Myanmar* Not Yet A Democracy But No Longer A Dictatorship." *Forbes*, Mar 31, 2016.

Beech, Hannah. *Burma's Backward Steps*. Time, Dec 1-8, 2014.

The Burma Environmental Working Group (BEWG). *Burma's Environment: People, Problems, Policies*. Published by BEWG, June 2011, Printed by: Wanida Press, Chiang Mai, Thailand.

Charbonneau, Louis and Megan Davies. *UN Admits 'Significant' Myanmar Exchange Rate Loss*. Reuters, July 28, 2008.

Myanmar's Transition. Edited by Nick Cheesman, Monique Skidmore and Trevor Wilson. ISEAS Publishing, Singapore, 2012.

Cockett, Richard. *Blood, Dreams and Gold – The Changing Face of Burma*, Yale University Press, New Haven and London, 2015.

Cockett, Richard. "Special Report *Myanmar*: A Burmese Spring," *The Economist*, May 25, 2013.

Ergreteau, Renaud. *Caretaking Democratization, The Military and Political Change in Myanmar*. New York: Oxford University Press, Oxford, 2016.

Fink, Christina. *Living Silence*. London: Zed Books, 2001.

Fuller, Thomas. *Profits of Drug Trade Drive Economic Boom in Myanmar*. The New York Times. June 5, 2015.

Global Witness, *Jade: Myanmar's 'Big State Secret'*. October, 2015.

Hanna, Willard A. *Re-Revving a Revolution*. American University Field Staff Southeast Asia Series, XI January 1963, 1-11.

Institute of Southeast Asian Studies, *Myanmar's Transition*, edited by Cheeseman, Skidmore, Wilson, ISEAS Publishing, Singapore, 2012

Johnstone, William C. *Burma's Foreign Policy*. Cambridge, Massachusetts: Harvard University Press, 1963.

Kearney, Vincent S. *Gourd Amid Cactuses*, America, CX March 14, 1964, 345.

Kenneth, V. *Burmese Small Arms Development. Small Arms Review, August 2009.* <http://www.smallarmsreview.com/display.article.cfm?idarticles=1154>

Kenneth, V. *Burma: Excluded from Public Eyes and Miscellaneous Mysteries*. Small Arms Review, July 2012. <http://www.smallarmsreview.com/inventory/detail.item.cfm?product_id=SAR.V13N7>

Khoo Thwe, Pascal. *From the Land of Green Ghosts*. New York: Harper Perennial, 2002.

Lall, Marie. *Understanding Reform in Myanmar*. London: Hurst & Company, 2016.

Lintner, Bertil. *Aung San Suu Kyi and Burma's Struggle for Democracy*. Chiang Mai: Silkworm, 2011.

Lintner, Bertil. *Burma in Revolt*. Westview Press, October 2000.

Lintner, Bertil. *Land of Jade: A Journey from India Through Northern Burma to China*. Orchid Press, April 2012.

Landry, Lionel. *Book in the News*, Saturday Review, March 17, 1962, 22.

Larkin, Emma. *Everything is Broken*. New York: Penguin Books, 2010.

Mahn Aung Lwin. *The Military Ties that Bind*. The Irrawaddy, August 2011. <https://www.irrawaddy.com/from-the-archive/military-ties-bind-2.html>

Mahtani, Shibani. *3 Digits Instill Fear*. WSJ, April 11, 2013, In *Myanmar*.

Montlake, Simon. *General Electric's Last Frontier*. Forbes, July 15, 2013.

U Myat Khine. *Interview with Thakin Aung Gyi*. Green Books Store, Pyi Zone Publishing, September 2009, Burma.

Pederson, Rena. *The Burma Spring: Aung San Suu Kyi and the New Struggle for the Soul of a Nation*, Pegasus, New York, 2014.

Popham, Peter. *The Lady and the Peacock*. London, Rider Books, 2011.

Richie, D. *Letter From Burma*, Nation, August 10, 1963, 77-78.

Rogers, Benedict. *Than Shwe: Unmasking Burma's Tyrant*. Chiang Mai, Thailand, Silkworm Books, 2010.

Rogers, Benedict. *Burma: A Nation at the Crossroads*. London, Rider, 2012.

Rose, Jerry A. *Burma and the Balance of Neutralism, The* Reporter, January 3, 1963, 24-29.

U San. *Thankin Aung Gyi (Paungde) Brigadier General Aung Gyi (ret)*. December 2012, Publisher U San, No 85, 164th Street, Tamwe Township, Yangoon.

Schrank, Delphine. *The Rebel of Rangoon: A Tale of Defiance and Deliverance in Burma*. Nation Books, New York, 2015.

Sein, Kyi Win (Malcolm). *Me and the Generals of the Revolutionary Council*. UK Book Publishing, 2015.

Steinberg, David I. *Burma/Myanmar, What Everyone Needs to Know*. Oxford University Press, 2010.

Stephens, Bret. *Aung San Suu Kyi's Narrow Road*. WSJ, June 11, 2014.

Studwell, Joe. *How Asia Works, Success and Failure in the World's Most Dynamic Region*. Published by Profile Books Limited, London, Grove Press, 2013.

Thant, Myint-U. *The River of Lost Footsteps: A Personal History of Burma*. New York: Farrar, Straus and Giroux, 2006.

Thant, Myint-U. *Where China Meets India: Burma and the New Crossroads of Asia*. New York: Farrar, Straus and Giroux, 2012.

Victor, Barbara. *The Lady Aung San Suu Kyi: Nobel Laureate and Burma's Prisoner*. Farber and Farber Inc., New York, 1998.

Wakeman, Carolyn and San San Tin. *No Time for Dreams*. Plymouth, UK, Rowman and Littlefield, 2009.

Walinsky, Louise J. *Economic Development in Burma 1951-1960*. New York: The Twentieth Century Fund, 1962.

Wilber, Donald N. *Burma*. Collier's Encyclopedia 1963 Yearbook. The Crowell-Collier's Publishing Company, 1963, 131-2.

Wintle, Justin. *Perfect Hostage: the Life of Aung San Suu Kyi, Burma's Prisoner of Conscience*. London, Arrow Books, Skyhorse Publishing, 2007.

Working People's Daily, Rangoon, March 21, 1966.

Working People's Daily, Rangoon, April 30, 1966.

Website References

http://www.irrawaddy.com

http://mizzima.com

https://www.mmtimes.com

https://www.globalwitness.org

Printed in the United States
By Bookmasters